The Infant Assembly Book

Doreen Vause MBE

SIMON & SCHUSTER
EDUCATION

Contents

Introduction   5

Term One: Autumn   **7-37**

A New Term   8
Time and Change   10
Trees   12
Autumn   14
Animal Harvest   16
Harvest of the Land   18
Bread   20
The Sea   22
Hallowe'en   24
Thanksgiving   26
Kind Deeds   28
Shepherds   30
Bells   32
Presents and Giving   34
Christmas   36

Term Two: Spring   **39-69**

The New Year   40
New Year Festivals   42
Shiny Things   44
Travellers   46
Winter   48
Birds   50
Candles   52
Our School   54
Morning and Night   56
Our World   58
The Sun   60
Water   62
Colours   64
Springtime   66
Eggs   68

Term Three: Summer   71-101

Big and Little	72
Animals	74
Small Creatures	76
Houses and Homes	78
Families	80
Me	82
Eyes	84
Ears	86
Hands and Feet	88
Air	90
Clothes	92
Summertime	94
Flowers	96
People Who Help Us	98
Children of Many Lands	100

Festivals   103-153

Christmas	106
Hogmanay	108
Chinese New Year	110
Islamic New Year	112
Passover	114
Easter	116
Holi	118
May Day	120
Pentecost and Whitsun	122
Sukkot	124
Yam Harvest	126
Diwali	128
Hanukah	130
Ramadan	132
Shrove Tuesday	134
Purim	136
The Buddha's Birthday	138
Baisakhi	140
St. Patrick's and St. David's Day	142
Mothers' Day	144

Raksha Bandhan	146
Weddings	148
Birthdays	150
One World	152

Index   154-158

Acknowledgements   159

Introduction

Although this book is intended to be a resource book for those who plan assemblies for the very young, I hope that it will prove useful to teachers in the classroom throughout the school year, and also to students in training. Many of the suggestions are capable of being extended so that they would be suitable for the junior age group.

I have provided a wide range of ideas for work in all curricular areas because all fields of study have something to offer in extending the child's capacity to grasp and to understand religious ideas. With the very young, such ideas and concepts can only develop alongside the child's growing experience of life.

I have chosen forty-five relevant themes which could be worked through systematically from the beginning of a school year. Alternatively, any one theme could be chosen in isolation, or themes could be taken in any sequence.

Much of the material is not new. There are many old favourites which, in many cases, have been slightly adapted to be more appropriate for use in the multi-ethnic, multi-religious society of today. In some cases, only one verse, or a few lines of the suggested material, could be used.

I have suggested suitable stories, songs, poems, hymns and other activities for each chosen theme. In making a selection, I have tried to keep in mind the wide range of ability which exists in infant schools. I have therefore attempted to include items suitable for older and younger children and also children for whom English is not their first language.

Stories given under a particular topic are often suitable for use with other topics too. Stories about the festivals of people of many faiths are included. In the multi-cultural society of today, I hope that children in infant schools will gain some knowledge of each other's cultures, and that this will lead to a greater understanding of people of different backgrounds. There are also many well-known stories from the Bible, and from other sources, which I have not included but which are appropriate. Some of the suggested stories lend themselves to being told by several children, each one being given a small part to read.

The activities I have suggested give various ideas for pictures, friezes and displays. These involve the development of skills and techniques appropriate for children in the infant age group. As is usual, teacher assistance is necessary in some cases.

In drawing together this material, I have referred to many sources, but in some cases the original source is unknown. Like many teachers, I have become acquainted with useful poems, stories and plays through working with other colleagues, and have then used these over a considerable length of time.

Every suggestion I have made has been carried out successfully with children in the infant age group. The number of children involved in an assembly, and the physical characteristics of the school building, will determine to a large extent what can be attempted. I regard these suggestions, therefore, as starting-points which teachers can adapt and supplement in order to meet their own requirements in their own particular schools.

I have envisaged that in some cases the assembly, based on a theme, may take place with suitable follow-up work in the classroom. Alternatively, work on the theme could begin in the classroom. The children could then bring their work into the assembly to act as a stimulus and thus make a meaningful contribution. In this way religious education becomes part of the whole curriculum, and an integral part of the life of the school and the relationships within it.

Term One
AUTUMN

A New Term

The first assembly of the new term should be an opportunity to greet new children and to welcome the other children back to school. It presents an opportunity to point out that there has been some change. Some children have left the school, and new children have taken their places.

The story of Confucius in 'The boy who loved to learn' gives many starting-points for discussion of friendliness, kindness, and consideration for others, which are appropriate at the beginning of the new school year.

The boy who loved to learn

Over 2000 years ago, in China, a little boy was born. His name was Kung Fu Tzu. When Kung Fu Tzu was only three years old his father died. His mother had very little money and they were very poor.

Kung Fu Tzu wanted to go to school so that he could learn interesting things. But in those days people had to pay to go to school and Kung Fu Tzu's mother did not have enough money to pay the fees. So Kung Fu Tzu could not go to school, but he still wanted to learn things, so he decided to find things out for himself. Kung Fu Tzu was a strange-looking little boy. He was tall and clumsy, his eyes were wide and staring, he had large teeth and he was rather ugly. The other children used to make fun of him, call him names and laugh at him, and sometimes would fight with him. All this used to upset Kung Fu Tzu, but he was a kind, gentle child and would not fight back.

Instead he used to wander off alone. He would go and talk to priests in the temple, and artists, and to the blind musicians on the streets. He was always trying to learn new things. If he tried to do something which he found difficult, he would try over and over again and would not stop trying until he could do it. It was in this way that the little boy learned lots of interesting things and grew up to become a very clever man. People all over the world now call the man Confucius and some believe that he was the wisest man who has ever lived.

Here are some of the many wise things that Confucius said:

Use your eyes and you will see many wonderful things.
Use your ears to listen and learn.
Always see that you have a friendly smile which tells other people that you are kind.
Always remember to be well-mannered and polite.
Always speak the truth.
Always play fair with others.
Do not do anything to other people that you would not like someone to do to you.

A greeting song

We'll sing to greet the morning
In weather dull or fine
For some may need the showers
And some the sun to shine
But we as happy children
Content at work and play
We'll sing to greet the morning
On every kind of day.
(adapted from 'a greeting song', Child Education 1958)

Action rhyme

See the little hands go clip, clip, clap
Then the feet go tip, tip, tap
I've some words to say to you
"Come shake hands – how do you do?"
Gaily we dance around just so
Then we bow – home we go.

Mary had a little lamb
(first two verses)
Mary had a little lamb,
Its fleece was white as snow;
And everywhere that Mary went
The lamb was sure to go.
It followed her to school one day,
That was against the rule;
It made the children laugh and play
To see a lamb at school.

Good morning

Good morning, good morning,
Good morning to you
And may it be a happy day
All the day through.

More ideas

STORIES
Danny's class *(Macdonald 1978)*
David's first day at school *(Hamish Hamilton 1981)*

HYMNS
Father we thank you for the night *(Someone's singing Lord, A&C Black 1973)*
One more step *(Come and praise, BBC Publications 1978)*

..Things to do............

Discussion

★ Discuss each of Confucius's sayings separately, and then ask the children which they feel is the most important one to remember and why.

★ What greetings do children use for different people? What do they say and do? When do people greet each other? How do people from other countries greet each other?

Library corner

★ Going to school *(Macdonald 1982)*

★ Going to school *(Methuen 1983)*

★ See all the things we share *(Lion 1979)*

Activities

★ Make a large 'welcome' poster for the school entrance hall (see instructions). Involve the parents in writing the word 'welcome' in their own language. These can then be added to the poster.

★ Divide the new children into groups, and allocate to each group a couple of older children, who will act as guides to show the new children around the school. A teacher should go with the group but should try to say as little as possible. Give the older children plenty of time to plan this. They will need to put themselves in the position of a new child, and consider how the new children will feel and what they would want to know.

To make a 'welcome' poster

Materials
A mirror
A sheet of paper/card
A large piece of card
Scissors
Pencils, crayons, paint brushes

1 Look carefully at your reflection in a mirror.
2 Draw a self-portrait on the card or paper. Write your name on a separate piece of paper.
3 Ask your parents to write 'welcome' in their own language on a piece of paper. Bring it into school.
4 Stick the faces, names and 'welcome' signs on a large piece of card and display it in the school entrance hall.

Look in a mirror

Draw your portrait and cut it out

Time and Change

Cultural and religious beliefs have their roots in the past. Because young children have difficulty in appreciating a time scale, this topic is introduced at the beginning of the new school year when the child has evidence of change all round. For example, new clothes, new pupils, new class.

The story of 'The peapod' offers the opportunity to develop the concepts of old and young, new and old. The story of 'The new moon' is about the passing of time.

The peapod

There was once a little boy called Paul. He was four years old and lived with his mummy and daddy in a flat in the centre of the town. His flat had no garden. Paul had a grandmother who lived in a small new bungalow, which had a big garden. Paul liked to visit his grandmother because they would go into the garden and granny would show Paul all the different things that grew there.

One day when Paul was at granny's house, she showed him her old photograph album. Paul was surprised to see that granny had once been a child just like him, although her clothes in the photograph were different from the ones children wear today.

After they had put away the photograph album, granny said to Paul, "I'm going to show you something so new that nobody has ever, ever seen it before." Paul wondered whatever it could be.

Granny led Paul into the garden to where some peas were growing in little green pods. "Look here," said granny. She opened a pod and put two small green peas from the pod into Paul's hand.
"Nobody had ever seen these two little peas until this very minute," said granny.
"How did they get into the peapod?" asked Paul. "That's another wonderful story," answered granny. "Can you guess?"

The new moon

Long ago, in North America there lived an Indian family. The father always looked very smart. He had reddish-brown skin, and always wore colourful feathers in his head-dress. The mother was small and also very fine-looking. She had long, thick dark hair which she wore in a plait. The baby was very small and all he could do was smile and cry.

They all lived very happily together until one day when Father Indian had to go away on a long journey. The mother Indian was worried that her husband might meet with some danger, for in that country there were big brown bears that roamed about and they were sometimes very dangerous. "I am afraid that you will not come back, said Mother Indian. "I shall worry all the time that you are away."

Father Indian turned to his wife and said "Don't worry. I will give you this rope. Can you see that I have tied three knots in it? Now look up at the moon. Can you see how big and round it is? It will become smaller each night, and then there will be a new, full moon again. Each time you see a new moon, untie one knot, and when you have untied the last knot I will be back with you."

So Father Indian left his wife and she did not worry. She watched the moon each night and untied the knots when she saw a new moon. On the night when she was about to untie the last knot she saw her husband coming over the hill. Carrying the baby with her, she ran to meet him. They were all very happy to be together again.

The little old lady

That little grey-haired lady
Is as old as old can be,
Yet once she was a little girl
A little girl like me.

She liked to skip instead of walk
She wore her hair in curls,
She went to school at nine and played
With other boys and girls.

I wonder if in years and years
Some little girl at play,
Who's very like what I am now
Will stop to look my way.

And think 'that grey-haired lady
Is as old as old can be,
Yet once she was a little girl
A little girl like me.'
(Book of a thousand poems, Evans 1959)

More ideas

POEM
New sights (*Book of a thousand poems, Evans 1959*)

HYMN
The golden cockerel (*Someone's singing Lord*, A&C Black 1973)

..Things to do..............

Discussion

★ Ask the children how they think they will look and behave when they are old women and men.

Library corner

★ How a seed grows *(A&C Black 1970)*

★ The seed *(Macmillan 1971)*

★ The seed *(Wayland 1978)*

★ Time & clocks *(Macdonald 1971)*

Activities

★ Make a moon chart. Observe the shape of the moon each night. Cut out the shape from a paper plate or circle of card. Keep a pictorial record of the change in shape, with the date underneath each picture.

★ Make a collection of old and new coins, pre-decimal and decimal money.

★ Take the children to visit a museum, monument or old building. Try to get old photographs of your local high street, railway station, etc.

★ Ask each class to keep a scrapbook of, for example, cars, ships, animals or clothes of long ago.

★ Have a grandparents' day when children invite their grandparents to come to school. Some of the grandparents could talk about their own childhood.

To make an Indian Head-dress

Materials
A corrugated paper strip
Feathers (real or home-made)
Scissors
A piece of cord
Decorations (milk bottle tops etc.)

1 Decorate a piece of corrugated paper strip with milk bottle tops etc.
2 Draw a feather shape and fold down the middle. Cut out round outline and snip triangular shapes out of the rounded edge.
3 Put a feather into each tiny hole in the corrugated strip.
4 Join the ends of the strip to make the head-dress.

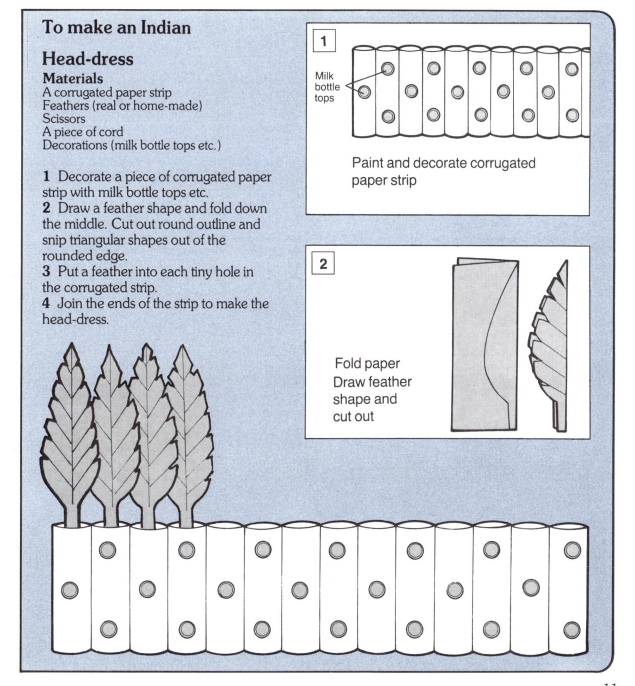

Trees

A study of trees is often undertaken during the autumn term because most children have access to trees. The story of 'New year for trees' demonstrates that people belong to different faiths and celebrate different festivals. A further aim is to promote ideas of conservation and friendship between different cultures, as in the story of 'Johnny Appleseed'.

Johnny Appleseed

Many years ago in America there lived a little boy called Johnny. When Johnny was a little boy he loved flowers, animals, and trees. He used to climb apple trees, pick an apple, and munch away until he came to the core. Then he would take out the little brown apple seeds and plant them.

When Johnny grew up, he roamed the countryside. Everywhere he went, he carried a big bag full of apple seeds and showed children how to plant them. Johnny made special friends with the Red Indians who gave him food and shelter. He was such a happy man that everyone liked him and called him Johnny Appleseed.

One night in winter Johnny became very ill. He fell down in the snow and while he lay there a bear came along and sniffed at Johnny. But because Johnny was friends with all animals, the bear did him no harm. It wandered off leaving its footprints in the snow. Some Indians saw the footprints and followed them. The prints led them to Johnny. They recognized Johnny as their old friend who had shown them how to plant apple seeds. The Indians carried Johnny back to their tepee where they took care of him until he became well again.

Johnny thanked his Indian friends and wandered off once more, planting apple seeds as he went. From time to time he returned to see his old Indian friends who had saved his life. Wherever he went he was always welcome because the people knew him as a man who had made their country rich with lovely apple trees where once there was nothing but brown earth.

New year for trees

Ilana woke up one day feeling very excited because it was the new year for trees, which is a very special festival for Israeli children. All the children of the small desert town where Ilana lived, were going together to the park in the town centre to plant trees.

Excitedly, Ilana ran downstairs and called for her friend, Zvi, who lived nearby and they rushed to school. Soon they were off on the short walk to the park.

When all the children were in the park, the mayor said a few words. He explained how Jewish people all over the world collected money to buy trees for Israeli children to plant on the new year for trees. He told them how important it was to plant trees and bushes in the desert so that their roots could grow down and stop the soil from blowing away. He hoped that one day the whole desert would blossom and that the town's little park would be full of beautiful trees.

When he had finished speaking, the children who had been chosen to plant came forward. They put each sapling into a hole and filled it up with sandy earth and water. Ilana and Zvi were very proud because they had been picked for the job!

When all the trees were planted, the children sang songs about the festival and the plants and animals of the country and danced in big circles on the grass. When it was time for the children to leave the park, Ilana looked at her little tree. It seemed very tiny! Never mind, she thought, she would visit it every day and make sure her tree was growing tall and straight and strong!

Tall trees

*With their feet in the earth
And their heads in the sky,
The tall trees watch
The clouds go by.*

*When the dusk sends quickly
The birds to rest,
The tall trees shelter them
Safe in the nest.*

*And then in the night
With the tall trees peeping,
The moon shines down
On a world that's sleeping.*
(Book of a thousand poems Evans 1959)

More ideas

HYMN
God who made the earth *(Come and praise, BBC Publications 1978)*

POEM
If I take an acorn *(Book of a thousand poems, Evans 1959)*

..Things to do............

Discussion

★ Encourage children to talk about their own place of worship and any special festivals they have attended.

★ Discuss the benefits we receive from trees and stress their importance in the balance of nature.

Library corner

★ Science from wood (Macdonald 1976)

★ The oak tree (Ward Lock 1979)

Activities

★ Make a small tree. Fold a circle of green cover paper in half, quarters, eighths, sixteenths. Cut small chips from the edges of the folds. Open out and raise alternate creases until the tree form emerges. Stick the folded pieces by inserting a piece of sellotape turned over on itself in each fold. Use a pencil in a plasticine base as the tree trunk.

★ Visit a park. Name the trees. Who can find the largest leaf? Who can find the most colourful leaf? Back in the classroom, find the area of each leaf using squared paper.

★ Draw round leaves, make leaf prints or leaf smudge patterns.

★ Plant a seed from a red apple and a seed from a green apple. Keep a growth chart.

★ Make a display of different kinds of wood.

To paste grain a tree

Materials
Thick card for 'comb'
Thick paste (flour and water mix)
Brown powder paint
Activity paper
Pencils

1 Make a thick paste from plain flour and water.
2 Take a small quantity of the paste and mix brown powder paint into it. Spread this on to a formica top.
3 Use a thick-toothed comb, or a piece of thick card cut out to make a comb, and comb the surface.
4 Press the paper to be printed on to the surface.
5 Use the printed paper to cut out the shape of trees and branches.
6 Take sheets of activity paper in gold, orange, brown. The children draw round their hands. These shapes are cut out and used for the foliage on the trees.

Spread the paste on to formica and then comb paste

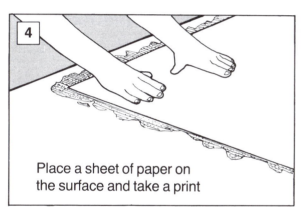

Place a sheet of paper on the surface and take a print

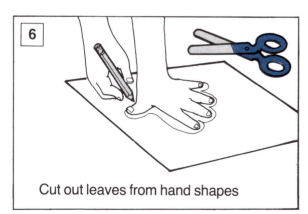

Cut out leaves from hand shapes

Autumn

By looking at certain events that are linked to a particular season we can help children to widen their experience of the world and arouse their sense of wonder. The two stories are of autumn festivals: the Chinese moon festival and the Jewish festival of Rosh Hashanah, which occurs in September or October.

Rosh Hashanah

David and his sister Rachel ran into school one morning and gave a note to their teacher. The note was from their mummy, and it said that the children would be absent the next day. David and Rachel's family were Jews and for them it was the New Year celebration called Rosh Hashanah.

That night their grandma told them that all over the world Jewish children would be hearing stories of Abraham, and so she told them this story:

A baby for Sarah

Long ago there was a man called Abraham. Abraham had many sheep and wandered from place to place so that he could find good grass for them.

Abraham had a wife whose name was Sarah. Abraham hoped that Sarah would have a child who could help him look after his sheep. But Abraham knew that Sarah was too old to be a mother, so he prayed to God to send them a baby.

Abraham's prayers were answered and a little later the baby was born. Sarah and Abraham called him Isaac which means 'laughter' because Sarah had laughed for joy when she heard she was going to have a baby! Abraham and Sarah loved Isaac more than anything else, and they cared for him as God wanted them to do.

When the children returned to school, the teacher asked them to tell the children all about Rosh Hashanah. Rachel told the children how friends of their family had visited them and how they had stayed up very late and eaten special food. There were apples covered in honey and special little plaited loaves.

The Chinese moon festival

Many years ago in China the people were very unhappy. Their land had been at war and a fierce tribe of people called the Mongols had become the masters of China.

The Mongols were so cruel that the people were very frightened and dared not even speak to each other. The Chinese wanted to win their own land back as this was the only way that they could live peacefully again.

So they made plans and passed secret messages to each other. They wrote the messages on scraps of paper and baked them inside little cakes which they passed to each other at night. In this way they kept their secrets from their cruel masters. Because they passed the cakes at night they called them 'moon cakes'.

Today the people of China remember this, and in the autumn they celebrate the moon festival. It takes place when the moon is full and bright. The people make special cakes which they call moon cakes and give them to their friends. The children stay up very late at night and then go out with their parents and friends and watch the moon rise in the sky. It is a very happy and joyful time.

An autumn song

(Tune: mulberry bush)

Oh what shall we do in autumn time
In autumn time, in autumn time,
Oh what shall we do in autumn time
On a misty moisty morning.

We'll watch the leaves turn gold and brown,
Gold and brown, gold and brown,
We'll watch the leaves turn gold and brown,
On a misty moisty morning.

We'll see the leaves (come tumbling down × 3)
We'll feel the wind (come blowing about × 3)
We'll go and sweep up (all the leaves × 3)
We'll pile them up in (a great big heap × 3)

Then we'll sing and dance around,
Dance around, dance around,
Then we'll sing and dance around,
On a misty autumn morning.

More ideas

SONG
Falling leaves (Sing a song 2, Nelson 1979)

HYMN
The farmer comes to scatter the seed (Hymns and songs for children, National Society 1969)

..Things to do............

Discussion

★ Talk about the seasons of the year in Britain and compare them with seasons in different parts of the world. Ask the children if any of them have travelled to a place where it was very hot at Christmas.

★ Discuss the changes which happen in the autumn: birds gathering in flocks prior to migrating; animals preparing for hibernation; leaves changing colour; trees bearing berries not blossom; simple seed dispersal (cones, acorns, etc.)

★ Discuss the seasonal festivals and celebrations that help us to remember things which happened a long time ago.

Library corner

★ Four seasons *(Franklin Watts 1983)*

★ Autumn days *(Macdonald 1979)*

★ What to look for in autumn *(Ladybird 1960)*

★ Autumn *(Evans 1979)*

Activities

★ Make little moon cakes from ordinary pastry. Use currants as eyes, nose and mouth to make a moon cake.

★ Make seed patterns using lentils, barley, peas, split peas and beans.

★ Display colour tables of autumn colours.

To make a seed pattern pendant

Materials
A circular cheese box
Thick white adhesive
An assortment of seeds and grains
An aerosol spray (gold or silver)
A length of floral ribbon

1 Cover the inside of a circular cheese box with thick, white adhesive.
2 Mark the centre of the circle with one large seed and work outwards arranging your seeds to form a pattern. Allow the adhesive to dry and see that all the seeds are fixed firmly.
3 Spray the pendant with gold or silver.
4 Attach a loop of floral ribbon to make a hanger. A calendar tab can be fastened to the bottom to make an attractive Christmas present.

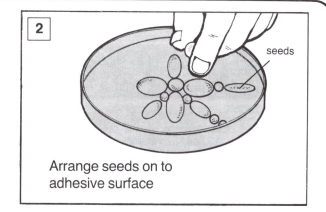

Arrange seeds on to adhesive surface

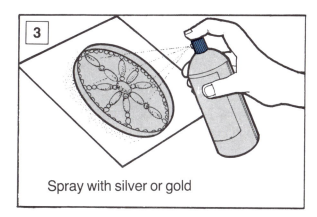

Spray with silver or gold

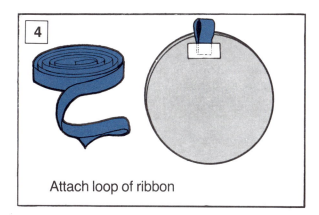

Attach loop of ribbon

Animal Harvest

The two stories are chosen to demonstrate that we all depend on each other. 'The story of Bushytail' shows how selfishness and greed are self-defeating; and the story of 'The grey squirrels and the red squirrel' reveals how all people have the same need for friendship and love regardless of their colour, creed or culture.

The story of Bushytail

Once upon a time there was a young squirrel who was called Bushytail, because he had a beautiful long, bushy tail.

When autumn came, Bushy rushed about collecting nuts and more nuts for his winter stores. Soon his home in the tree was so full of nuts that he could hardly shut his door.

When the other animals went to call on him, he did not let them in, and he changed from being a kind, helpful squirrel into a selfish, greedy one. He would not play with the others, nor would he help them. If they called on him, he would say, "Go away, I don't need you!"

One night, during the winter months, when all the squirrels were sleeping, the wind began to blow fiercely. It tossed the branches of the trees and woke most of the squirrels. Suddenly, the bough on which Bushy had built his home was torn from the tree, and Bushy fell down, down, down, into the cool waters of the stream below.

"Help! Help!" shouted Bushy. Luckily, the other animals of the wood heard his cries. They rushed to the river bank to see Bushy being swirled around in the water. They knew that although Bushy had told them that he did not want them, he needed them now. They all joined together to try and save him.

Soon Bushy was pulled from the water. He was covered in bruises and looked a terrible sight! For several days the other squirrels thought he would die, but they looked after him very carefully. They brought him food and built him a new home.

Bushy soon began to think about how kind his friends were being to him. He decided he had been greedy and horrible to his friends. He knew now that everyone needs friends and that being a friend means being kind to others.

When Bushy was well enough he invited all his friends to his new home and gave them nuts. He told them that he was sorry and said a big "THANK YOU!"

The grey squirrels and the red squirrel

Deep in a wood lived a family of grey squirrels. One day as the three young squirrels were playing together, they noticed a strange creature nearby. He looked rather like them. He had two ears, two eyes, and a bushy tail, but his coat was not the same colour. Timidly, the grey squirrels asked the stranger, "Who are you?"

"I am a red squirrel," said a kind voice. "A red squirrel? How can you be a squirrel when your coat is not the same colour as ours?" said the grey squirrels.

The red squirrel asked if he could join in their games as he was rather lonely and had no friends with whom he could play. The grey squirrels whispered together but decided that he could not join in their games because he was stranger and might not play fairly. So the red squirrel had to play on his own, and he felt very lonely.

One day one of the grey squirrels was chased by a big brown dog. The grey squirrel was so frightened that it ran and ran without knowing where it was going until finally it was trapped by a falling branch. The young, grey squirrel lay there all night, injured, frightened and very cold.

The next day the red squirrel was walking through the wood and heard faint squeakings. Soon he found the little grey squirrel. "Can I help you?" he asked. He tried to lift the branch but he was not strong enough. So he ran to the other end of the wood to get help from the grey squirrel's family.

The whole grey squirrel family ran as fast as they could to the place where the red squirrel took them. Soon they had moved the big branch and they all helped to carry the poor, injured grey squirrel to safety.

Since that day, the young grey squirrels always invite the red squirrel to join in their games and they play very happily together.

More ideas

POEM
Winter (*Infant teachers' prayer book*, Blandford 1974)

HYMN
I love God's tiny creatures (*Someone's singing Lord*, A&C Black 1973)

..Things to do............

Discussion

★ To demonstrate how humans are dependent on animals, talk about the role of animals and birds in seed dispersal. Show how all living things are interdependent.

Library corner

★ *What to look for in autumn* (Ladybird 1960)

★ *The squirrel* (Macdonald 1978)

★ *The hedgehog* (Macdonald 1978)

★ *The red squirrel* (Philograph 1958)

★ *The hedgehog* (Philograph 1958)

★ *A book for autumn* (Wheaton 1972)

Activities

★ Visit a park to collect acorns and horsechestnuts. Use them for counting, experience of more and less, and weighing.

★ Make displays of autumn berries, acorns, pine seeds, hazel nuts, horsechestnuts etc.

★ Make masks for squirrels and other animals and act out either of the suggested stories.

★ Frieze work: make an autumn seasonal collage.

To make a hedgehog

Materials
A normal size paint pot
Powder paint
Cold water paste powder
A shallow dish or saucer
Coloured or plain straws
Large piece of white paper
Strong adhesive

1 Put a tablespoon of cold water paste powder into a paint pot. Add cold water gradually to almost fill the paint pot. Add powder paint to bring up to a rich colour. Pour some of the mixture into a shallow dish.
2 The child coats her hand with the paste.
3 The child places her flat hand, fingers closed together and thumb tucked in, on to the paper.
4 Cover the printed form with strong adhesive and lay down small pieces of straw to make the 'prickles'.

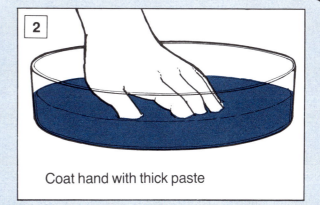
Coat hand with thick paste

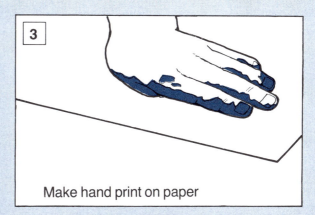
Make hand print on paper

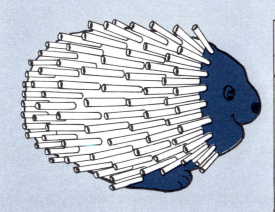

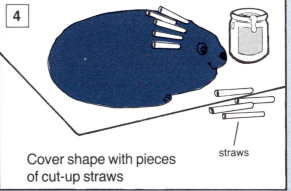
Cover shape with pieces of cut-up straws
straws

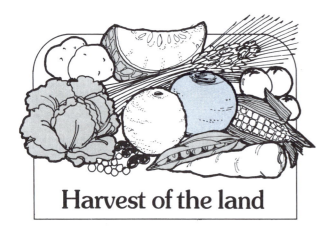

Harvest of the land

The harvest theme is used to develop the idea of the interdependence of peoples of the world. The topic also presents opportunities to demonstrate ideas of kindness, loyalty, sharing and helping those in need.

The church mouse

There was once a tiny brown mouse that lived inside a very old church. It was a poor little mouse for there was often nothing to eat inside the church. So the little mouse had to make many dangerous journeys into the fields nearby in search of food. It was often so dangerous that the little mouse dare not venture out and therefore went without food.

One evening in September lots of excited people came into the church bringing all kinds of food. There were apples, oranges, nuts, sheaves of wheat, a huge loaf of bread, and lots of colourful flowers.

That night, when all the people had gone, the mouse nibbled away at all the delicious food until his tummy was so full that he could hardly creep back to his little hole. Once there he slept very soundly and did not wake up until the next day.

It was Sunday. But this Sunday was different. The church was very full, and everybody seemed to sing so joyfully. The mouse heard that this was a harvest festival.

Little mouse said, "I wish these people would have a harvest festival every week, not just because I could enjoy a good meal more often, but because I have never seen them looking so happy."

The next day all the food was taken away. Little mouse heard the people say that some of it would be taken to hospitals, and some to old people and some to sick and poor people. Little mouse said, "I wonder if the people know that they have also given some of their food to a poor little church mouse!"

The story of Ruth

Long ago there lived a man whose name was Elimelech. He had a wife called Naomi, and two sons. Before long their sons married. One married a girl called Orpah and the other married Ruth. Orpah and Ruth went to live with Elimelech and Naomi and her sons. All went well at first, but then everything started to go wrong. Elimelech became ill and died. Soon afterwards the two sons also died.

Naomi was so sad that she decided to return to Bethlehem where most of her friends lived. She told Orpah and Ruth to go back to their own mothers. Orpah went back to her own home, but Ruth told Naomi that she would always look after her. So Ruth went back to Bethlehem with Naomi.

When they returned it was the time of harvest. In those days, after the reapers had cut the barley, the farmers let the poor people go round the field and pick up some of the leftover grain. So Ruth went out into the fields to pick up some grain to feed Naomi and herself. As Ruth was doing this Boaz, the rich farmer, came by. Boaz did not know Ruth and he asked someone who she was. The people told him how Ruth cared for Naomi. Boaz was pleased to hear about Ruth's kindness to Naomi and told his workmen to let Ruth pick as much barley as she wanted. Ruth and Boaz became great friends and later they married. They soon had a baby son. Naomi loved the little boy and helped Ruth to look after him.
(for a more detailed account of this story see page 122).

Every day

*There are so many things to do today
In city, field and street,
And people are going everywhere
with quickly hurrying feet.*

*Some are ploughing and sowing the seed
And some are reaping the grain,
And some who worked the whole night through,
Are coming home again.*

*Over the hills the shepherd goes,
While in the busy town,
People and carts and motor cars
Are running up and down.*

*And everywhere they come and go
In sun and rain and sleet,
That we may have warm clothes to wear,
And food enough to eat.*
(Book of a thousand poems, Evans 1959)

More ideas

PRAYER
Thank you, God, for harvest time. *(Infant teacher's prayer book, Blandford 1974)*

HYMN
Join with us to sing God's praises *(Come and praise, BBC Publications 1978)*

..Things to do............

Discussion

★ From the concept of interdependence of peoples of the world, move on to talk about the harvests of other countries – rice in India and China, citrus fruits in Spain, coffee in South America, wheat in Canada. How do different climates affect these crops? How are they transported around the world?

Library corner

★ The rice farmer *(Macdonald 1982)*

★ Bananas and oranges *(Schofield and Simms 1964)*

Activities

★ Take the topic of harvest time in other lands for a school project. Each class in the school takes one aspect of the theme (e.g. harvesting rice in India) and develops it. The work of all the classes is brought together to produce a larger piece of work, 'harvesting crops around the world'. The work can include drawings, paintings, writing, models, displays of clothing and traditional costume, simple maps, reference books, food wrappers and empty cartons and packages.

★ Draw the outlines of various fruit and vegetables (these outlines can be enlarged using an episcope or overhead projector). These are then coloured, using crayon or paint, cut out and mounted to produce colourful wall friezes. Very large outlines may be painted and hung as mobiles.

To make a target chart (to raise money for less fortunate people in other lands)

Materials
A large piece of paper
Blu-tack (or similar adhesive)
Scissors
Drawing/painting materials

1 On a large piece of paper, draw an outline showing land to the left and the right of a stretch of sea. Include a scale on the seabed to correspond to the number of coins it is hoped will be collected.
2 Draw a boat on a piece of cardboard. Cut it out. Attach a small piece of Blu-tack (or similar adhesive) to the back. Stick it on the chart in such a way that it is clear how many coins have been collected at any one time.
3 On separate pieces of paper, paint the sun, clouds, palm trees, houses and figures. Stick these on the target chart.

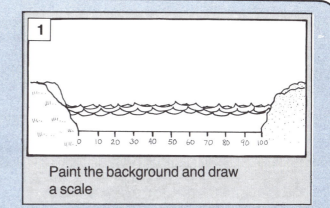

Paint the background and draw a scale

Draw, colour and cut out a simple boat shape

Bread

Bread is a basic food which is eaten in many lands. But there are many countries where there is not enough bread to go round. 'A story for today' reminds children of the hunger that many people suffer, and encourages them to think about those who are less fortunate than themselves. This section is also intended to help children make a connection between the source of our food and the finished product, in this case, a loaf of bread. Furthermore, the practical tasks of baking are rich in scientific and mathematical activity and demand cooperation on the part of the children.

A story for today

Mrs Martindale is a school cook. She works very hard to see that the children have a good meal but some boys and girls always throw some of their dinner away. The children who bring food from home often leave crusts of bread.

We are very lucky in our country because most children have plenty of food to eat. We sometimes feel hungry but we know that it will not be for long. We have many different kinds of food and there is always enough for us all.

But in some countries of the world there are many boys and girls whose parents cannot give them food. They get only a tiny piece of bread to eat each day. Sadly there are some children who get less than that. They are always hungry and their tummies are empty and swollen. Sometimes they are so poorly that they die.

Half the people in our world do not have enough to eat. Many die each year because there is not enough rain to make their crops grow. Sometimes there is too much rain, and the crops are ruined by floods.

There is enough food in our world for us all, but we still have not learned how to share it properly. There are some people who go to different lands to take food to the many hungry people. But more help is needed. When you eat today, or if you are tempted to waste food, think about the poor hungry children in other lands and about the people who are helping them. Perhaps one day you will be able to help them too.

The mouse, the frog and the little red hen

Once a mouse, a frog, and a little red hen,
Together kept a house;
The frog was the laziest of frogs,
And lazier still was the mouse.

The work all fell on the little red hen,
Who had to get the wood,
And build the fires, and scrub, and cook,
And sometimes hunt the food.

One day, as she went scratching round,
She found a bag of rye;
Said she, "Now who will make some bread?"
Said the lazy mouse, "Not I."

"Nor I," croaked the frog as he drowsed in the shade,
Red hen made no reply,
But flew around with bowl and spoon,
And mixed and stirred the rye.

"Who'll make the fire to bake the bread?"
Said the mouse again, "Not I,"
And, scarcely op'ning his sleepy eyes,
Frog made the same reply.

The little red hen said never a word,
But a roaring fire she made;
And while the bread was baking brown,
"Who'll set the table?" she said

"Not I," said the sleepy frog with a yawn
"Nor I," said the mouse again.
So the table she set and the bread put on,
"Who'll eat this bread?" said the hen.

"I will!" cried the frog. "And I!" squeaked the mouse,
As they near the table drew,
"Oh, no, you won't!" said the little red hen
And away with the loaf she flew.
(Book of a thousand poems, Evans 1959)

More ideas

HYMN
Loving heavenly Father *(Hymns and songs for children, National Society 1969)*

POEM
Bread *(Book of a thousand poems, Evans 1959)*

SONG
Oats and beans and barley grow *(Sing a song 1, Nelson 1978)*

..Things to do............

Discussion

★ Have you ever bought bread? What kind of bread did you buy? Where did it come from and how was it made?

Library corner

★ Bread *(Macdonald 1971)*

★ A loaf of bread *(Macmillan 1974)*

Activities

★ **Recipe for chapatti:** Stir water into 300 g of wheatflour until the dough is of a consistency to make small balls. Take each small ball and press between the hands. Toss from palm to palm to flatten. Cook on a metal plate over a gas ring. Turn frequently. Cover one side with melted butter.

★ **Recipe for bread:** 460 g flour; 20 g dried yeast; 1 teaspoon salt; 5 ml sugar; 300 ml warm water.
Mix yeast, sugar and 75 ml of water. Leave for 15 minutes until frothy. Put flour and salt in the mixing bowl. Add the rest of the water to the yeast mixture. Now pour all the liquid into the flour and mix well. Knead the dough for 5 minutes and then put it into a greased mixing bowl. Cover the bowl with a damp cloth. Leave in a warm place for an hour to let the dough rise. Knead the dough again and shape into 2 loaves. Put them on a greased baking tray and put them in a warm place until they double in size. Bake in a hot oven for 30 minutes.

To make a windmill

Materials
Cardboard cartons
Glue/Sellotape
Tube of card
Thick white paint
Blu-tack (or similar adhesive)
A piece of coloured card
Another piece of card
Paint and paint brushes
Scissors

1 Stick three or four cardboard cartons together and paint white.
2 Cut out the roof from a sheet of coloured card. Stick it on to the boxes so there is an overhang.
3 Cut out the sails from another piece of card. Take a tube of card and paint it black.
4 Cut circular holes in the sides of the windmill. Push the tube through. Fasten the sails to the tube, and bind sellotape very close to the sails.

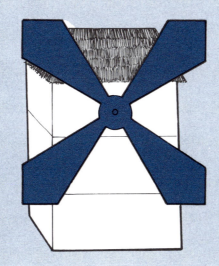

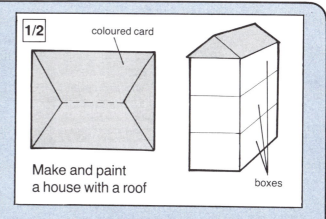

Make and paint a house with a roof

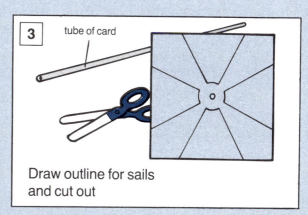

Draw outline for sails and cut out

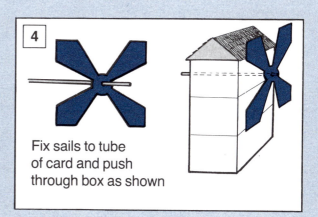

Fix sails to tube of card and push through box as shown

The Sea

The aim of this topic is to bring children's attention to the fact that the oceans are full of riches. 'Sea festivals' tells of a continental thanksgiving festival for the harvest of the sea. The story of 'Grace Darling' presents opportunities for discussion of bravery and consideration for the needs of others.

Grace Darling

Long ago a family lived in a lighthouse on a little rocky island close to the shore. There was Mr and Mrs Darling and their daughter, Grace. Every night Grace helped her father to light the oil lamp at the top of the lighthouse, and to keep it lit all night long.

One night a great storm raged. The wind howled and the waves crashed on the rocks. Grace and her father worked all night to keep the little light burning brightly. When morning came, Grace looked out from the top of the lighthouse. She saw that a ship had been wrecked and that some people were standing on the rocks quite a way out at sea.

Grace called her father, and they decided that they would row out their little boat and try to rescue the people who had been ship-wrecked. Mrs Darling did not want them to go, because the sea was still very rough and she thought they might be drowned if their little boat overturned.

Grace knew that it would be dangerous. But she also knew that she must be brave, for if she did not help her father, he could not go alone, and the poor people would die. So Mr Darling and Grace pushed their little boat into the rough sea. Their boat was tossed about by the big waves but they still rowed towards the rocks where the people were standing.

At last they reached the rocks. There were nine people standing there. They were very wet and very cold. Grace and her father were able to take five people in their boat and then go back for four more. All the nine people were saved because Grace had been such a brave girl on that stormy night.

Sea festivals

In Spain, and many other countries there are villages along the coasts where people have been fishermen for years. Each village has a special festival when the people from all the villages nearby come to join in the fun. Bands play music and people dance through the narrow streets from the churches to the seashore. Then the sea is blessed and thanks are said for all the wonderful things we get from the sea – fish to eat, and oil which we use for all kinds of things.

Sometimes special prayers are said by people who go out in a little boat on the sea. They know that the sea can be very dangerous. So they ask God to take care of all the people who sail on the sea. Prayers are also said on the shore, and in the fish markets. Often as the day ends and darkness falls there are firework displays.

There are big waves

There are big waves and little waves
Green waves and blue
Waves you can jump over
Waves you can dive through
Waves that rise up
Like a great waterwall
Waves that swell softly
And don't break at all
Waves that can whisper
Waves that can roar,
And tiny waves that run at you
Running on the shore.
(Book of a thousand poems, Evans 1959)

Two in a boat (a singing game)

Children make a circle and join hands. Two children make a rocking boat in the middle of the circle. Each of the two chooses a new partner at the appropriate point in the song.

Two in a boat and the waves run high, (× 3)
Get me a partner by and by.

(Each child chooses a partner now giving two boats)

Two little boats and the waves run high, etc.
Four little boats and the waves run high, etc.
Eight little boats and the waves run high, etc.
Wave to your partners and say goodbye.

More ideas

HYMN
Thank you Lord (*Come and praise*, BBC Publications 1978)

SONGS
Jackie the sailor boy; the big ship sails (*Sing a song 2*, Nelson 1979)
Bobby Shaftoe (*Music for the nursery school*, Harrap 1966)

..Things to do............

Discussion

★ Have you ever been to a fish and chip shop? How did the fish come to be in the shop? Discuss the work of deep sea, and inshore, fishermen around the world.

★ Have you ever been to the sea? What was it like on the seashore? What did you do? Did you enjoy being near the sea? Did you see a lighthouse or a lifeboat? Have you ever seen a rescue helicopter? Tell the children about the R.N.L.I.

★ Discuss pollution of the sea and rivers.

Library corner

★ The seashore *(A&C Black 1983)*

★ By the sea *(Macdonald 1976)*

Activities

★ Set up a fish and chip shop. Make chips from rolls of paper and paint them. Make fish (*see instructions*) and stuff them with newspaper. Make peas from plasticine. Collect containers, provide a scoop, aprons and a money till.

★ For a display, find pictures of the seaside, oil rigs, ships and fish for the background and shells etc. for the foreground.

★ Examine a globe and a large map. See how much of the world's surface is covered by the sea.

★ Paint pictures of a sea rescue.

To make a fish mobile

Materials
A sheet of A4 paper
Scissors
A piece of string or cotton
Coloured pens or pencils

1 Fold a sheet of A4 paper and draw outline. Cut out the shape, and along the line, X to Y.
2 Open out the fish shape and make folds for tabs, A, B, C and D. Draw the eyes, the fins and the scale pattern.
3 Fold back A and B. Bring A and B together and fasten.
4 Fold back C and D. Join them together.
5 Make a hole in the top of the fish and attach a piece of string or cotton for hanging the fish as part of a mobile.

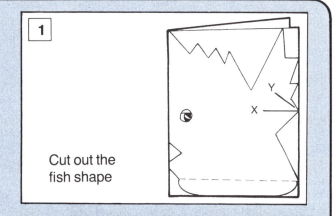

Cut out the fish shape

Open out the fish shape, fold A and B back and join them

Fold C and D back and join them together

Hallowe'en

The beliefs of people long ago were often based on ignorance, fear and misunderstanding. If an event should happen which could not be understood, it was attributed to magic or witchcraft. Beliefs based on ignorance, fear or lack of understanding are still prevalent today. Many people hold preconceived ideas about people of different races and cultures which stand in the way of friendship. The stories below are both about witches, and offer opportunities for discussion of preconceived ideas and the effect of our actions on others.

The witch in the wood

Once in a small tumbled-down cottage in a dark wood there lived an old woman dressed in ragged clothes. She had two black cats and a goat which she kept in the garden. The children from the nearby village were very frightened of the old woman. Whenever they saw her they called out "witch, witch!" and then ran away.

In that same village there was a little girl named Pat. One day as she was walking with her sister near the wood she saw a goat. Pat took hold of the rope around its neck and said to her sister, "This goat must belong to someone. Shall we try to find its owner?"

Soon they came to a cottage and knocked on the door. It was opened by the old woman. The two girls were rather frightened when they saw the old woman with long black hair and black ragged clothes. But they were not frightened for long because the old woman was so pleased that the girls had brought her goat back. "I have only three friends in the whole world," said the woman, "my two black cats and this little goat. My husband died a long time ago and I live here all on my own." Pat and her sister felt so sorry for the old woman that they promised to visit her again the next week.

On the next Saturday they visited the old woman. She was so pleased to have visitors that she had put on her best dress. The girls found that she was really a sweet and kind old lady.

Pat and her sister told the other children about their visit to the old lady, so the other children were no longer afraid of her. Instead of shouting "witch, witch!" they decided to go and help her. They went and weeded the garden, fed the goat and sang songs for her. The old lady was very pleased that the children no longer thought she was a witch, and that they were now her friends.

Wanda the kind witch

In a house in the forest lived Wanda the kind witch. She had a black cat called Simon and a long broomstick. Wanda was tired of her old broomstick for it did not fly fast enough. One day she told Simon that she was going to make a spaceship. With Simon's help she made the spaceship. It had a signal for danger and a large box of magic spells. Their spaceship was faster than an aeroplane, and much faster than the broomstick.

10, 9, 8, 7, 6, 5, 4, 3, 2, 1, Zero! Off went Wanda and Simon until their spaceship was over the forests of North America. Simon sounded the alarm – "DANGER BELOW". Wanda looked down to see a little Indian girl caught in the deep, dark forest with all the trees blazing around her. "Time to cast a spell," said Wanda. She waved her wand and there was the little girl safe in the spaceship. They took her back to her people who thanked them for saving the girl's life.

Wanda had many more adventures in their spaceship. They helped all kinds of different people all over the world, which just goes to show that not all witches are bad!
(adapted from Wanda the kind witch, Reading with rhythm, Longman 1961)

There was an old witch

There was an old witch,
Believe it if you can,
She tapped on the window
And she ran, ran, ran.
She ran helter, skelter,
With her toes in the air,
Cornstalks flying
From the old witch's hair.

"Swish," goes the broomstick,
"Meow," goes the cat,
"Plop," goes the hop-toad
Sitting on her hat.
"Wee," chuckled I,
"What fun, fun, fun!"
Hallowe'en night
When the witches run.
(traditional)

More ideas

SONG
When I needed a neighbour (*Someone's singing Lord*, A&C Black 1973)

..Things to do..........

Discussion

★ (Before story) What is a witch? What kind of things do you think witches do? (After first story) Was the witch the sort of witch you had thought about? Was the witch kind to children? Were the children kind to the witch?

Library corner

★ *Witches and wizards (Macdonald 1980)*

★ *Sorcerer's apprentice (Ladybird 1983)*

★ *Meg and Mog stories (Heinemann 1982)*

Activities

★ Language work: ask the children to write spells, good spells and bad spells.

★ Shadow puppetry, using an overhead projector. Simple outlines of witches, cats, cauldrons can be used very effectively on an overhead projector.

★ Make a classroom cavern from frame and black paper. Provide masks, hats and black cloaks for a fantasy play.

★ Make a simple witch. Fold a rectangle of white card lengthwise. Keep the card folded. On the outside of the card, draw a line from the top left-hand corner to the bottom right-hand corner, incorporating a pointed shape for the brim of the hat. Hold the card together and cut out the symmetrical shape. Open out and draw a face and hands and decorate as you wish.

To make a classroom witch

Materials
Paper bag
Newspaper
Adhesive tape, or string
A brush handle
Bucket full of sand and bricks
Large pieces of card
Black sugar paper

1 Fasten head and cone to a brush handle. Put it into a bucket with sand and wedge with bricks.
2 Wrap corrugated paper around the bucket to form a cylinder.
3 Make two cylindrical sleeves from black sugar paper. Attach them, plus hat and cloak, to figure.

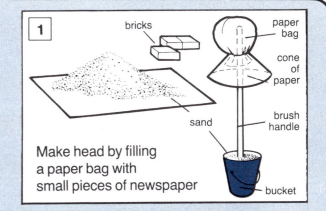

Make head by filling a paper bag with small pieces of newspaper

Wrap around with corrugated paper to make body

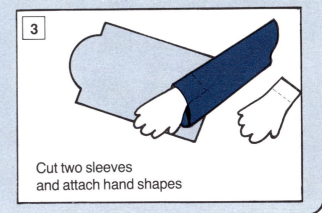

Cut two sleeves and attach hand shapes

Thanksgiving

The American festival of Thanksgiving is a happy time when people praise and thank God for all his gifts. It offers the opportunity to discuss with the children the social skills of saying please and thank you to those who help them each day. 'The story of William Penn' demonstrates the richness of the earth, the benefits of making friends with people of different cultures, and of living together peacefully.

The Pilgrim Fathers

In our country today live many different people who worship God in different ways. Some people go to chapel, others to mosques or temples, some go to synagogues and some to churches.

Long ago, people could not choose how they worshipped God. One group of people decided that they wanted to leave this country and go to America, where they could praise God in the way they wished. About one hundred people set sail in a tiny boat called the *Mayflower*. They were called the Pilgrim Fathers.

When the Pilgrim Fathers arrived in the new land, life was very hard for them. They had few tools to help them build homes. They were very short of food and often very hungry until their crops had grown.

When their first harvest was gathered in they thanked God because they were so pleased to have enough food for the winter. They invited the Indians to come and join in their thanksgiving festival. The Indians brought with them ducks and venison and other different kinds of food.

Since that time the American people have held a special Thanksgiving every year, on the fourth Thursday in November. Families come together and thank God for their homes, their food and their friends. Everyone has a happy time eating special food – turkey and pumpkin pie – and dancing and singing together.

The story of William Penn

Many years ago the people who left England to make new homes in America found the life very hard. But their lives were made easier by using what they found on the land. Rivers gave them water to drink, and fish to eat. Trees were used to make houses. Crops grew quickly in the fertile ground. Cattle gave them milk, from which they made cheese and butter, and hens gave them eggs.

But still the newcomers were in great danger because the tribes of Indians did not want to share the land with others. Often they came to the small camps by night and set fire to the huts and sometimes killed the animals and the people.

One man called William Penn decided that he must try to talk to the Indians. Everyone told him that he would be killed if he went near the Indian camp. But William Penn was very brave. He went and made friends with the Indian people and showed them that people can live on the land and share its riches. After that the people were able to live in peace. They were no longer afraid that they would be attacked because the Indians became their friends. At the time of Thanksgiving the Indians joined in the feast and the people enjoyed these happy times together. They all realized that it was far better to be friendly than to fight each other.

Land of the silver birch

Land of the silver birch, home of the beaver,
Where still the mighty moose wanders at will.
Blue lake and rocky shore, I will return once
    more.

CHORUS (children tap chests like Red Indians)
Boom de de boom boom,
Boom de de boom,
Boom de de boom boom,
Boom!

Down in the forest, deep in the lowlands,
My heart cries out for you, hills of the north,
Blue lake and rocky shore, I will return once
    more.

CHORUS

High on a rocky ledge, I'll build my wigwam,
Close by the water's edge, silent and still,
Blue lake and rocky shore, I will return once
    more.

More ideas

HYMN
Thank you Lord for this new day (*Come and praise*, BBC Publications 1978)

SONG
Yankee Doodle (*Sing a Song 1*, Nelson 1978)

..Things to do.............

Discussion

★ Do you know any people who have come to live in this country from lands across the sea? Which countries have they come from? Has anyone been to a land across the sea? What was it like there? Would you like to live there?

★ Do you go to a mosque, temple, church, chapel or synagogue? What do you do when you go there? When do you go?

★ Imagine that a little girl from the planet Mars arrived in our playground today. Although she looked very different from us she came up to you and said she wanted to be your friend. How would you feel? What would you say to her?

Library corner

★ *Indians* (Macdonald 1980)

★ *People and customs* (Macmillan 1979)

★ *Different peoples* (Macdonald 1982)

Activities

★ Dress up as cowboys and Indians and perform two American country dances: Skip to my Lou and Sandyland.

★ Make plates of model food, e.g. chips: roll long strips of newspaper and paint golden brown; baked beans: use tiny pebbles from a builder's yard, paint these orange and apply a coat of varnish.

To make a wigwam

Materials

Coloured activity paper
Printing materials (potatoes, bottle tops etc.)
Crayons
Straws or pipe cleaners

1 Cut out a semi-circle from paper radius 20cm. Fold and fold again.
2 Open out and mark guidelines for younger children. Start at the lower edge and print pattern at base, using a printing method of your choice. Leave space above free. Print in alternate spaces. When dry, make crayon patterns in the interim spaces.
3 Stick straws or pipe cleaners along the folds on the inside. Draw the shape round to raise the form.

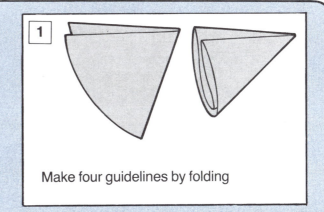

Make four guidelines by folding

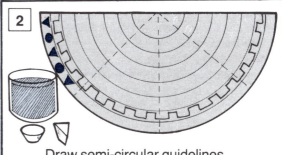

Draw semi-circular guidelines
Print and crayon patterns alternately

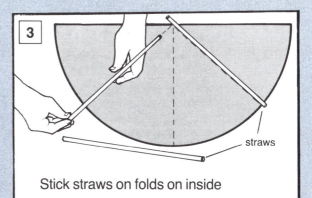

Stick straws on folds on inside

Kind Deeds

The aim of this topic is to show that there are people in our world today who dedicate their lives to performing kind deeds and serving the needs of others. Mother Teresa is a shining example of a life dedicated to caring for the welfare of poor people.

Mother Teresa

Far away, in the town of Calcutta in India, there are many poor people. Some of these people have no homes and live on the pavements. Often new-born babies are found among the rubbish because their mothers are too poor to feed them. Mother Teresa works to help these poor people.

Mother Teresa was born in Yugoslavia. When she was eighteen, Teresa left her family. She was sent out to Calcutta in India. Teresa taught girls in a big school during the daytime. After school was over she would visit hungry, sick and lonely people.

Teresa went to live in an old shack so that she could be with the poor people. She did not want to wear rich clothes. Instead she wore a simple white cotton sari. She started a little school for the children and she asked one or two people to help her. They all asked their friends to help Teresa. Some gave food and some gave money for medicines. The town council gave Teresa two large rooms to house sick people, so that they could be nursed properly.

Since then, Mother Teresa and her helpers have started hospitals for disabled children who have no parents, or whose parents are too poor to feed them. Today Mother Teresa's helpers work in many places: the Middle East; Australia; Peru; and even in London, Rome, and New York where there are poor people too.

Junaid Baghdadi, a kind man

Once in Baghdad in Iraq there lived a very wicked robber. One night he went to rob a house. Once inside the house he saw many big bundles of rich cloth. He began collecting up the bundles and tied them together. Just as he was ready to leave with the cloth, he heard someone coming into the house. At first he was frightened but when he looked up he saw an old man with a candle. The old man began to talk to him in a friendly way and said that he would help the robber to carry the cloth. Each man took a bundle and they went off together.

After a little while the old man became very tired and started to stumble. The robber shouted at him angrily, "Do not stumble, we must reach my hide-out before sunrise, or we will be caught." The old man was weary but he carried on until they reached the hide-out.

The robber then said, "Now take a few pieces of the cloth and get out of here." The old man replied, "I do not wish to take any of the cloth. The house you robbed was my house, and you must be very poor if you need to steal cloth. If it will give you some comfort, keep all the cloth. If you need help from me again come back to my house." Then the old man went back home.

The robber was astonished. He thought to himself, "How can anyone be so kind? That old man helped me to rob his own house, he carried a heavy load for me, he listened to my angry words and now he has said he will help me and I can go to his house at any time." The robber felt so ashamed that he went back to the old man's house. Outside the house he met a woodcutter.

The robber asked the woodcutter if he knew who lived in the house. The woodcutter told the robber that Junaid, a very kind man, lived there. The robber went inside the house and put his head on Junaid's knees and cried many tears. He told the old man Junaid how sorry he was and asked to be forgiven. Junaid forgave him and ever after the robber lived a better life.

More ideas

HYMN
Kum bah yah my Lord (*Someone's singing Lord*, A&C Black 1973)

POEM
Kind deeds (*Book of a thousand poems*, Evans 1959)

Contact the following charities:
Save the Children Fund
157 Clapham Road
London SW9 0PT

Oxfam
274 Banbury Road
Oxford OX2 7DZ

Christian Aid
240 Ferndale Road
London SW9 8BH

TEAR Fund
11 Station Road
Teddington
Middx. TW11 9AA

..Things to do............

Discussion

★ Have you ever seen anyone being kind to someone else? Has anyone ever been kind to you? What did they do for you? What sort of things can you do to show kindness to others?

Library corner

★ Food

★ Families

★ Working

★ Learning

The above four titles are in the Round the World series published by the Save the Children Fund, *(Macmillan 1981)*. They show how an agency helps in different ways in many different lands.

Activities

★ Write letters to charitable organizations, e.g. Save the Children Fund and Oxfam, for posters and educational literature.

★ Pay a visit to an old people's home and entertain the elderly with songs.

★ Make a full-size cut-out of Martin, the Roman soldier who gave half his cloak to a poor beggar (see instructions). Follow this up with displays of Roman history – soldiers, roads, camps, milestones – and visit a museum which covers the Roman period.

To make a Roman soldier

Materials
Large piece of cartridge paper
Strips of material
A large piece of material (cloak)
Tin foil

1 Spread the paper on the floor. Draw round an adult with one arm extended. Paint the shape. Cover lower part with strips of material to make a tunic.

2 Make a breastplate and a helmet from tin foil. Attach to figure. Decorate with milk bottle tops. Draw face and add shavings for hair and beard.

3 Fasten the cloak with staples. Draw footwear. Mount the whole shape on a coloured background.

Draw round an adult to give basic shape

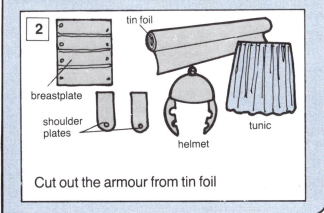

Cut out the armour from tin foil

Shepherds

The aim of this topic is to introduce the role of the shepherd as one of caring. The stories also offer opportunities for discussing obedience and truthfulness.

The naughty little lamb

Once upon a time there was a shepherd who had many sheep. The shepherd cared for his sheep and each day took them up the hillside to find fresh new grass for them to eat. Each night he brought them back down the mountain and counted them as they went into the sheep fold.

Some of the sheep had baby lambs. One day a little lamb left its mother's side and wandered away. It went on and on and took no notice of its mother's calls. Soon it was too far away to hear its mother calling.

That night the shepherd counted his sheep into the fold. He had noticed that one of his sheep had been bleating all the time as they came down the hillside. When he had finished counting he knew that the mother sheep was unhappy because her little lamb was missing.

The shepherd put his sheep safely in the fold and then went back up the hillside. He looked everywhere for the missing lamb and was about to go home when he heard a faint bleating noise. He went to the spot where the noise was coming from. There, at the bottom of a deep hole, something moved. It was the little lamb.

The shepherd used his crook to get the lamb out of the hole. He wrapped it in his cloak and carried it safely all the way back to the fold. Mother sheep was pleased to see her lamb and was so glad that they belonged to a shepherd who really cared.

Florence and the shepherd's dog

There was once a girl called Florence who was very kind. One day she met an old shepherd who was very sad. She asked him why he was so sad. The shepherd told her that he had a sheep dog whose name was Jip. Jip had been such a good friend and had helped the old shepherd for many years, but now Jip had hurt his leg so badly that he would not get better.

Florence asked the old shepherd if he would let her try to make Jip's leg better. Jip's leg was very bad but Florence bathed and bandaged it and took great care of him. Soon he was well enough to stand up again and as his leg became stronger he could go out with the old shepherd and the sheep. The shepherd was very pleased and thanked Florence very much for all the care which she had shown to Jip.

Many years later the little girl called Florence became a nurse. She looked after people and she taught other young people how to care for sick people too.
(adapted from Stories for infants, Blandford 1967)

The boy who cried wolf

There was once a shepherd who had one son. One day the shepherd said to his son, "My boy, you are old enough now to look after my sheep. Tomorrow you must get up early and take the sheep up on the hills to graze. Care for them well as I have always done. If any wild beasts should come near, call out loudly. The village people will come to help you. You need not be afraid, we always help each other."

Early the next day the boy took the flock of sheep to the hills. He watched them carefully all day and brought them home safely in the evening. He did this for several weeks and his father was pleased with him.

One day the boy thought that it would be fun if he played a trick on the village people. So he cried out in a loud voice, "wolf! wolf!" The village people heard his cry and ran quickly to his rescue. But when they got near the boy, he just laughed and they saw that there was no wolf at all.

A few weeks passed and the people down in the village heard the boy cry again, "wolf! wolf!" But this time they did not help him. "Ah! ah!" they said. "It is that boy again. We will not let him trick us this time." But up in the mountains a wolf had attacked the sheep, and had carried one of the lambs away.

When the boy came home at nightfall with some injured sheep and one lamb missing, his father was very angry with him and said, "Because you told a lie and said there was a wolf when there was no wolf at all, my friends did not believe you when you were telling the truth. That is why they would not help you."

More ideas

POEMS
The sheep; the wolf and the lambs (*Book of a thousand poems,* Evans 1959)

..Things to do.............

Discussion

★ Talk about the work of sheep farmers today and long ago, in this country and in other lands.

Library corner

★ Thank you for a woolly jumper *(Lion 1980)*

★ Hot and cold *(Macdonald 1973)*

★ David and Goliath *(Macdonald 1983)*

Activities

★ Science: fill three containers with very hot water. Cover one with woollen material, another with cotton, and the third with nylon. Show the children a thermometer and discuss its use. Record the temperature of each container early in the day, at lunchtime and late in the afternoon. Record the results.

★ Tell the story of David and Goliath of Gath (Bible reference: 1 Samuel 17).

★ Mathematics: measure other objects using the non-standard measure of cubit and span. Who has the widest span? How wide is your span in centimetres?

★ Display woollen garments, (a sheepskin rug, shepherd's crook, raw wool etc.). Also display pictorial evidence of shepherds long ago; different breeds of sheep; and shepherds and herdsmen in different parts of the world.

To make figures of David and Goliath

Materials
Large roll of paper
Paint and paint brushes
Collage materials

1 Measure the forearm of an adult to make a cubit and the outstretched hand of an adult to make a span.
2 Cut out six cubits and place them end to end. Cut out one span.
3 Spread out the large roll of paper and draw Goliath to the measurement, six cubits and one span.
4 David can be drawn by outlining a child. These templates are then painted, cut out and decorated with tin foil and other collage materials.

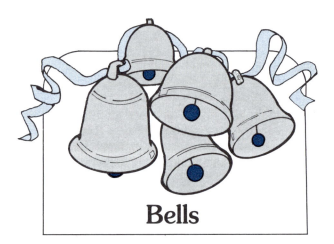

Bells

There are many kinds of bells which are used to give different aural signals. They also act as visual symbols. This topic is chosen to introduce children to the concept of 'sign', 'signal', or 'symbol', especially in religion. The story of 'The bell of Atri' encourages discussion of fair play and kindness to humans and animals. The story of 'Columba rings the bell' is about obedience and helpfulness to others in need and offers an opportunity to talk about the power of prayer.

The bell of Atri

There once lived a king who was wise and good and wanted all his people to live happily. So he decided that a bell should be put in the market-place and that anyone who was lonely, hungry or afraid could ring the bell and he would hear it.

A large wooden frame was built and the bell was hung up high. It had a long rope fastened to it. People came and rung the bell and the good king tried to help them all. Soon all the people were living happily together.

One day the king went into the market-place and saw that the rope on the bell was very worn. He told the bell-keeper to go and buy a new one. The bell-keeper took off the old rope. In its place he fastened a long piece of hay until he could bring a new rope. Off went the bell-keeper to get a new rope and while he was away he heard the bell ringing. He ran back quickly to the market-place.

All the people were gathered in the market-place to see who was ringing the bell. The king himself came to see what was happening. There was a poor, old horse pulling at the long piece of hay. The bell-keeper ran forward to shoo him away, but the wise king stepped forward. "Do not turn this old horse away," he said. "See how thin and hungry he is. He needs our help."

The king turned to all the people and asked who owned the poor horse. A rich man came forward and said that once the horse had belonged to him, but now that the horse was old he no longer wanted him. The king was very cross that the rich man was being so unkind to the poor horse. He told the man that he was not fit to have any animals to care for and that any he had would be taken from him and given to someone who would take care of them.

The king then sent for his stable boy and told him to take the old horse and care for him, feed him and see that he was never hungry or unhappy again.

Columba rings the bell

Long ago there lived a man whose name was Columba. He went to live on a small island called Iona. Some of his friends went with him and he called them his brothers. The brothers lived together in a big house. Next to the house they built a little chapel which had a bell and a bell rope. Columba and his brothers helped the people of the island to farm the land and sometimes would go out on the sea with them to help them catch fish.

One day as the brothers were working in the fields a fisherman came running to the house of the brothers. He told Columba that across the sea there was a small island, and on that island there was a poor man who was very sick and needed help. Columba called one of the brothers, whose name was Cormac, and told him to go to find a boat and sail out to the island and help the sick man.

Cormac had just set sail when a very strong wind began to blow, and soon a fierce storm was raging. Columba was very worried about his brother Cormac for he knew that he was in danger, and that if he was shipwrecked by the storm he would never reach the sick man.

Columba went and rang the bell. The other brothers heard the bell and came running to see why it was ringing. Columba told them what had happened and asked them to pray that Cormac would be safe and be able to reach the island. The brothers did pray and then went back to their work.

Sure enough, not many days later, Cormac's little boat came sailing to the shore. The brothers all ran down to welcome him. Cormac told them how he had been afraid but how he had suddenly felt that God was helping him. He had been able to reach the island and help the sick man who was now much better. The brothers all smiled for they knew that their prayers had been answered.

More ideas

POEMS
Silver bells; the donkey (Book of a thousand poems, Evans 1959)

HYMN
Bells (Sing a new song, REP 1969)

..Things to do............

Discussion

★ There are many different kinds of bells and they convey many different meanings. Door bells call one's attention; school bell signifies time; cowbells, place; bicycle bells, warnings; church bells, important occasions; fire bell, alarm; etc.

★ Discuss the need for, and importance of, visual signs and symbols such as road signs, washing symbols on clothing etc.

Library corner

★ Sounds *(A&C Black 1968)*

★ Noises *(Macdonald 1973)*

★ Hearing *(Studio Vista 1975)*

★ Listen and hear *(Burke 1973)*

★ The highway code

Activities

★ Science: set up a circuit to show how a doorbell works.

★ Make bottle bells and experiment with different sounds according to water levels.

★ Make a collection and display of bells (cow bells, alarm clock, school bells, bicycle bell, ornamental bells, percussion bells etc.).

★ Tell the tale of 'Dick Whittington and his cat'.

To make a bell decoration

Materials
Egg cartons
Tin foil
Floral ribbon
Gummed paper
A piece of card

1. Cut out three bell shapes from egg cartons. Cover with tin foil. Push the foil well over into the inside. Thread floral ribbon of differing lengths through the holes in the top of each 'bell'. Knot the ends.
2. Make a template and cut out holly leaves, and berries, from gummed paper.
3. Cut a circle of card and cut out an inner circle. Keep the outer ring. Stick holly leaves and berries on to the outer ring. Staple the floral ribbons holding the bells to the top of the ring.
4. Use raffia or floral ribbon to cover staples and make a bow.

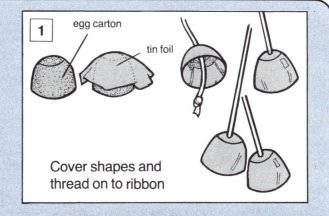

Cover shapes and thread on to ribbon

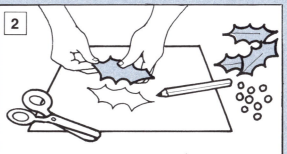

Use templates to draw and cut out holly leaves and berries

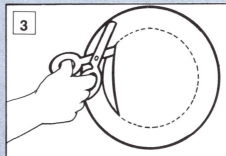

Cut a circle of card for basic shape

Presents and Giving

Everyone loves to receive presents and therefore this topic has immediate appeal. The aim is to display customs of giving in other lands. At the time of religious festivals, gifts are often exchanged to show love, thought and consideration for others. The gift may be very small, but the kind thoughts are much more important.

The spirit of giving takes different forms in different lands: St. Nicholas or Sinter Klaus in Holland, Père Noël in France, Santa Claus in the USA, Julienese (a tiny elf) in Norway, der Weihnachtsmann in Germany, Yul Tomten (a dwarf) in Sweden, Baboushka in Czechoslovakia and parts of Russia, and La Befana in Italy.

A poor boy gives a present

Long ago in India there lived a teacher known as the Buddha. He walked from village to village teaching people how to live happily. In one of the villages lived a little boy, who had heard all the people saying that the great teacher was coming to visit their village. The little boy waited by the road, and soon he saw the Buddha coming along the road with some friends. The Buddha was dressed in a simple robe. He went to the centre of the village. The people gathered to hear the great teacher. He told them that if they wished to live happily, they must follow these rules:

They should not be greedy or selfish.
They should not steal.
They should not tell lies.
They should hurt no living thing.
They should work hard.
They should think of others before themselves, and always be kind to everybody.

After the teacher had finished speaking, the people of the village went to get little gifts of food for the Buddha and his friends. Everyone brought a gift except the little poor boy, who had nothing at all to give. He wanted to give something to the Buddha so he knelt down and scooped up in his hands some grains of sand, which he gave to the great teacher. The Buddha smiled at the little boy and said 'thank you' because he knew that the little boy was trying to be kind.

Baboushka

Long ago in Russia, there was an old woman named Baboushka. She lived in a small hut in the middle of a forest. It was wintertime and the ground was covered with snow. As Baboushka sat in front of her fire she heard a knock on her door. Baboushka was afraid. "Who are you?" she called. "We are travellers from a far country," was the reply.

It was such a cold night that Baboushka felt very sorry for the travellers, so she opened the door and invited them into the warmth of her poor little house. The three travellers wore very rich clothes. They told Baboushka that they were kings who were following a bright star which they knew would take them to a place where a baby king had been born. Baboushka gave the travellers a place to rest for the night.

The next day the three kings asked Baboushka if she would like to go with them to find the baby king, but Baboushka said that she was very busy. So the kings set out and Baboushka went about her work. But she was not happy. "I should have gone with them to help them find that baby king," she said. "I will go tomorrow." That night she packed a bag with all kinds of little things that children like so that she could take it to the baby king.

The next morning she set out on her journey. She asked everyone she met if they had seen a bright star, or if they knew the way to the baby king. She walked on for many days, still carrying her little bag, but she did not find the baby king.

On her journey she met many children who were sad, hungry and unhappy and she gave each a little present from her bag to try to make them happy. Some people believe that Baboushka is still travelling around the world at Christmas time. Everywhere she goes she carries her bag and gives presents to children who are kind and bring happiness into the world.
(In Italy the children know this story but instead of the woman being called Baboushka she is named La Befana.)

More ideas

STORIES
The story of St. Nicholas (traditional)

POEMS
The little tree (Nursery song and picture book, REP 1947)
The Christmas party (Book of a thousand poems, Evans 1959)

..Things to do............

Discussion

★ Have you ever received a present? When did you receive it? Who gave you the present? Why did they give it to you? Have you given presents to anyone?

★ In multicultural schools encourage children to talk about their own particular festivals and customs of giving.

Library corner

★ *Festivals* (Macdonald 1984)

★ *Festivals around the world* (Macmillan 1983)

Activities

★ Make a collection of parcels of different shapes and sizes. Use multicoloured decorative wrapping paper. Some of the presents should be small, some large. Some should be heavy, and some light. The parcels can be used for display, to introduce 3-D shape recognition and to assist the development of concepts of relative weights and sizes. The parcels can be filled with everyday objects from the classroom. The children should be encouraged to guess what is inside them.

★ Ask the children to make up stories about the elf Julienese or the dwarf Yul Tomten.

★ Make gift tags (see instructions) and ask the children to write or to say to whom they would give a present, and what they would write on the gift tag.

To make a gift tag

Materials
A small piece of card
Coloured pens and pencils
A piece of cord
Scissors
Staples or tape

1 Draw the outlines for each shape on the card. They are symmetrical so just draw one half of the shape.
2 Fold the paper along the dotted line and cut out around the shape. Open out and punch a hole in the hat.
3 Draw a face, hat and clothes. Colour in.
4 Put a double piece of cord through the hole in the hat and attach the tag to a present with staples or tape.

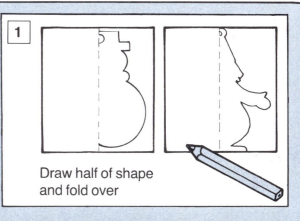
Draw half of shape and fold over

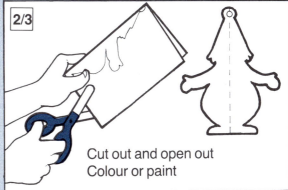
Cut out and open out
Colour or paint

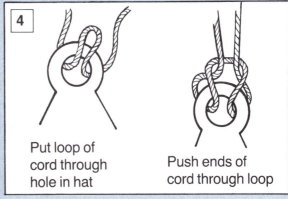
Put loop of cord through hole in hat
Push ends of cord through loop

Christmas

Christmas is celebrated in many lands but there may be children in our schools who come from homes where Christmas is not celebrated. Christmas is presented here as the birthday of Jesus, a time of goodwill and happiness when people show kindness in words and deeds; a time of greeting and good wishes; and a time for giving presents as the three kings did long ago.

The bright star (a play)

ALL SING: first verse of 'Winds through the olive trees' (from Third 60 songs for little children, OUP 1933)

Child dressed as a star stands centre, and says:
A twinkling star was shining and bright
And down it looked on the earth one night.
[Enter Mary and Joseph]
It saw mother Mary and Joseph so poor
An ox and an ass and a stable door.
[Innkeeper opens door]
The stable door was opened wide
And Mary and Joseph went inside.
[Shepherds enter and sit round fire]
A twinkling star was shining and bright
And what did it see on the hills that night?
Some poor old shepherds were minding their sheep,
Whilst the baby lambs were fast asleep.
[Angels enter and stand round shepherds]
A twinkling star was shining and bright
What did it hear on the hills that night?
It heard a choir of angels sing
They told the shepherds, "Good news we bring."
[Exit angels. Shepherds get up and walk round the stage]
The shepherds got up and left their sheep
A baby king they went to seek.
As down the road the shepherds walked
To one another they gently talked
Of a baby king, and the angels' song
And they came to a stable before very long.

ALL SING: 'Come in, come in the stable door stands wide.' (Hymns and songs for children, National Society 1964)

[Innkeeper opens the door. Mary and Joseph and the manger centre stage]
The stable door was opened wide
And so the shepherds went inside.
They were glad they had found the way
To a little baby who had slept in the hay.
[Enter a second bright star and the three kings]
Now over the desert another star shone
This star in the sky was a very bright one
Three kings from the east saw the very bright star
And came riding on camels from great lands afar.

ALL SING: the carol, 'We three kings'

They followed the star and saw that its beam
Shone down on a stable or so it did seem
They knocked on the door
With the gifts in their hands
Which they brought for the baby
From far distant lands.
[A group of children then say:]
So when we wake up on Christmas Day
And see presents, candles and trimmings so gay
We too will remember these wonderful things
The shepherds, the manger, and the three kings.
We'll think of all children in lands far away
And wish for each one a happy Christmas Day.
(adapted from 'A twinkling star', Child Education 1959)

When the littlest camel knelt

Long ago in a faraway land, a little camel went on a long journey with three men who were going to find a king. For many days they followed a bright star, until they saw the star shining down on a very poor stable. The travellers took presents from their bundles and went inside the stable. The little camel went forward and peeped inside. There he saw a mother, a father and a lovely little baby whom they had named Jesus. There were some poor shepherds, an ox and an ass. The travellers were giving presents to baby Jesus and were very happy. The little camel knew that he had seen a very wonderful thing. Very quietly he knelt down and when he looked at the other animals they were kneeling too. Although that was a long time ago, children all over the world think of that poor stable at Christmas time.

More ideas

SONG
Song of Christmas (Sing a new song REP 1969)

..Things to do.............

Discussion

★ What sort of weather do we usually have at Christmas? Would you like to spend Christmas in a hot country? What would you like to do if the weather was hot?

Library corner

★ The Christmas book *(Macdonald 1978)*

★ Christmas *(Macdonald 1981)*

★ The Christmas book *(Methuen 1964)*

Activities

★ School frieze: 'Christmas or winter customs in other lands'. Each class should take a Christmas or winter custom from a different land.

★ A school project to make a nativity scene. Each class makes one figure, e.g. a king.

★ Make a simple Father Christmas. 1. Take a toilet roll. 2. Cut a piece of paper, (5.5cm long, 3.4cm deep). 3. Fold sides back to meet and draw a smiling face. 4. Stick face round tube. 5. Take piece of red crêpe paper (9cm × 11cm) and gather it round tube. Fasten with an elastic band just under the face. 6. Turn back frill. 7. To make hat, join ends of a piece of red crêpe paper (5.5cm × 5cm) and sellotape together. Pull top together and tie. Turn up bottom edge. 8. By sellotaping inside the brim, fasten hat to figure. 9. Add tiny pieces of cotton wool for hair and beard, and bobble on hat.

To make a Christingle

Materials
An orange
A small piece of tin foil
Four cocktail sticks
A mixture of nuts and dried fruit
A candle
A piece of red ribbon

1 Choose an orange that stands firmly and will not roll. Cut a hole in the top to hold the candle. Cut a circle of foil to line the hole and turn back.
2 Put the candle in position.
3 Put the fruit and nuts on the cocktail sticks and place near the top of the orange. Tie a red ribbon round the orange.

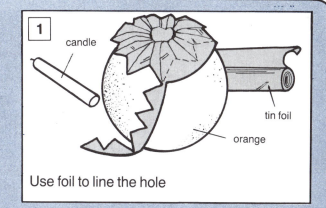

Use foil to line the hole

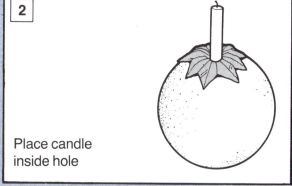

Place candle inside hole

Make up the four cocktail sticks and insert into orange

The New Year

By using the theme of new year, the children are made aware of new year customs in many lands and also of religious new year festivals which do not fall on 1 January. Most of these festivals are a time of 'new beginnings' – a time for saying sorry for past wrongs and trying harder to do things better in the future.

New year customs

1 January is the beginning of the new year. In England, some people go to watchnight services in churches. At midnight, the church bells ring to welcome the new year. In some families, one member of the family goes outside just before midnight on 31 December, and when midnight strikes comes back into the house to bring in the new year. In the north of England people light fires and hold torchlight processions. Some bring in the new year with symbols of coal, bread, salt and money. In Scotland people celebrate Hogmanay and visit the homes of friends to wish them happiness.

In Switzerland there are bell-ringing contests to welcome the new year. In many countries, Old Father Time walks hand-in-hand with a young child to represent the old year and the new. In Japan the new year festival is known as Ganjitsu. The people celebrate for six days. They pay their debts and say sorry to anyone with whom they have quarrelled. On New Year's Day the first thing they do is to drink water from a well for they believe that this will keep them healthy throughout the year.

Religious new year festivals

People of different religions hold their New Year festivals at different times.

For Jewish people, Rosh Hashanah is the time for new year celebrations. They say sorry for things they have done wrong and make a fresh start.

For Christians, Advent Sunday is the beginning of the religious year. Advent is a time when Christians get ready for the coming of Jesus. Children hear the story of how the angel Gabriel told Mary that she was going to be the mother of Jesus. Advent Sunday is in late November or early December. There are four Sundays in Advent. Some people make an Advent wreath with four candles and light one on each Sunday before Christmas.

Muslims celebrate the religious new year on the first day of Muharram, the first month in the Muslim calendar. It is called Hijrah, and is a time when Muslims tell stories about the life of the prophet Muhammad.

For Hindus, the new year festival is called Diwali.

The kind man and the wolf

Long ago there was a man who lived by himself in the desert. He was a kind man who loved all the animals that lived in the desert. There was one big wolf who was his special friend. Each day the man shared his dinner with the wolf.

One day the man made his dinner ready and then heard the cry of an animal. He went to see if the animal was injured. While he was away the wolf came and saw the dinner. He did not know whether he should begin to eat it or not, but he felt so hungry and the food smelt so good that he ate it all. Then the wolf hurried away as fast as he could.

When the kind man came back he knew what had happened. For several days the wolf did not come because he knew that he had done wrong. The man wished that the wolf would return, for he missed his friend. One day the wolf did come back. He was walking very slowly with his head hung down. He was ashamed and sorry. He went and stood in front of the kind man who said, "You have been a bad wolf but I can see that you are sorry, so I will forgive you."

The man and the wolf were friends again because the wolf was brave enough to come back and say that he was sorry.
(adapted from 'The monk and the wolf', stories for infants at home and school, Blandford 1967)

A calendar rhyme

Thirty days hath September,
April, June and November
All the rest have thirty-one
Except February alone
Which has twenty-eight days clear
And twenty-nine in each Leap Year.

More ideas

STORY
Onito's hat (A&C Black 1978)

HYMN
One more step (Come and praise, BBC Publications 1978)

..Things to do............

Discussion

★ Through discussion, establish what is meant by new year. Discuss the months of the year, new year customs in different lands and religious new year celebrations which fall on dates other than 1 January.

Library corner

★ The new year *(Wayland 1985)*

★ Festivals *(Macdonald 1981)*

★ Festivals and customs *(Wheaton 1979)*

★ People and customs *(Macmillan 1979)*

★ Onito's hat *(A&C Black 1978)*

★ The year around us *(Dinosaur 1982)*

Activities

★ Make a classroom wall calendar for the month of January. Incorporate a weather chart *(see instructions)*

★ Use a calendar to encourage mathematical skills by counting the days, weeks and months.

★ Draw a bar chart graph to show in which months birthdays fall. In which month are the most birthdays celebrated?

★ For a school project each class should work on one new year project. Write about it, draw and paint it and then display your results for discussion.

To make a weather chart

Materials
A piece of card or paper
Squared paper
A brass paper clip
Pencils
Paint and paint brushes

1 Cut out a circular piece of card. Divide it into six segments. Add a needle pointer by attaching a brass paper clip to the centre. Stick this on to a large piece of paper. Write the six climatic conditions – cloud, rain, sun, snow, wind, fog/mist – on six separate pieces of paper.
2 Draw the weather symbols on to the weather chart. The pointer is moved each day as the weather changes.
3 Duplicate a 18cm × 18cm square, or use squared paper. Write the days of the week across the top line of squares. The rest of the squares are divided diagonally. The children write the numerals in the top half of the square and each day place a weather symbol in the bottom half of the square.

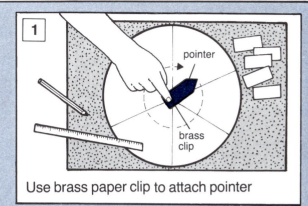

Use brass paper clip to attach pointer

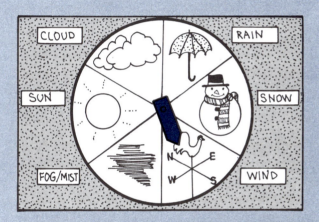

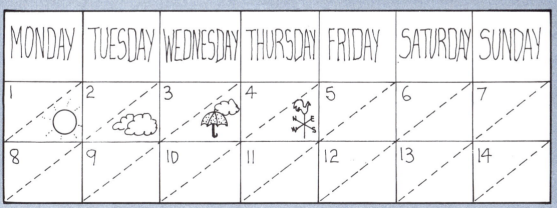

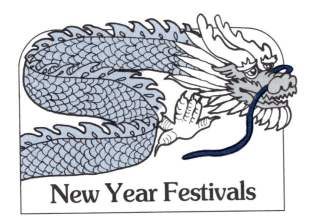

New Year Festivals

The aim of this topic is to promote understanding of people of different creeds and cultures by introducing the children to their festivals, beliefs and folklore. In 'The story of Diwali', where good triumphs over evil, the children are introduced to Diwali, the New Year festival for Hindus.

'The monster and the red doors' is a story about the Chinese New Year. Towards the end of the old year, offerings of sweet things are made to the kitchen god, Tsao Chun. Pictures of Tsao Chun are then burnt in the hope that he will give a good report to the great god, Emperor Jade. On the last day of the old year, Tsao Chun returns and a new picture of him is placed in the kitchen. In the streets there are processions, with musicians and dancers. On the last night of the festival, when there is a full moon, the festivities last all night long until the moon disappears from the sky. There is a great parade in which a huge dragon dances through the streets protected by people dressed as lions (see also pages 110-111).

The story of Diwali

In the land of India there once lived a handsome prince whose name was Rama. Rama married a very beautiful girl called Sita and all the people were very happy.

Rama's father was an old man so he decided that he would give his throne to Rama. Rama had several brothers and they were all happy that Rama was to become the next king. But someone was not happy. The old king had a wife who thought that her son, Bharata, should be the next king. So she tricked the old king into sending Rama away and making Bharata the ruler.

Rama told Sita to stay at the palace where she would be safe. But she followed him, and they went away together into the forests.

Not far away, on an island called Lanka, there lived a demon king called Ravana. He was a very wicked creature with ten heads. While Rama and Sita were roaming the forests the demon king Ravana captured the beautiful Sita whom he wanted for his wife and took her back to Lanka.

Rama was helped by some monkeys who built a bridge so that Rama could cross to the island of Lanka and kill the wicked demon Ravana. Rama shot an arrow which killed Ravana and then found his beautiful Sita once more. They were so happy to be together again.

Rama and Sita went back to their own land where Bharata was waiting for them. He was very pleased that Rama and Sita had returned. Bharata took them to the throne where he had put a pair of Rama's shoes to remind all the people that Rama was the true king (for a more detailed account of this story, see pages 128-129).

The monster and the red doors

Long ago in China there was a small village where the people were very frightened. A large monster prowled about in the hills nearby. Each night he came down to the village at nightfall and captured one of the villagers to eat for his supper. The villagers did not know what to do. They were too frightened to try to fight the monster.

One afternoon a young girl was washing her clothes when she saw the monster coming towards her. She had just hung a piece of red cloth on a tree to dry. She was too frightened to scream and could not run away. The monster came nearer until suddenly the breeze blew and the red cloth moved and began to flap about so that it looked like red flames. At that moment the monster let out a shriek and turned on his heels and fled towards the hills.

The monster has never been seen since. At the time of the new year all the people remember the monster and put red paper on their doors so that no evil monster will try to get inside their homes and no good luck from the inside will escape.

Chinese New Year

The lanterns are out and our street is all gay,
The people are having a festival day
We'll have fireworks and crackers and
  dumplings to eat
And tonight a huge dragon will come down
  our street.
Our friends come to visit from far and from
  near,
For today is so special, it's Chinese New
  Year.

More ideas

SONG
Puff the magic dragon (*Sing a song 1, Nelson 1978*)

..Things to do..............

Discussion

★ Compare and contrast the different ways in which New Year festivals are celebrated in different parts of the world.

Library corner

★ Festivals and customs *(Wheaton 1979)*

★ Festivals and celebrations *(Blackwell 1979)*

★ Festivals *(Macdonald 1981)*

Activities

★ Draw or paint Ravana, the wicked ten-headed creature, or Chinese dragons.

★ Make Chinese fans.

★ Display willow pattern crockery, fans, Chinese writing, pictures of Chinese people and cities.

★ Make a Chinese dragon. Create the basic shape of the head from chicken wire. Cover the structure with newspaper soaked in cold water paste. Last coat is of small pieces of tissue paper to give skin effect. Paint. Use white card for teeth, paint eyes and nostrils. Use bright orange/red card for flames from mouth. To make the body, dye a long piece of material. Decorate it with 'scales'. Stitch the edges together and insert hoops to give 'body'. Add a tail and legs and join the body to the head. Suspend from the ceiling.

To make a lantern

Materials
Coloured activity paper
Decorative paper (wallpaper or gift wrap)
Glue
Scissors

1 Paste a sheet of decorative paper on to a piece of coloured activity paper leaving 3cm at each edge uncovered.
2 Draw dotted lines along the width of the decorative paper, about 1cm apart. Fold and cut from fold to the edge of the decorative paper.
3 Open out, and fold round so that the edges form a small overlap. Stick down and glue.
4 Cut a small strip for a handle and paste it into position at the top of the lantern.

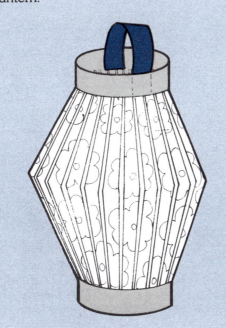

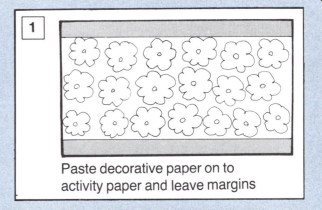

Paste decorative paper on to activity paper and leave margins

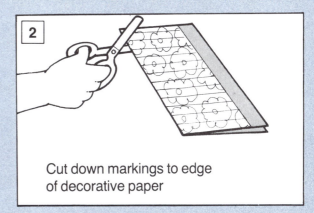

Cut down markings to edge of decorative paper

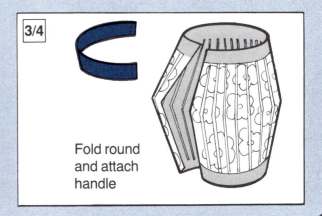

Fold round and attach handle

43

Shiny Things

Throughout the ages shiny things have been considered synonymous with beauty and goodness. The aims in introducing this topic are to help children to observe differences in properties and to appreciate beauty in the world around them. 'The woodman and his axe' highlights the importance of honesty and the story of 'The king who wanted gold' shows that the beauties of nature are as valuable as gold and other riches.

The woodman and his axe

One day a woodcutter was chopping down some trees by the side of a river. As he swung his axe he let it go and it fell into the water and sank to the bottom. The woodcutter was poor and this made him very sad because he did not have enough money to buy a new axe. He sat down on the river bank and wondered what his family would do, for if he had no axe he could not work and they would all go hungry.

Suddenly he looked up and there he saw a sprite who lived at the bottom of the river. The sprite asked the woodcutter if he could help him. The woodcutter told the river sprite what had happened and, without saying another word, the sprite dived into the water and brought up an axe made of shining gold.

"Oh! That is not my axe. My axe was an old iron axe," said the woodcutter. The sprite dived into the river again and this time brought up another axe, made of silver. It was a beautiful shiny axe too. The woodcutter again said, "Oh! That is not my axe. My axe was an old iron axe." Once more the sprite dived deep into the river and this time brought up the old dull iron axe. "That is my axe," said the woodcutter. The sprite handed the woodcutter the axe. Then he said, "You are a truthful and honest man so I want you to have the shiny gold and silver axes also." The woodcutter could not believe what had happened and went home and told his friends.

The next day one of his friends went by the river and pretended to chop down some trees and dropped his axe into the water. The river sprite came as before and asked if he could help the man. When the river sprite brought up a shiny gold axe the man said that it belonged to him. The river sprite was very cross. He threw the axe back into the river and said to the man, "You have not told the truth so you shall not have the shiny golden axe and what is more you shall not have your own back either."

The king who wanted gold

Long ago there was a king in Greece whose name was Midas. King Midas was very rich and had many lovely treasures but he was very greedy and always wanted more gold.

One day King Midas met one of the Greek gods, whose name was Dionysius. Dionysius told King Midas that he could have whatever he wished for. Without thinking, King Midas asked that everything that he touched should turn to gold.

King Midas touched the flowers and they turned to gold, he touched trees and they turned to gold, he touched his tables and chairs and they became shiny gold. Everything went well for a short time. But when he began to eat and drink, the food and drink turned to gold and his clothes turned to gold and were very uncomfortable.

As evening came, the king's beloved little daughter came to say goodnight. As soon as she touched her father she became a little gold statue. King Midas was now very sad and rushed out of his palace to take the steep pathway that led to the top of Mount Olympus. He went to Dionysius and asked if he could take away the power of the wish. Dionysius listened to the king's story and knew that Midas realized how greedy he had been and that he was sorry, so he took away the power of the wish.

King Midas went back down the mountain and realized that gold is not the only lovely thing. There are many beautiful things to see, and hear and touch. He saw the colours of the grass, flowers and trees, he heard the songs of the birds, he touched things and found that some were dry, some wet, or soft, smooth, rough. When he arrived back at the palace gate his little girl was waiting for him and she ran into his arms and hugged him. So Midas then knew that having all these different living things around him was far better than everything being made of gold.

More ideas

HYMNS
All things bright and beautiful (Songs of praise, OUP 1931)

POEM
The silver house (Book of a thousand poems, Evans 1959)

..Things to do.............

Discussion

★ Do you prefer days when the sun shines or dull days? Are we usually happier when the sun shines? Can we 'shine'? Can we make people happy? When you see a dark sky, a shining moon and lots of twinkling stars, what do you think about?

Library corner

★ *Light* (Lion 1984)

★ *Stars* (Macdonald 1979)

★ *Batteries and bulbs* (Macdonald 1973)

Activities

★ Mathematics: do shape work on pentagons and decagons.
Science: experiment to show loss of heat. Fill four similar bottles with hot water. Cover each with a different material – wool, cotton, nylon and tin foil. Take the temperatures at different times, record and discuss the results.

★ Give experience of reflections – use of kaleidoscopes, mirrors, and other shiny surfaces.

★ Make a display of articles sorted according to properties of shiny and dull.

★ Display the sign of the crescent moon and star with artefacts of the Muslim religion, e.g. prayer mats; pictures of mosques; the books Muslims use when they attend the mosque.

To make a five-pointed star

Materials
A sheet of A4 activity paper
A pencil
Scissors

1 Fold the piece of A4 activity paper once and letter A, B, C, D. D is the midpoint of AB.
2 Take C and fold forward to rest on D.
3 Fold the triangle OAC backwards. Then fold in towards C along the line OP.
4 Turn the form over completely and mark a point Z, as shown. Cut from A to Z. The shorter the line OZ, the more pointed the star. (To cut along AX gives a pentagon.)
5 Open out, and you will have the five-pointed star.

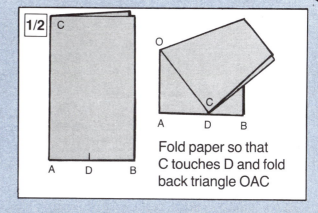

Fold paper so that C touches D and fold back triangle OAC

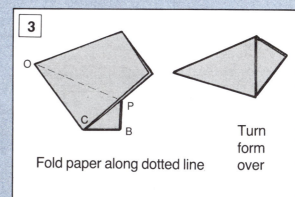

Fold paper along dotted line

Turn form over

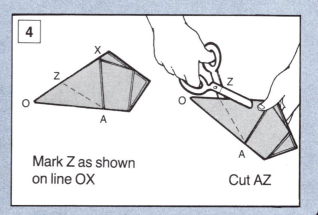

Mark Z as shown on line OX

Cut AZ

45

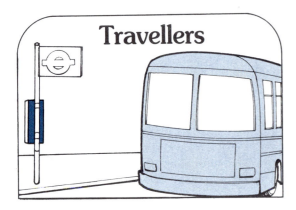

Travellers

Since early times people have been travellers. Long ago, travelling was very hazardous and even today there is still an element of risk. Travellers today often need help from others in order to reach their destination. The aim of 'The poor traveller' is to demonstrate that cooperation and helpfulness should be extended to all people irrespective of differences in colour and creed. The story of 'The Indian boy and the robbers' reiterates the importance of truthfulness.

The poor traveller

Long ago in a faraway land a poor old man had to travel along a lonely road. In those days, people travelled together in groups because there were many robbers who lay waiting by the roadside. The old man was travelling alone and knew that it was very dangerous. He came to a lonely part of the road and suddenly robbers jumped out from behind some rocks and beat the old man, snatched his purse and ran away. The old man was left badly injured by the roadside.

After a little while a man came along that way. He saw the injured traveller and said, "Oh dear, someone is hurt but I cannot stay because I'm in such a hurry. Someone else will help him." The man went on his way.

Soon another rich man came along. He looked at the injured traveller and said, "Oh dear, someone is hurt but I don't know him. He is not one of my friends," and he also went on his way.

Much later that day another man came along riding on a donkey. He saw the poor man. "Oh dear, this poor traveller is injured," he said. "I don't know him, he is not a friend of mine, he doesn't live in my village, he doesn't dress in the same kind of clothes as I do, but he needs my help."

The man got off his donkey, gave the injured traveller a drink, bandaged his wounds and then lifted him onto his donkey and took him to the nearest inn. When they arrived at the inn the kind man asked the innkeeper to feed and take care of the injured man until he was well again, and he paid the innkeeper to do this.

The Indian boy and the robbers

Long ago in India there lived a boy who wanted to learn as much as possible about the world. One day he asked his mother if he could leave the family home and travel to a big town where there were many schools.

His mother agreed and made some food for the boy to take with him on his journey. She also gave him forty coins which she had saved. She knew that travellers could be stopped by robbers, so she put the coins into a little bag and sewed it into the boy's coat under his arm.

When the boy was ready to leave, his mother called him to her and said, "My boy, one thing you must always remember. Always tell the truth. It will save your life."

The young boy set out on his journey with some other people, but as they were travelling along, robbers came down from the hills. The robbers stole everything they could find. One of the robbers then went up to the boy and asked him if he had anything else. The boy replied, "Yes, I have forty coins." The robber thought that the boy was joking and took him to his chief. The chief asked the boy where the forty coins were and the boy told the truth. "They are in a little bag under my arm. I am not going to tell a lie for forty coins. Take them if you wish."

The chief robber was so amazed because the boy had been so honest that he did not take the coins. He even ordered the robbers to give back all that they had taken from all the travellers. The robbers were so ashamed of themselves that they asked the travellers to forgive them and promised not to rob again.

Down at the station

Down at the station, early in the morning,
See the diesel engines, standing in a row.
See the engine driver pull a little lever,
All aboard, all aboard, and off we go!
Down at the bus stop, early in the morning,
See the bright red buses standing in a row,
See the bus conductor ready on the platform,
Ding, ding, ding, ding, and off we go.
Down in the High Street, early in the morning,
See the shiny taxis standing in a row,
See the taxi driver start up the engine,
Peep, peep, peep peep, and off we go!
(traditional)

More ideas

SONGS
The happy wanderer; the runaway train (*Ta-ra-ra boom-de-ay*, A&C Black 1977)
The train is a'coming (*Apusskidu songs for children*, A&C Black 1975)

..Things to do.............

Discussion

★ How did you come to school this morning? How many different kinds of travel do you know? Why do people travel? Have you ever been on a long journey? What do you know about travelling long ago?

Library corner

★ Land travel *(Macmillan 1979)*

★ Things that go *(Usborne 1981)*

Activities

★ Act out the story of 'The poor traveller' and then a modern version of a traveller needing help.

★ Display pictures and books of travel by land, sea and air, through the ages.

★ Explore different ways of 'travelling', e.g. walk, run, hop, skip, jump, roll, crawl.

★ Mathematics: measurement of hops, jumps etc. Look at the workings of a simple timetable.

★ Science: how can we make things move? Wheels, levers, pulleys. Make a collection of wheels (from clocks, toys, bicycles etc.) and things with wheels (pastry cutters, toy cars, egg whisks etc.).

★ Arrange for a talk on road safety. Invite the lollipop person, or a member of the police force, into the school.

To make a street scene

Materials
Card
Matchboxes
Small rectangles of sponge
Paint
Gummed paper
Frieze paper roll
Glue
Corrugated paper
Other collage material

1 Make brick effects by printing with small rectangles of sponge.
2 Cut out house shapes from the printed paper. Add gummed paper for roofs, doors and windows.
3 Cut out shapes of cars, lorries, buses etc. in card. Stick a matchbox on the underside to make them stand out from the frieze.
4 Stick houses at the top of frieze, vehicles in the middle, overlapping the houses, and people, cut from card, along the front.

Print brick shapes with sponge dipped in paint

Add roof shape windows and doors

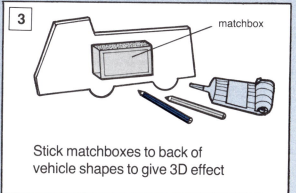
Stick matchboxes to back of vehicle shapes to give 3D effect

Winter

Winter can be presented as a time when there is much beauty to be seen although the world is 'sleeping'. The aim in introducing seasonal topics is to encourage observational skills and foster a sense of wonder. A further aim is to remind children that old people often need help during the long winter months, as in 'The story of King Wenceslas', and that winter can be a difficult time for animals and birds.

The story of King Wenceslas

There was once a good king named Wenceslas. He always tried to help everyone. One evening in wintertime he was looking out of his window. It was a very cold night. The silver moon shone down and the stars twinkled brightly in the sky. Snow had fallen and lay very deep on the ground. As the king looked out he saw a poor man in ragged clothes. The man was gathering sticks of wood to take home for his fire. Wenceslas knew that the poor man was very cold and wondered what he could do to help him.

Wenceslas sent for a young boy who worked in the palace and asked him if he knew the old man. The boy said that the man lived in a little cottage at the foot of the mountain.

Wenceslas wanted to help the old man so he said to the boy, "Go and get some food, some drink and some logs to take to the home of this poor man. We will see that he has something to eat, something to drink and a fire to keep him warm." The boy and the king then set out together in the bitter cold. The wind was blowing very hard and it was difficult to walk in the snow.

Soon the boy said, "Oh! Master, I cannot go any further." The king said, "We must go on. Walk behind me and I will shelter you from the wind. Put your feet into my footprints and you will find it easier."

The boy did this and they reached the cottage of the poor old man. They went inside and gave the man the food, the drink and the logs they had brought. The poor man and his family were able to make a warm fire and have a good meal because King Wenceslas had been so kind.

A Greek myth

Long ago people believed that there were many gods and goddesses who ruled the earth and the universe. One of these gods was called Hades who was ruler of the underworld. There was also a goddess called Demeter who was the earth goddess. The Greek people used to tell this story of how winter ends and spring arrives.

One day, Persephone, the daughter of Demeter the earth goddess, was picking flowers when Hades, the god of the underworld, came along in his chariot driven by four black horses. He took Persephone in his chariot and carried her back to the underworld. Demeter was so sad that she let all the flowers on earth die and the cold winds of winter blow over the earth.

Demeter searched for Persephone and found that Hades had taken her away. Demeter asked Hades to give back her daughter but Hades would only allow Persephone to return to Demeter for part of the year.

When Persephone is with Hades in the underworld it is wintertime and the world is sad and bare. But when Persephone returns to her mother, spring comes and the flowers grow again because Demeter is so happy.

Jack Frost

Look out! Look out!
Jack Frost is about
He's after our fingers and toes;
And, all through the night,
The gay little sprite
Is working where nobody knows.
He'll climb each tree,
So nimble is he,
His silvery powder he'll shake;
To windows he'll creep,
And while we're asleep,
Such wonderful pictures he'll make.
Across the grass
He'll merrily pass
And change all its greeness to white;
Then home he will go,
And laugh, "Ho! Ho! Ho!
What fun I have had in the night!"
(Book of a thousand poems, Evans 1959)

More ideas

POEM
Ritsch, ratsch, filibom! *(Sugar plum Christmas book, Hodder and Stoughton 1977)*

SONG
The north wind doth blow *(Sing a song 2, Nelson 1979)*

..Things to do............

Discussion

★ What kind of clothes are you wearing today? How do birds and animals keep warm in winter? What are the signs that tell us that it is wintertime? Will it always be winter? What will the next season be? Do old people like wintertime? Why do they find winter a hard time? Who else finds winter a difficult time?

Library corner

★ Animals in winter *(A&C Black 1979)*

★ A walk in the snow *(Macdonald 1984)*

★ Winter *(Dinosaur 1978)*

★ Winter *(Evans 1979)*

Activities

★ Make symmetrical snowflake cut-outs from white paper. Spot with white adhesive and sprinkle with glitter dust. Suspend at different heights.

★ Mathematics: look at the hexagon and other symmetrical shapes.

★ Science: investigate freezing and melting.

★ Make drawings of bare twigs. Notice the buds, leaf scars etc.

★ Grow bulbs.

★ Make scrapbooks of pictures cut from magazines about life in cold lands.

To make and dress a doll

Materials
Card
Scissors
Collage materials (cotton, nylon, felt etc.)
Glue

1 Cut out a basic shape suitable for a boy or a girl.
2 After cutting out the basic shape, make small templates in card. The children can use these to help make clothes which will fit the form.
3 Use the form to make the patterns of different articles of clothing. Include patterns for winter and summer clothing and clothing of people of varied cultures.
4 Use all kinds of collage material to make the figures more life-like.

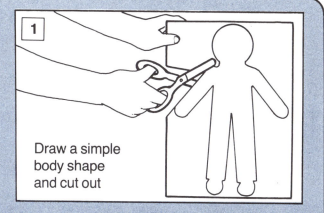

Draw a simple body shape and cut out

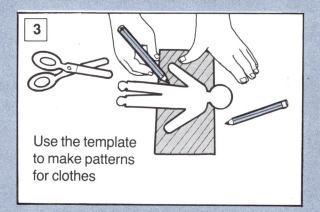

Use the template to make patterns for clothes

Use collage materials to dress the shape

Birds

This topic presents opportunities to discuss migration, and the different climates of the world. It also encourages children to appreciate how difficult it can be for birds to survive during a harsh winter and stresses the importance of caring for, helping and protecting the weak.

A little bird in Africa

A man and his wife lived in a small house in a village in Africa. They had grown some plants on a shelf which ran along one side of the small house, and in among the plants a little bird had built a nest. In the nest the bird had laid four small eggs. Soon the eggs hatched out into baby birds.

One warm afternoon the man and his wife heard the little bird giving a very loud call. It went on calling and then came up to the door of the house still calling very loudly. The man went to the door and the little bird flew a short distance as if it wanted the man to follow. The bird called again loudly so the man followed and it went back to its nest. There the man saw a snake that had come to kill and eat the baby birds.

The man shooed the snake away. One little bird was already dead but the others were safe. The little bird had asked for help and the man had been able to help her and save three of her babies from the snake.

Piccola and the baby bird

In a small village by the sea there lived a little girl called Piccola. Piccola lived with her mother and father. Father was a fisherman but he had been very ill and had been unable to go to sea. His family had become poorer and poorer, but Piccola was a happy little girl and even when there was little to eat she always found something to smile about.

It was wintertime and almost Christmas when Piccola's father said, "My dear Piccola, although we love you very much, we are too poor to buy a gift for you."

Christmas Eve came and Piccola took off her small wooden shoes and put them by the fireplace. The next morning when Piccola awoke she went to put on her shoes, and there inside one of them was a tiny, helpless baby bird which had fallen from its nest and dropped down the chimney. The poor little creature was dirty and shivering with cold. Piccola called out, "Father, mother, come quickly and look at my Christmas gift." Piccola was full of joy. "What a wonderful gift," she said. The tiny bird was very weak but Piccola loved it and cared for it so well that it was not very long before it grew into a strong bird that could chirp and sing. The bird made Piccola and her family very happy.

The blackbird

(A three-part verse that can be used by three groups of children speaking the different parts)
First child (or first group of children):
Out in the garden, up in a tree
There is a blackbird, singing to me.
Second child (or second group of children):
What is he singing, up in the tree?
What is he piping, so merrily?
First child:
Come out in the garden,
Come out and hear!
Stand still and listen,
(But not too near).
Blackbird (third group of children):
I love the wind, and the stars, and the moon.
I love the sun when it shines at noon;
I love the trees, but I love best
My little brown wife in our cosy nest!
First child:
That is the song he's singing to me,
That's what he's piping – so merrily.
(Book of a thousand poems, Evans 1959)

Birds

Two little brown birds
Sitting on a twig
Both very plump
But neither very big.
"Tweet!" said the first one,
"Cheep!" said his brother
Wasn't that a funny way
To talk to one another?
Both little brown birds
At the set of sun
Flew into a big tree
Because the day was done.
Cuddled in a warm nest,
Cosy as could be,
Mustn't it be lovely
Sleeping in a tree?
(Book of a thousand poems, Evans 1959)

More ideas

HYMN
Little birds in wintertime (*Someone's singing Lord*, A&C Black 1973)

..Things to do.............

Discussion

★ Have you seen any birds today? What kind of birds? What were the birds doing? Some birds gather in flocks in autumn to fly to other lands. Why do they go? Do any birds come to this country in winter? Where do they come from?

Library corner

★ *The birds from Africa* (Macdonald 1980)

★ *Migrating birds* (Dinosaur 1982)

Activities

★ Make and set up a bird table. Children take turns to feed the birds. Keep records of the birds which come to the table.

★ Arrange for a walk in a park to feed the ducks. Point out how their feet are adapted for swimming and their beaks for feeding.

★ Produce duplicated sheets of bird outlines for the children to colour in, using authentic colours, and cut out. Name the birds and make a class picture.

★ Make bird mobiles. Cut out the basic bird shape and make a cut where the wings will go. Decorate the flat shape and add tinsel to head and tail. Pleat a piece of coloured paper or tissue and push flat. Insert it into the cut to give equal length each side of the bird shape. Open the pleats out and push upwards. String from between the wings and hang the birds as a mobile.

To make a hand-printed peacock

Materials
A large sheet of paper
Powder paint
Coloured tin foil
Scissors
Glue

1 Draw the basic shape of a peacock for children to paint and cut out.
2 Children make handprints on paper and cut them out. Use blue, turquoise and green colours.
3 Stick the basic shape on to a large sheet of paper leaving space all round.
4 Stick the handprints into the space. Overlap. Add circles in green and blue and gold foil. Add tiny foil circles to the top of the crest.

Cut out and paint basic shape

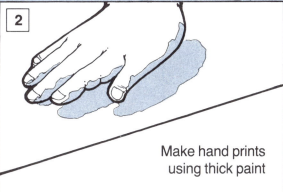
Make hand prints using thick paint

Stick cut-out hand prints and foil circles to backing sheet — foil circles

Candles

Candles have been used for a very long time by people of many different faiths because light has been associated with good, and darkness with evil. The Jews, Hindus, Buddhists and Christians all use candles during worship. The candle is regarded as a symbol of light, life and truth, and the triumph of good over evil.

Festivals of light.

Christian – candles are used at Christmas because Christians think of Jesus as the light of the world. They are also used at Candlemas each 2 February. This is to remember the time when Jesus was received as a young child in the temple by Simeon, an old priest, who called Jesus, "a light to lighten the gentiles."
Buddhist – at Magha Puja, 1250 candles are lit in the largest of Buddhist temples as Buddhists remember a time when 1250 people were enlightened, i.e. began to follow the teachings of the Buddha.
Hindu – during the New Year festival of Diwali, Hindus light up their homes to welcome Lakshmi, the goddess of prosperity, into their homes.
Jewish – candles play a big part in the eight-day festival of Hanukah, in December.

Hanukah

Long ago the Jews had a very cruel ruler named Antiochus. Antiochus would not allow the Jews to worship God as they wished and he took their temple from them.

The Jews were very angry about this. They banded together under a leader called Judas Maccabeus, fought off the army of Antiochus and won the temple back. When they went inside the temple they found that it needed to be cleaned. They found the temple lamp and were about to light it when they noticed that there was only a little oil left.

When they lit the lamp they expected it to burn for one night but it went on burning for eight days. Judas Maccabeus said that every year all Jewish people should remember this miracle and celebrate for eight days. The Jewish people call this festival Hanukah.

In Jewish homes a large candlestick called the Menorah, or Hanukiah, is put on a windowsill so that the light of the candles can shine out for all to see. It has nine branches. Prayers are said as a candle is lit each night. The people thank God for keeping them safe and caring for them.

Jewish children love this festival because they eat special food and get presents on each of the eight days. The families sing songs and play games with little spinning tops called 'driedles', and everyone has a happy time (for a more detailed account of the festival of Hanukah, see pages 130-131).

St. Lucia

In Sweden the people have a special festival on 13 December. They remember a girl who lived a very long time ago on the island of Sicily in the Mediterranean sea. The girl's name was Lucia which means 'light'. The people on the island of Sicily were ruled by the Romans who would not allow people to worship as they wished. Lucia became a Christian and gave away money to the poor. The Romans said that Lucia was a witch and they captured her and put her to death.

Now there are processions each year in the big cities of Sweden to remember Lucia. A girl is chosen to be Lucia and with her attendants she leads the procession through the streets to the big town hall. The girl has a crown of candles on her head and is dressed in a long, white dress.

Within each family the eldest girl dresses up as Lucia. Very early in the morning she gets out of bed and takes little cakes, like ginger biscuits, and a drink to the other people in the house. Later in the day, they give presents to each other.

Each school chooses its own Lucia. She is dressed in white, sometimes with a red sash, and she always wears the crown of candles and evergreens. Lucia and the girls who are chosen to be her attendants walk in a procession round the school. Sometimes boys are attendants and are called star boys. During the procession the other children sing a song called Santa Lucia. After the procession there are usually parties and everyone has a happy time as they remember Lucia of long ago.

More ideas

HYMN
Give me oil in my lamp, keep me burning (Come and praise, BBC Publications 1978)

POEM
A giant's cake (Book of a thousand poems, Evans 1959)

..Things to do............

Discussion

★ If you go into a dark room, what is the first thing that you want to do? What did people use long ago to light their houses? Why do people use fewer candles today? Have you ever had a birthday cake? Why did you have candles on your cake? Have you seen any candles which were not on a birthday cake? Where did you see them? What were they used for?

Library corner

★ *Light* (Lion 1984)

★ *Candles* (Macdonald 1976)

Activities

★ Make a class picture of St. Lucia. Use fairy lights to protrude through the backing paper.

★ Mathematics: make candle clocks. Place two side-by-side in identical candle holders. Make sure they are safe. Light one candle. After a set period of time, part of the candle will have burned down. Place a mark on the second candle which represents that period of time. Light the second candle and test to find if it burns at the same rate as the first candle.

★ Science: examine torches and batteries to find out how they work. Make a simple circuit. Discuss good and bad conductors.

★ Make scrapbooks of utensils we use to heat and light our homes today.

How to make a candle

Materials
A toilet roll holder
Clay or plasticine
Small pieces of spruce or evergreen
Paint and paint brushes
Pipe cleaner
Glue
A piece of paper

1 Cut a shape for a flame. Use two of these and stick each one on either side of a pipe cleaner.
2 Paint (or cover) a toilet roll holder. Wedge the toilet roll into a piece of clay or plasticine, pushing clay securely around the base.
3 Put the pipe cleaner through the toilet roll and push it into the base. Adjust the length if necessary.
4 Add small pieces of spruce or evergreen. Tiny cones can also be pressed into the clay. Small baubles on wire add colour to the base.

Make a flame shape and attach to pipe cleaner

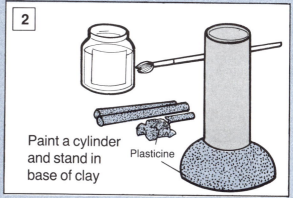

Paint a cylinder and stand in base of clay

Insert pipe cleaner through cylinder and into base

Our School

The school should be presented as a small interdependent community where the children can find opportunities for caring, sharing and helping others on a day-to-day basis. From the school we look outwards, firstly to people who visit the school from the immediate community and then to children in other parts of the country, and beyond to other lands.

Schools in other lands

Schools in hot lands begin their day very early. Children often walk long distances to school, sometimes barefoot. Some children in Australia live so far away from a school that they have to listen to lessons on the radio.

In some African schools lessons are held out-of-doors. The children sit on the ground and draw letters in the sand. In big towns there are schools like our own but in the villages they may be built of mud bricks and roofed with corrugated iron. Often there are very many children in a class. More schools are being built but there are still not enough.

Many children do not go to school or have to leave school when they are very young to work on farms. Some schools have farms attached where children learn all about how to farm.

The boy who disliked school

Long ago in China there was a little boy called Mencius. He lived with his mother. They were very poor. When Mencius was old enough his mother took him along to school. Mencius soon found that he would rather play than work but he made no friends because he was unwilling to take turns and share things with the other children.

Mencius's mother felt very sad that her boy no longer wanted to go to school to learn. So she decided to teach him a lesson. At that time she had a lovely piece of weaving on her loom. "Come here, Mencius," she said. "Look at my work. This has taken a great deal of time and effort. Tomorrow I shall take it to market and I shall sell it. I shall spend some of the money on food that you will eat and clothes that you will wear. I am ready to work and share my things with you and so you must do your work and be ready to share your things with others."

So Mencius went back to school, and worked hard at his lessons. He found that it was fun to make friends, to play games, to take turns and to share things with others. He grew up to be a clever man who was able to help many people.

Alfred learns to read

Once upon a time there lived a queen who had three young sons. The queen hoped that they would be good and wise so she decided that she would try to teach her sons to read. In those long ago days there were very few books and not many people could read.

So one day the queen told the boys that she would give a beautiful copy of the Bible as a prize to the one who learned to read first. The three princes all tried hard at first but soon the eldest boy grew tired and went off to play with his bow and arrow. The second prince preferred to be out-of-doors fishing in the ponds, so when the reading became difficult he also gave up. The youngest one liked to play games with his brothers but each day he spent some time learning to read the book.

After a time the queen called her sons to her and asked each one to read the book to her. The eldest said that he could not read; the second son said that he could not read; but the youngest son, whose name was Alfred, was able to read a story to his mother. The queen gave Alfred the book as his prize.

The years passed and it was Alfred, the youngest prince, who became king. When Alfred was king he did all he could to help more people to read. He was such a wise king that he is now called Alfred the Great.

A school creed

This was found inscribed on the back of a door in an old school in Canada:
This is our school.
Let peace dwell here.
Let the rooms be full of contentment.
Let love abide here:
Love of one another,
Love of mankind,
Love of life itself,
And love of God.
Let us remember
That as many hands build a house,
So many hearts make a school.

More ideas

SONG
The work calypso (*Sing a song 2*, Nelson 1979)

..Things to do............

Discussion

★ Talk about the various people who work in the school and the different tasks they perform. Also discuss the people who visit the school, and the reasons for their visits.

★ When, how and by whom was the school built?

★ Discuss different kinds of schools, schools of long ago, and schools in other lands. How do they compare with your school?

Library corner

★ David's first day at school *(Hamish Hamilton 1981)*

★ Going to school *(Macdonald 1981)*

★ At school *(Evans 1982)*

Activities

★ Create a school portrait gallery. Ask the children to paint portraits of the people they meet in school (friends, teachers, dinner ladies, lollipop persons etc.).

★ Mathematics: graph work to illustrate 'things I like to do best in school'; number of children in each class; number of boys and girls; number of children of different ethnic origins.

★ 'People who help us' booklets: make illustrated booklets about the different occupations of people who in some way help towards the life of the school.

To make a weaving mat

Materials
Gummed paper
Strips of coloured paper
Scissors
Glue

1 Take a 20cm square of gummed paper and prepare with slits, 3cm apart.
2 Also prepare strips of coloured paper, the same width as strips in base mat, but of varied colour.
3 Thread the loose strips under and over the strips in the frame. Stick loose ends at the edges.
4 This weaving mat technique can be used on different shapes, e.g. a Martian.

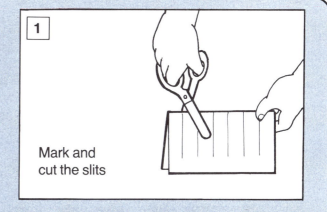

Mark and cut the slits

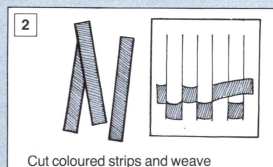

Cut coloured strips and weave them in and out of base

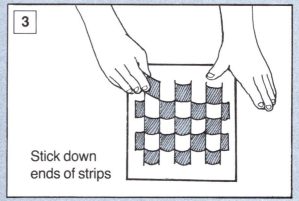

Stick down ends of strips

Morning and Night

There are many things for which we should be thankful. A new day is one of them, but this happens so often and so regularly that we take it for granted. Each day there are people all over the world who worship God as they wake up in the morning for they think of every day as being a gift from God. The aims are to demonstrate how we share the sun with children in other lands, and to show how some people are willing to work during the night to care for the needs of others.

A traveller calls at night

A long time ago in India there lived a wise man named Guru Gobind Singh. He taught the people that God loves all men and women the same whether they are rich or poor. He told the people that they should care for everyone, and that if any travellers should come to their door, whether it was during the night or during the day, they should always show them kindness and be ready to offer them a meal.

Very early one morning when it was still dark, the guru dressed himself up as a poor old traveller and went around the city in disguise. He wanted to see if the people were following his teaching and whether they would give him a meal.

He knocked on one door but the people were still in bed and there was no reply. He knocked on a second door and heard voices telling him to go away. He then came to a third house and when he knocked on the door he was invited inside. He was treated very kindly and given something to eat. Guru Gobind Singh knew that the family who lived at this house were trying their very best to be friendly to those in need.

Guru Gobind Singh was the leader and teacher of the people we call Sikhs. In our towns and cities today we often see Sikhs. Many wear a type of head-dress which we often call a turban. They worship at a place called the gurdwara and all gurdwaras have a kitchen where food can be prepared for those who need it.

The lady with the lamp

Many years ago there lived a little girl called Florence Nightingale. She was a kind girl and loved to help other people. She did not like to see any living creature in pain. When she was old enough she told her parents that she was going to become a nurse. Her mother and father did not like the idea but Florence persuaded them that she would be happy helping others. Florence had to work hard and learn how to bathe and bandage wounds and many other things so that she would be able to nurse her patients properly.

When Florence had finished her training there was a terrible war which took place in a land far over the sea. Many men were wounded and nurses and doctors were needed to go and help them. Florence set out with a few other young women. When they arrived at the hospitals where the wounded soldiers lay, they worked very hard to nurse the men who were in great pain because of their terrible wounds.

The soldiers all knew how kind Florence was. She worked very hard all through the day. When night came and all was quiet she walked around the hospital carrying a little lamp so that she could see her way. She went quietly from one soldier to the next to see if she could help them. Even when the men were very ill they could see the tiny lamp shining in the darkness and because of this they called Florence "The Lady with the Lamp".

That was many years ago but doctors and nurses today sometimes work all through the night while we are sleeping so that those who are ill are properly cared for.

Someone

Someone came knocking on my wee small door
Someone came knocking I'm sure, sure, sure
I listened, I opened, I looked to left and right
But nought there was but a stirring in the still dark night.
Only the busy beetle tap tapping on the wall,
Only from the forest the screech owl's call
Only the cricket whistling while the dewdrops fall,
So I know not who came knocking,
At all, at all, at all.
(Book of a thousand poems, Evans 1959)

More ideas

HYMNS
The golden cockerel; morning has broken (*Someone's singing Lord, A&C Black 1973*)

SONG
Sing a song of morning (*Sing a new song, REP 1969*)

..Things to do............

Discussion

★ What are the differences between daytime and night-time? Does everyone go to bed at night? Would you like to work during the night? What time is your bedtime?

★ Do all creatures sleep at night? Do some animals come out only at night? Why do they prefer to be awake at night?

Library corner

★ *The Sikh world* (Macdonald 1985)

★ *My day begins* (Macdonald 1980)

★ *My morning* (Macdonald 1980)

★ *My afternoon* (Macdonald 1980)

★ *My bedtime* (Macdonald 1978)

Activities

★ Science: demonstrate how we experience daytime and night-time by using a torch and a globe.

★ Mathematics: discuss the different times in a child's day (e.g. getting-up time, lunchtime, bedtime etc.). Illustrate these and display alongside a clock face at the appropriate times.

★ Make a display frieze showing nocturnal animals (badgers, owls, foxes etc.). Use this to stimulate free writing on topics 'I am a badger', 'I am an owl', 'a night in the forest'.

To make an owl

Materials
An egg-box
Brown paint
Brown and orange pieces of tissue (or gummed) paper
Paint and paint brushes
Glue

1 Paint an egg-box brown. Place the blank side uppermost. Cut two large circles, and two smaller circles of different colours, for the eyes. Stick these as shown.
2 Cut many small triangles from brown tissue (or gummed) paper. Two different shades of brown give the best effect.
3 Begin at bottom edge and stick the small triangles to the carton so that they overlap. Use lighter brown shade on breast.
4 Cut orange triangles of appropriate size and stick on to form a beak, feet and wings.

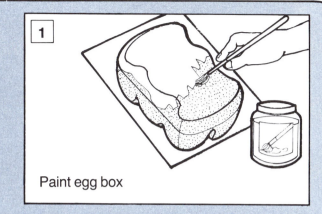
Paint egg box

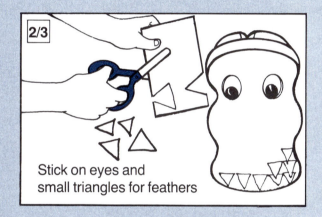
Stick on eyes and small triangles for feathers

Add a beak, wings and feet

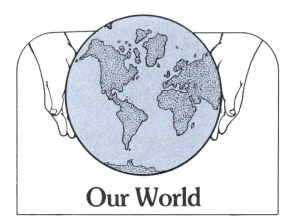

Our World

The aim of this topic is to broaden children's perceptions of our world. The two stories introduce children to the ancient belief that God is the creator of all things. The activities section encourages conservation, which is presented in terms of caring for our world and keeping it beautiful.

How Krishna saved the world

The great god Brahma made the world. It was very beautiful but after a time the men who lived on the earth became wicked. In India there ruled a very wicked king whose name was Kansa. He did so many evil things that the people believed he must have been a demon. They asked the great god Brahma to help them and this is what happened.

Kansa had a sister named Devaki and her husband was named Vasudeva. One night Kansa thought that he heard a voice telling him that Devaki would have eight sons and that the eighth son would kill him. When Kansa heard this he tried to kill his sister Devaki. But Devaki's husband, Vasudeva, grabbed Kansa's arm as he tried to strike her with his sword. Vasudeva then promised Kansa that they would give the king any baby boys as soon as the babies were born, if he did not harm Devaki.

As the years passed, Devaki had seven little boys. Vasudeva and Devaki kept their promise and gave each one to the bad Kansa. The bad Kansa killed each baby boy as soon as he saw it.

When Kansa learned that Devaki was going to have her eighth baby he cast Devaki and Vasudeva into prison. He told the guards to stand outside the prison cell and as soon as they heard cries to rush inside and kill the baby if it was a boy.

That night a great thunderstorm arose. As the thunder roared, Devaki's baby was born. They named him Krishna. The storm was so bad that the guards did not hear the baby's cries. The great flashes of lightning had made their eyes so tired that they had gone to sleep.

Brahma then spoke to Vasudeva and told him to wrap the baby Krishna up and take him to a farmhouse where a poor farmer's wife had just given birth to a new baby girl. Vasudeva did this. He exchanged the baby boy for a baby girl.

In this way Krishna was saved from the sword of evil Kansa. The baby Krishna was brought up by the poor farmer and his wife. When Krishna grew to be a man he knew he had to fight the wicked demon who was spoiling the world with his cruel ways.

Kansa had found out that he had been tricked, and he tried to kill Krishna, but his plans did not succeed. So Kansa asked Krishna to go to his palace. When Krishna went inside he saw there a very old man who had been the king before Kansa, and also his own mother and father, Devaki and Vasudeva. The evil Kansa said, "Now I will kill you all." Just at that moment Krishna ran forward and the wicked Kansa fell dead. The kind king who had ruled before Kansa, came back to his throne and ruled his people wisely and well.

The people of India were glad that the great god Brahma had sent Krishna to defeat the wicked Kansa. Every year Hindus in India celebrate the birthday of Krishna.

How God made the world

This is a very old story. It is a story which we can find at the beginning of the Bible. It tells us about how God made the world.

Long ago people believed that at the beginning of time there was no world, no sun, and no stars. So God made lightness and darkness and called the light, day and the darkness he called night. God then made the skies and the clouds and the earth.

God then covered part of the earth with seas and part of it with dry land. The earth was dry and bare so God commanded that grasses, trees and plants should grow on the earth and that they should have seeds so that new plants could grow.

God then made all living creatures. He made the fishes of the sea, the birds to fly in the skies, and the animals to roam the earth.

Last of all God made a man and a woman. The first man God called Adam and the woman he called Eve. They lived in a beautiful garden called the Garden of Eden. The world was very beautiful and God blessed the world which he had made.

More ideas

POEM
The wheel around the world (*The wheel around the world*, Macdonald 1978)

SONG
I'd like to teach the world to sing (*Apusskidu songs for children*, A&C Black 1975)

..Things to do............

Discussion

★ Where do you live? Do people in different countries live in the same way as we do? Do they live in houses like ours? Do they dress like we do? Do they eat the same kind of food?

★ What do you know about outer space? Is our world a planet? Do you know the names of any other planets of the sun?

Library corner

★ Peoples of the world *(Usborne 1978)*

Activities

★ Involve the children in a litter project. Children collect litter from a small area around the school. The litter is examined and sorted. Where did it come from? Has the school enough litter bins? Children then form 'litter teams', make badges for themselves, select a leader and try to solve the problem of litter.

★ Make a class wall frieze of the Creation (Genesis Chapter 1). Include darkness and light, sun, moon and stars; oceans, rivers and mountains; plants and trees; fishes, reptiles, insects, animals and humans.

★ A school topic: each class takes an appropriate theme e.g. our world, and other planets. The work of different classes is brought together. One assembly time is given to each class to explain their work to others. Suitable hymns, songs and poems are used with each topic.

To make a model African village

Materials
A strip of card 20cm × 6cm
Modelling tray
Sand, tiny pebbles
Plasticine
Green crepe paper
Newspaper
Glue
Corrugated paper
Floral wire

1 Make a cylinder from a strip of card.
2 Cut a circle from corrugated paper radius 6cm. Snip out a sector and raise to form a shallow cone. Mount the roof on to the base. Make a doorway.
3 To make the trees, roll newspaper to make trunks. Paint these brown. Cut out several leaf shapes. Stick two leaf shapes over a piece of floral wire. Group several leaves together. Insert the wires into the centre of the trunk. Push the bottom of the trunk into a knob of plasticine.
4 Arrange as a village on a modelling tray.

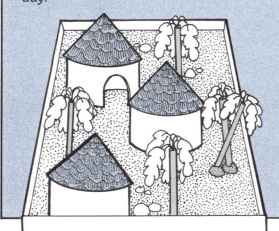

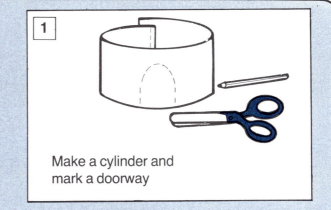

Make a cylinder and mark a doorway

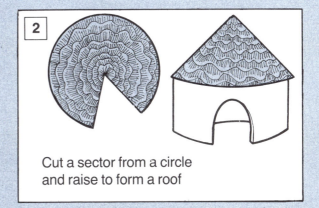

Cut a sector from a circle and raise to form a roof

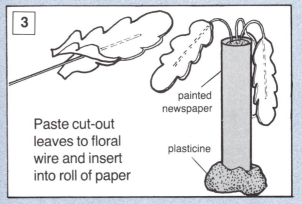

Paste cut-out leaves to floral wire and insert into roll of paper

The Sun

Superstition often blocks the way to true understanding and many beliefs based on old knowledge change as new knowledge becomes available. The aim here is to introduce the child to the beliefs of people long ago and to contrast these with our beliefs about the sun today. This offers opportunities for discussion of modern inventions, many of which make our everyday lives much more comfortable than the lives of our ancestors.

The sun god

Long ago people used to watch the sun move across the sky each day. They thought that the sun was a god who rode in a mighty chariot pulled by great horses. They called him Sol.

The people noticed that sometimes the god Sol seemed much stronger than at other times. In summer he was much hotter than he was during the winter. They thought that they could help to keep up Sol's strength by lighting big bonfires.

On 21 June they had a special celebration called Midsummer Night. On this night they had processions when people carried torches which burned brightly. Great bonfires were lit and the light from their flames shone up into the sky. The people thought that this would please the god Sol and make him stronger so that he could shine longer in the sky.

Today we know that nothing we can do can affect the sun. We know that our world is one of several planets which travel around the sun. The sun is in fact a big star which gives its light and its heat to the earth even though it is 93 million miles away.

We know these things today because people with clever minds have invented wonderful things. One of the instruments which help people to know more about the sun and the moon and the stars is called a telescope, but there are many things which people have invented which help us today. Can you think of some of them?

The house with the golden windows

At the edge of a little town stood a tiny house. It had walls made of red bricks, a roof made of grey slates, a green door and four windows. A little boy called Adam lived in this house with his mother and father and three brothers. One day in the summer, when the sun was shining brightly, Adam was sitting on the garden gate. He looked up the road and noticed that there was a house at the very top of the steep hill. The house looked like his own but the windows were very beautiful. "I have never seen windows like that before," thought Adam. "They are made of gold."

Adam fetched his brother to see the golden windows. They decided to visit the wonderful house. The house was such a long way away that the walk took them a long time. By the time they arrived it was late in the afternoon. As they approached the house they saw that it was just an ordinary house like their own. The windows no longer shone like gold. They were just glass windows like in their own house.

The boys were very disappointed. But, as they turned around to go back down the hill, they looked at their own little house. What did they see? They could not believe it. Their own house had golden windows! Yes, golden windows, or so it appeared, for the sun had moved round in the sky and was now shining down on the front of their little house.

The boys realized their mistake. The windows had not been made of gold at all. They now knew that each day everyone shares the sun's rays as they move across the sky. When they told their mother she said, "Yes we all share the sun's light and even when we are in bed at night, the sun shines on us all."

Five little spacemen

Five little spacemen sitting on the stars,
The first one said, "Let's all fly up to Mars."
The second one said, "There are rockets in the air,"
The third one said, "But we don't care."
The fourth one said, "Let's fly away so high."
The fifth one said, "Let's go up in the sky."
Then swish went the ship and out went the light,
And the five little spacemen flew right out of sight.
(Sing a song 2, Nelson 1978)

More ideas

STORY
The story of the sun and the wind
(Aesop's fables)

HYMN
The sun that shines across the sea
(Someone's singing Lord, A&C Black 1973)

..Things to do............

Discussion

★ If you are outside and look up at the sky, what kind of things do you see? (smoke trails, clouds, sun etc.). Why do we see different things during the day than at night?

★ How do we keep warm? Talk about the sun as the original source of all heat on earth.

Library corner

★ Sun calendar (*A&C Black 1983*)

★ Let's find out about the sun (*Franklin Watts 1977*)

Activities

★ Mathematics: make shadow clocks in the playground and measure the length of the shadows throughout the day.

★ Science: place one thermometer in the sun and another in the shade. Take readings at different times of the day.

★ Set up a display table of inventions. If possible, include binoculars, telescope, microscope, portable radio, computer, tape recorder, wheel, lever etc.

★ Make a wall frieze of the god Sol in his golden chariot riding across the sky. Use coloured dyes for good sky effects; metal foil papers which reflect the natural light; crepe paper and gummed paper in rich colours of gold, orange and yellow.

To make a sun bird mobile

Materials
Bright yellow activity paper (two squares, 25cm × 25cm)
Two pieces of orange gummed paper
A hoop
Fine wire
Yellow and orange crepe paper
Gold tinsel
Glue

1 Fold a piece of yellow activity paper into pleats about 2cm wide. Bend over in the middle to make a fan. Stick inside edges, A and B, to make a semi-circle.
2 Make two of these and join together to form a circle. Add eyes and a diamond shape folded over for a beak. Add legs from two concertina strips of yellow, plus orange feet.
3 Cover a hoop with strips of orange and yellow crepe paper. Run fine wires from circumference to circumference. Fasten the birds to circumference and diameter wires.

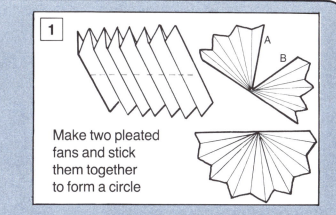

Make two pleated fans and stick them together to form a circle

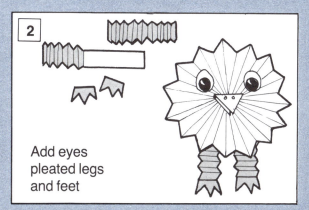

Add eyes pleated legs and feet

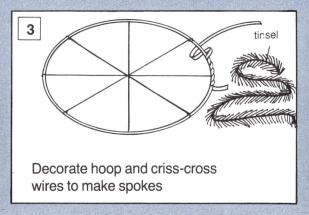

Decorate hoop and criss-cross wires to make spokes

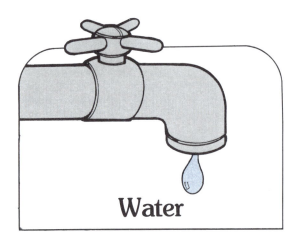
Water

The aim of this topic is to make the children aware that water is a very precious commodity which we in this country often take for granted. In many lands where the climate is different from our own, the people often have insufficient water, so that crops fail and famine results.

Muhammad and the well

Far away in the Arabian desert there is a city called Mecca. Long ago in this city there lived a man called Abdullah who had a wife whose name was Amina. Amina was very worried because there had been no rain for a very long time and the wells were running dry. All the people were hungry, some were very ill and there was no sign of rain. Amina knew that she was going to have a baby and she wondered how she would be able to feed the baby if the drought went on any longer.

One day Abdullah set out on a journey. Not long afterwards Amina heard that Abdullah had died. She was very sad. A few days later Amina had a little son. She named the little boy Muhammad. As soon as Muhammad was placed in Amina's arms rain started to fall very heavily. The people began to dance and sing for they were so happy to see the rain after such a long time. Amina thought that this must be a sign that her little son would grow up to be someone special.

When he was much older Muhammad married a very rich lady named Khadijah. Khadijah and Muhammad gave away most of their money to the sick and the poor. Muhammad always remembered how he had been poor when he was a young boy and was always ready to do all he could for those who were poorer than himself.

One day a young man came to Muhammad and told him that his mother had died and left him a lot of money and that he wanted to spend the money wisely. He asked Muhammad what he should buy with the money. Muhammad told the man to dig a well as a monument. Muhammad said that a well would be useful to all people, for the rich and the poor. The man did make a well and when the people went to fetch water they remembered the man's mother whose money had paid for the well.

Hagar and Ishmael

This is a story about a little boy named Ishmael who lived long ago in a desert land far across the sea. Ishmael's father was called Abraham and his mother's name was Hagar. In those days the people who lived in the desert lived in tents and kept sheep. They travelled about over the hot desert to find water for their animals.

One day Abraham and Hagar had been to the city of Mecca and had taken little Ishmael with them. On their way home it was very hot and the little boy, Ishmael, was very thirsty. Hagar tried to find water for her little boy but all the streams and wells were dry for there had been no rain for many months. Ishmael began to cry and Hagar knew that he could not go on for much longer without water.

Hagar searched everywhere for water. She became very thirsty too and the hot sun made her feel unwell. She held her little son in her arms and as she sat down to rest against a huge rock, Ishmael's mouth touched the rock. Immediately a spring of fresh, cool water began to trickle down the side of the big boulder and both Hagar and little Ishmael were able to drink.

Much later a well was built around the spring. It is called the well of Zamzam. Today Muslims who make a pilgrimage to Mecca drink at the well and remember how Hagar looked for water for her little boy Ishmael so long ago.

Insey winsy

Insey winsy spider
Climbed up the spout
Down came the raindrops
And washed the spider out
Out came the sunshine
Dried up all the rain
So insey winsy spider
Climbed up the spout again.
(repeat with actions alone, and end with a clap)

More ideas

STORIES
The stream; saying 'thank you' *(Stories for infants at home and school, Blandford 1967)*

HYMN
Have you heard the raindrops drumming on the rooftops *(Come and praise, BBC Publications 1978)*

SONG
There's a hole in my bucket, dear Liza *(Apusskidu songs for children, A&C Black 1975)*

..Things to do............

Discussion

★ Why do you need a tap in your house? Have houses always had taps? Look at other ways of obtaining water. In hot lands, how do people obtain water? What happens when there is not enough water?

★ Talk about the importance of pure water and the number of people involved in providing us with pure water. This is also an opportunity to discuss pollution of seas and rivers.

Library corner

★ *Things wet and dry (Franklin Watts 1978)*

★ *Wet and dry (Macdonald 1973)*

★ *Things outdoors (Usborne 1981)*

Activities

★ Make a simple rainfall gauge. Take a liquid soap container and cut off the top section. Invert the top part and fasten with four strips of sellotape. Surround with bricks to prevent tipping, or sink into the soil.

★ Science: conduct simple experiments in absorbency. Collect several articles, e.g. a sponge, piece of towelling, a log of wood. Weigh each one, then leave in water for an hour. Weigh each one again and record differences.

★ Science: set up experiments to show water in various states – ice (solid); water (liquid); steam (gas).

To make a flower posy

Materials
A circle of card 20cm diameter
A doyley 15cm diameter
Glue/staples
Tissue paper
Pencil
Blue, green coloured pens

1 Cut four strips of paper 8cm long and 1cm wide. Curl each one around a pencil. Glue or staple at the centre.
2 Screw tiny pieces of tissue to make a centre for the flower.
3 Take the circle of card, and stick a doyley on to it.
4 Cut four leaves from light-green gummed paper and mark the leaf veins in dark green or blue. Stick them, and the flower shape on to the doyley.

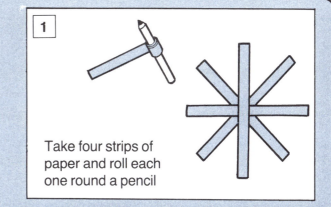
Take four strips of paper and roll each one round a pencil

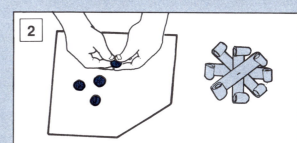
Roll tissue to form balls to decorate centre of flower

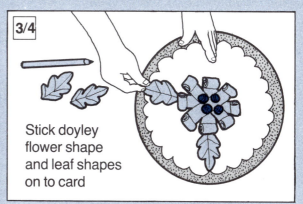
Stick doyley flower shape and leaf shapes on to card

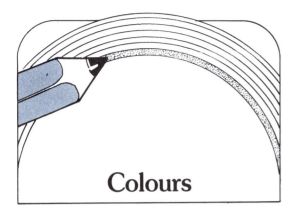

Colours

The children delight in bright colours in their environment. The aim is to show that colour adds great beauty to the world and also has many uses in everyday life. The two stories introduce the children to the Old Testament figures, Noah and Joseph, and offer opportunities for discussing feelings, attitudes and behaviour towards others, e.g. making promises, obedience, favouritism, jealousy, fair play and truthfulness.

Joseph and the coloured coat

Long ago in Canaan there lived an old man whose name was Jacob. Jacob had twelve sons who helped him to look after his sheep and goats. There was one son called Joseph whom Jacob loved more than the other sons. One day Jacob gave Joseph a very beautiful coloured coat. This made the other brothers very jealous of Joseph.

One day Joseph told his brothers that he had a dream and that in the dream they had all bowed down to him. When the brothers heard this they were so angry that they decided to put him down a dried-up well.

So the brothers took off Joseph's beautiful coloured coat and put Joseph down the well. Very soon some men came that way riding on camels. They were going to the markets in Egypt. One of the brothers said, "Let's sell Joseph to these merchants and then we will be rid of him." This they did. The merchants went off, taking Joseph with them and the brothers thought that that was the last they would see of him.

The brothers then dipped the beautiful coat in the blood of an animal and took it to their father. When Jacob saw the coat he was very sad because he thought that some animal had killed his son Joseph. But Joseph was not dead. He was alive and well in Egypt. After many years had passed, the ruler put Joseph in charge of the food supplies. At that time there was a famine in Canaan. There was no food for anyone, and Joseph's brothers were forced to travel to Egypt to beg for grain. Joseph saw his brothers but they did not know who he was. In the end he told them that he was their brother Joseph and asked them if their father was still alive. When he learned that Jacob was still alive, Joseph sent waggons to bring him to Egypt. Jacob was glad to know that Joseph, his favourite son, was still alive and they were very happy when they finally met after so many years apart.

Noah and the rainbow

A long time ago there lived a good man called Noah. One day Noah heard God speaking to him. Then Noah called together his wife and his three sons. He told them that they must build a very big boat because God had told him that there were going to be great floods on the earth. The boat was to be very large because he was going to build a house on it with room for lots of animals.

Noah's family worked hard to build the boat. When the other people saw them making a boat on dry land they thought it was a very silly idea.

Soon, however, drops of rain began to fall. Noah knew that this was the time for his sons to lead two of every kind of animal into the boat. When all the animals were aboard, Noah's family went aboard.

The rain came down for forty days and forty nights. Water covered the earth but Noah and his family were safe in their house on the boat. At the end of the forty days and nights the rain stopped. Noah looked out and said to his sons, "I think that the water is slowly sinking. I will send out a raven and we will see if it comes back. If it does not return we will know that it has found some branch or tree." Noah sent out the raven but the raven came flying back to the boat.

Several days later Noah sent out a dove which soon returned, carrying a branch of an olive tree in her beak. Noah knew that the water was going down. A few days later Noah sent out the dove a second time and this time she did not return. He knew that the dove must have found some dry land. Several days later the big boat came to rest on dry land at the top of a mountain. The three sons let all the animals out of the ark.

As the family left the ark a beautiful rainbow appeared in the sky. Noah heard God's voice telling him that whenever he saw a rainbow he would know it was a sign that God was keeping his promise to care for his people.

More ideas

SONG
The green dress (*Sing a song 2, Nelson 1979*)

..Things to do............

Discussion

★ Why do animals and birds have different coloured coats? Why do flowers have bright colours?

★ How do we use colour to help us? Discuss uses of colour, as a warning, a means of identification and a means of decoration. Talk about colour and safety: the use of arm bands, cones, zebra and pelican crossings, traffic lights, belisha beacons etc.

Library corner

★ Colour *(Ward Lock 1980)*

★ Shapes and colours *(Hamlyn 1981)*

Activities

★ Mathematics: graph work on the subject of favourite colours.

★ Science: experiment with prisms, oil on water and torchlight on white paper to produce the colours of the spectrum.

★ To make sequencing patterns, stamp tiny shapes at random on a sheet of paper. Give the children three colours and ask them to draw concentrically around each shape, keeping the colours in sequence. The lines gradually begin to overlap giving a pleasing overall effect.

★ Make gaily-coloured beads using multi-coloured gift wrapping. Thread these to make necklaces etc. or use them for counting practice.

To make a balloon seller
(to be made individually, or as a class wall picture)

Materials
Pieces of card
Collage materials
A pencil
Paint and paint brushes
Scissors

1 Use a symmetrical shape to make the figure of the person. Cut out and open out.
2 Paint the figure and decorate it, using a variety of collage materials.
3 Cut out the balloon shapes and attach each to the figure with a piece of string glued to the outstretched hand.

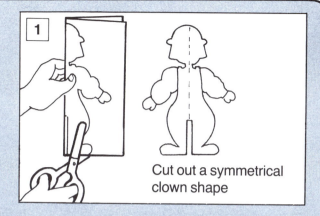

Cut out a symmetrical clown shape

Paint and decorate using bright colours

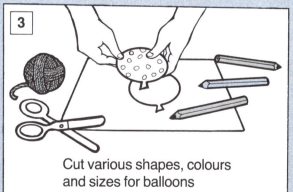

Cut various shapes, colours and sizes for balloons

Springtime

Although 21 March is officially the first day of spring we see signs of spring from February until the end of May. Since early times, people have celebrated the coming of spring after the dark days of winter. Today, in countries all over the world, people celebrate the spring and welcome new birth in the world with festivals and carnivals.

Springtime customs and festivals

People of many different religions have special times of fasting. Fasting usually means that people stop eating for a period of time. During the season of Ramadan, Muslim people do not eat between sunrise and sunset. During springtime Christians have a period of fasting called Lent. Today, Christians don't usually fast. Instead they give up something they like to do, or some food they like to eat. Lent begins on Ash Wednesday, the day after Shrove Tuesday.

Long ago Shrove Tuesday was a day of great feasting when people ate all the delicious foods that they were not allowed during Lent. In France today a great carnival, which means 'without meat', is held. The name of the carnival is Mardi Gras (Fat Tuesday). Processions are held with floats, and there is a battle of flowers. There is dancing in the streets and music and firework displays. But on the next day, which is called Ash Wednesday, the people begin the season of Lent and fasting which will last until the great Christian spring festival of Easter.

In our country today there are many children who have come from islands in the Caribbean. In their home lands there are special celebrations on Shrove Tuesday. The people gather together at spring carnival time and the bands play their music which they will have practised all year, and the people dance to welcome the spring.

A spring festival for the Jewish people is the Feast of the Passover. This is a happy time because the Jewish people remember when Moses led their people away from the bad kings (pharaohs) of Egypt.

An Indian festival in spring

Wheat is grown in some parts of India and in the early springtime it is ready to be harvested. About this time the Hindu people have a special festival which is called Holi. The festival usually lasts for five days and is a very happy time. Large statues of the god Krishna are carried through the streets in the towns and villages and people play pranks, throwing coloured water and red powder at each other. At the time of the festival of Holi the people tell this story:

Long ago there was a very wicked king. He sent out a message to all his people telling them that they must not worship any gods at all. They were to worship him alone. The people knew how wicked the king was and were very frightened.

The king's name was Hiranyakasipu and he had one son whose name was Prahlada. The boy Prahlada was very good and kind. He loved the god Vishnu and decided that he would go on praying to Vishnu and singing his praise each morning as he had always done. When the wicked king heard that his son was still worshipping Vishnu he was very angry. He told his soldiers to torture Prahlada and to throw him into the palace dungeon. After a time Prahlada was allowed out of the dungeon and left the palace. He went around the town telling everyone that he would carry on worshipping Vishnu, and not the king. The king tried several times to have his son killed but he always failed.

Hiranyakasipu had one sister, named Holicka, who was just as wicked as he. "I will ask my sister Holicka to do the job for me," he said. Holicka came to the palace and they made plans. Holicka tricked Prahlada into sitting next to her on a pile of wood. She wore a fireproof cloak to protect her from fire because she had asked someone to step forward and light the wood, so that Prahlada would burn in the flames.

The fire was lit and burned fiercely but the fireproof cloak was no good in the heat and it was Holicka who was burnt. Prahlada was able to leap from the fire and was saved. When the people heard this they were glad that it was the good person, and not the wicked one, who had been saved. (See also pages 118-119).

More ideas

SONG
Gipsy in de moonlight *(A singing game from Trinidad) (Sing a song 2, Nelson 1979)*

HYMN
Little baby Moses *(Come and sing, Scripture Union 1971)*

..Things to do.............

Discussion

★ Have you seen any signs which tell you that winter is nearly over? What have you noticed about the birds, and the plants? Have you seen any insects about? What do you think is happening in the ponds and streams? What is happening in the fields and woods?

Library corner

★ *Spring on the farm* (Wayland 1985)

★ *First day of spring* (Macdonald 1978)

★ *Louisa's garden* (Macdonald 1981)

Activities

★ Springtime display: divide the children into groups and give each group one topic, e.g. birds, plants, insects, ponds and streams, fields and woods in springtime.

★ Springtime celebrations: as above, but children take topics of Valentine's Day, Holi, the Feast of the Passover, Shrove Tuesday, Caribbean Carnival, Mardi Gras, Mothering Sunday, May Day.

★ Collect twigs (catkins, pussy willow, horse chestnut, beech, ash etc.) and draw them. Note leaf scars, rings, sticky buds etc.

★ Grow seeds in eggshell containers (see instructions). Grow them under different conditions in the classroom, e.g. without water, without light, and record the different rates of growth.

To make an eggshell seed box

Materials
An eggshell
Paint and paint brushes
Peat, fibre or cotton wool
Mustard and cress seeds
A strip of card
A brass clip

1 Paint a face on an empty eggshell.
2 Fill the shell with damp peat, fibre or cotton wool.
3 Scatter mustard and cress seeds on the surface.
4 Make a holder by using a strip of card fastened by a brass clip. Draw a bow tie on the card.
5 Stand the eggshell in the holder and wait for the hair to grow!

Paint a face on the eggshell

Fill with peat and sprinkle seeds

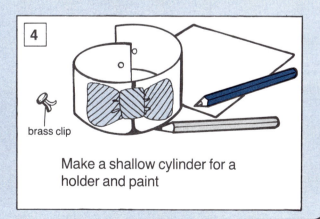

Make a shallow cylinder for a holder and paint

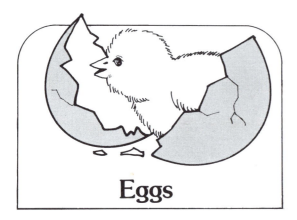

Eggs

The aims of this topic are to tell the story of the most important Christian festival, Easter, and to introduce the children to some of the customs associated with eggs.

The story of the Easter egg

People who lived long ago believed that there was a very beautiful goddess whose name was Eostre. Eostre visited the earth at the end of winter. When she arrived, the earth became warmer. As she walked over the ground, tiny shoots began to grow, birds began to sing, make nests and lay eggs, and life came back again to a world which had been sleeping through the wintertime. In early spring the people of long ago had a great festival for Eostre. It is from her name that we today have the word Easter.

In many countries of the world, eggs are a special symbol of Easter. Easter is the most important festival for Christians because they remember how Jesus came alive again after dying on a cross. The egg is a sign of new life because baby birds hatch out of eggs. Today at Easter, children receive chocolate eggs beautifully wrapped in fancy-coloured paper and foils.

In Greece the people have a special Easter custom. Eggs are painted in different colours and every person carries a decorated egg. When friends meet they take out their eggs and knock them together. Then they say, "Christ is risen". The children play a game with the eggs. They knock the pointed ends together and see who can crack the most eggs without breaking their own.

In our own country there are egg rolling competitions. People decorate eggs by painting them and then gather together in parks. They choose a grassy slope and the egg rolling begins. It is like a race. The winner is the person whose egg arrives at the bottom of the slope first.

In many places special Easter cakes are used which need many eggs. There are bonfires, processions and plays about how Jesus died on a cross.

The Easter story

Once there lived a man whose name was Jesus. He spent his time telling people about God, showing them how to be kind to each other and helping the sad, the sick and the lonely. He loved children and told them stories. He was a good man and people followed wherever he went but he had twelve special friends who were called the disciples.

Now the rulers at that time became very jealous that the people were listening to Jesus and not to themselves. One night Jesus was with his disciples when the soldiers captured him. They took him to a judge who decided that Jesus should be crucified. The next day Jesus was taken to a hill just outside the city and was hung on a cross to die. That night a friend of Jesus took Jesus's body to his lovely garden. He placed it in a little cave and covered the doorway with a big stone.

The next morning two friends of Jesus, who were both named Mary, came to the garden. When they came to the little cave they saw that the great stone had been rolled away and Jesus was no longer there. Jesus had come alive again. This is what Christians celebrate on Easter Day.

The Easter rabbit

Long ago in Germany there were several families who lived in a small village. The people of the village were always very happy and always tried to help each other. Easter was a specially happy time when all the children were given beautifully decorated Easter eggs.

A little boy named Hans lived in the village. One year at Easter time, Hans's mother felt very sad because they were too poor to buy an Easter egg for little Hans. That night the family went to bed. When the light went out, a kind person from the village crept into the garden, and made a little nest from straw. Into the nest he put a beautiful big Easter egg. Then he wrote Hans a little note which said, "Search your garden because the Easter rabbit has been there during the night."

When Hans woke he found the note. He ran into the garden and found the lovely gift from the Easter rabbit. No one in the village knew who left the egg but all the people agreed that he was very kind.

More ideas

HYMNS
Happy Easter *(Come and sing, Scripture Union 1971)*
Very early in the morning *(Hymns and songs for children, National Society 1969)*
Songs of praise; Easter Day; my garden; morning carol *(Sing a new song, REP 1969)*

..Things to do..........

Discussion

★ Discuss the different kinds of eggs: hen, duck, goose, swan, ostrich; insects; frog and toad spawn; and turtle eggs. How do the parent creatures protect their eggs? How do the young get out of the egg?

Library corner

★ The Easter book *(Macdonald 1980)*

★ Baby animals *(Franklin Watts 1983)*

★ The little chick *(Wayland 1976)*

Activities

★ Make Easter bonnets and decorate with tiny buds, new green leaves and/or new spring flowers.

★ Set up an incubator and hatch some eggs; or bring some young chicks into the classroom; or visit a poultry farm.

★ Examine a bird's nest and note the construction materials: twigs, grasses, moss, feathers, clay or mud.

★ Discuss, learn and illustrate the nursery rhymes 'hot cross buns' and 'Humpty Dumpty'.

★ Make Easter cards.

★ Bring frog spawn into the classroom. Observe the different stages of development from spawn (egg) to adult. Make drawings to record observations.

To make a soldier
(from Humpty Dumpty poem)

Materials
A pencil
Scissors
Pieces of gummed paper (red, blue, yellow and black)
Toilet roll holders

1 Fold a piece of paper. Draw the symmetrical shape as shown and cut out.
2 Open out flat and paint face. Stick on a small piece of black material for the helmet (shape A); a piece of red gummed paper (shape B) for the jacket; and blue gummed paper (shape C) for the trousers.
3 Fold backwards around a toilet roll holder and glue X to Y.
4 Draw a line down the trousers. Add a yellow belt and buttons, and black boots. Bend the arms forward.

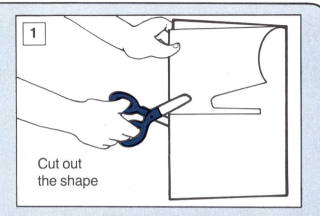

Cut out the shape

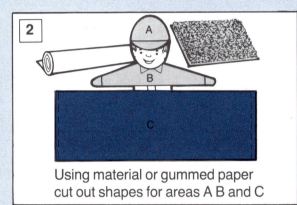

Using material or gummed paper cut out shapes for areas A B and C

Fold X on to Y and stick firmly

Big and Little

When young children first come to school they are often intimidated by the size of the school buildings, as well as the size of the older children. The aim of this topic is to develop the confidence of children who feel small by stressing that personality is more important than physical size and appearance.

The lion and the mouse

There was once a big and fierce lion who lived in Africa. One day he had eaten such a huge dinner that he fell asleep in the sun. As he was sleeping, a tiny mouse came along and touched the lion's paw. The lion woke up. He was very cross that the mouse had disturbed his sleep.

The little mouse was very frightened. "Please do not eat me! I am only very small but one day I may be able to help you". The lion gave a big roar. "How can a little fellow like you help a big lion like me? You are far too small to be helpful!" But because the lion was not hungry, he let the little mouse go.

A few days later the lion was walking in the jungle when suddenly he was caught in a big rope net which some hunters had set as a trap. The lion struggled and struggled but he could not break free.

Just then, along came the little mouse. The mouse saw that the lion was caught and said, "Let me help you." So the little mouse began to gnaw the ropes. He chewed and chewed with his sharp teeth until some of the ropes were cut through and there was a hole big enough for the lion to escape.

When the lion was free, he said to the little mouse, "You were right, little mouse. Little things like you can be very helpful. Thank you for saving my life."

Kind Cinder Joe

A long time ago and a long way away, there was a country where everyone was happy. In this happy land the kindest person was always chosen to be the king. In this land there lived a family – a mother, a father and three boys. The two older boys were big and strong but the youngest boy was very small. The two older boys teased the little boy, and would not let him play with them. So the little boy spent his time helping the neighbours or stayed at home and helped his mother and father. The two older boys called him Cinder Joe because he often sat by the fireside.

One day, the king died. Everyone gathered in the village square to see who would be the new king. The two big brothers went but they refused to take Cinder Joe with them. "You are too small," they said.

After they had left the house, Cinder Joe decided to go to the village square to see what was going to happen. At the side of the village square was a cottage and in the garden there was a pigsty. Cinder Joe was too shy to mix with the crowds, so he hid inside the pigsty, peeping out now and then to see what was happening.

In this land there was a magic crown which could find the kindest person. That night the crown was brought into the village square on a beautiful silk cushion and everyone wondered on whose head it would rest at the end of the evening. When the bells began to ring, all the people watched as the crown rose up in the air. It flew over the village square towards the little cottage, and disappeared into the pigsty.

The crowd ran to see what was happening to their magic crown. When they got to the pigsty, they saw little Cinder Joe wearing the crown. The people lifted Cinder Joe onto their shoulders and carried him to the king's throne. Everyone cheered and the bells rang even louder. The two big brothers could not believe their eyes when they saw their little brother sitting on the big throne. How small he looked, but that did not matter. Although he was small, he was the kindest person in the land and that is why he had been chosen as king.

If

If I were oh, so very small,
I'd hide myself away,
And creep into a paeony cup
To spend the summer's day.
If I were oh, so very tall,
I'd walk among the trees,
And bend to pick the topmost leaf
As easy as you please.
(Book of a thousand poems, Evans 1959)

More ideas

HYMN
All things bright and beautiful *(Songs of praise, OUP 1931)*

STORY
The David and Goliath story *(Bible: 1 Samuel 17)*

..Things to do............

Discussion

★ Have you any brothers or sisters? Is it fun having brothers and sisters? Who has a brother or sister who is bigger than they are? What sort of things can they do? Who has a small brother or sister? What can big children do to help little children?

★ Name an object which can be big or small, e.g. a clock on the wall and a wrist watch. Would you wear a clock on your wrist, or put a watch up on the wall? Why not?

Library corner

★ Estimating *(A&C Black 1971)*

★ Bigger and smaller *(A&C Black 1972)*

★ Size *(Macdonald 1971)*

★ Big dogs and little dogs *(Hulton 1970)*

★ Big cats and little cats *(Hulton 1970)*

Activities

★ Mathematics: make comparisons of big and little, tall and short, fat and thin, wide and narrow.

★ Draw graphs of children's heights, head measurements, foot measurements. Who is the tallest? Who is the smallest?

★ Language work: find as many words as possible to describe size, e.g. tiny, large, big, enormous, huge, tall, small, fat, thin, wide and narrow.

To make 'big and little' patterns

Materials
Shape templates
Chalk
Powder paint/paint brush
Liquid soap
A large piece of paper

1 Mix powder paint and add a small quantity of liquid soap to thicken. Using a paint brush, 'wash' a sheet of paper.
2 Select two templates of different sizes. Place on to a sheet of newspaper. Rub chalk thickly along the edges. Use a different colour on each shape.
3 Place the larger template on to the painted paper. Smudge chalk outwards on to the paper with a finger. Remove template. Place the smaller template so that it partially overlaps the larger, and do the same.
4 Repeat the process, chalking the edges where necessary. Spray with hair lacquer to stop the chalk smudging.

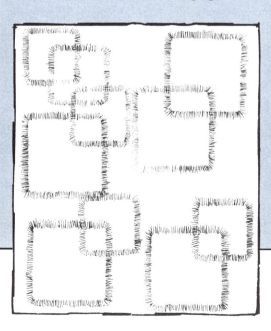

Use thick paint to make a 'wash'

Rub chalk thickly on to the edges of two shapes

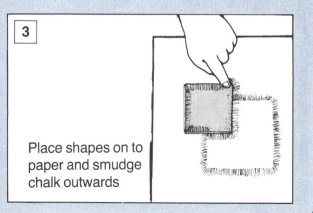

Place shapes on to paper and smudge chalk outwards

Animals

Children show a natural interest in living things and animal stories are always popular. The aims of this topic are to develop concepts of kindness and fairness. The story of 'The cat and the tortoise' is included to develop sensitivity to the fact that, although living things are different, each has something to offer to others.

The bullock's festival

In the villages of India the people work hard growing crops on the land. Some of the crops they eat, and some they take to market. Very few of these farmers can afford to buy a car or a lorry to take their crops to market. Most of them use bullocks to pull their little carts along the dusty roads. Bullocks are big animals and they work very hard. Sometimes they walk round and round in circles all day pulling a heavy wheel which helps to lift water from a well deep in the earth.

The farmers know that the bullocks are their friends because they help them and their families by working hard. So, on one day each year, they say a special thank you to these animals. This special day is called the bullock's festival.

On this day, the bullocks are given a holiday. They are washed and then they have flowers placed around their necks. The farmers and their families walk into town alongside their bullocks.

In the town they meet other families and there is music and dancing. The people even sing a little song for the bullocks to thank them for all the hard work they do on the farms. After the festival is over, the bullocks go back to the farms and the next day are hard at work once again.

The cat and the tortoise

It was a fine sunny day. A cat was curled up in the sun ready to go to sleep when he heard someone coming. Who was it?... It was a tortoise.

The cat did not like the tortoise because the tortoise had a shell on his back. The cat said, "You are a silly creature to carry that shell on your back." The tortoise said, "I love my shell. It is my little house and it keeps me safe." The cat said, "I have lovely soft fur. You should have soft fur like me. I can run and I can jump, but you can only walk." The tortoise said, "I do not want to run or jump. I want to walk s-l-o-w-l-y." The cat started to call the tortoise nasty names which made the tortoise very sad.

Just then, some boys came along carrying sticks. The tortoise pulled his head and his little legs inside his shell. He looked just like a stone. The boys left the tortoise alone but chased the cat. The cat was very frightened. He ran off and the boys chased after him.

The cat climbed up a tree but the bad boys threw sticks at him. One of the sticks hit the cat's leg and it started to bleed. After a while the cat jumped down from the tree but the boys ran after him. The cat hid among some big rocks and the boys went away.

It began to thunder and then large drops of rain started to fall. Soon the poor injured cat was wet through. After a while, the tortoise came along. "Are you in trouble my friend? I will help you," he said. "Brrr! Brrr! Brrr! I am wet and cold. I can't stop shivering," said the cat. "I am all right," said the tortoise, "my house keeps me warm and dry." "Yes, you are very lucky," said the cat.

The tortoise told the cat to follow him and they went along to see a friend of the tortoise. The friend was a kind dog. The dog took the cat and the tortoise into his house and gave the cat some warm milk to drink. The cat told the tortoise that he was very sorry for quarrelling with him, and said a big thank you to the dog for the warm milk.

The dog looked at the cat and the tortoise and said, "We are all different from each other, but we must love one another and be happy just as we are." After that, the cat, the dog and the tortoise were friends and spent many happy hours together.

My dog

I have a dog, his name is Jack.
His coat is white, with spots of black.
I take him out, most every day,
Such fun we have, we run and play.
Such clever tricks, my dog can do.
I love my Jack, he loves me too.
(Book of a thousand poems, Evans 1959)

More ideas

POEMS
The elephant; the tiger (*Sing a song 1, Nelson 1978*)

SONGS
Zoo time; Wiggley Woo (*Sing a song 1, Nelson 1978*)
Ferdinando the donkey (*Apusskidu songs for children, A&C Black 1975*)

..Things to do.............

Discussion

★ Who has a pet at home? Tell us about your pet. What does your pet do during the day? What does your pet do at night-time? What does your pet need? Are you sure that you are always kind and fair to your pet?

★ Do you know of any animals that help us to do our work? (e.g. horses, bullocks) Some animals are very helpful for other reasons. Can you think of any? (e.g. guide dogs)

Library corner

★ Cold-blooded animals *(Macmillan 1979)*

★ Warm-blooded animals *(Macmillan 1979)*

★ Baby animals *(Franklin Watts 1983)*

★ My friend the elephant *(Hamlyn 1984)*

★ My friend the crocodile *(Hamlyn 1984)*

★ Animal world series: bear, dolphin, duck, hedgehog, hippo, kangaroo, panda, penguin, squirrel, tiger, zebra *(Macdonald)*

Activities

★ Make animal masks

★ Make a Noah's Ark frieze.

★ Science: make a wormery.

★ Visit a zoo or a farm.

To make a lion

Materials
Yellow card
Toilet roll holder
Coloured gummed paper
Dark pipe cleaners
Brown wool

1 Paint a toilet roll holder light brown. Cut out a circle of card, diameter 6cm. Cut strips of gummed paper (2cm × 10cm). Cut fringes.
2 Cover the card circle with glue. Start at outer edge and wind the fringing round the card circle, working towards the centre. Cut out features in gummed paper. Stick on top of fringing. Add two ears, and whiskers from pipe cleaners.
3 Glue a small strip of card (6cm × 2cm) to head. Glue the remainder to the toilet roll holder.
4 Cut two strips of card for legs. Stick shaded part to underside. Bend down the feet. For a tail, stick on a plait of wool and tie a knot at one end.

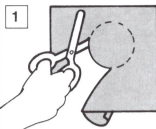
Cut circle of card and make fringes in several strips of gummed paper

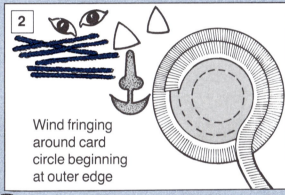
Wind fringing around card circle beginning at outer edge

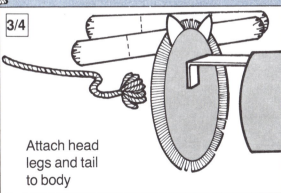
Attach head legs and tail to body

Small Creatures

The aims of this topic are to introduce children to the world of small creatures and to encourage them to show kindness to all creatures, however humble. In 'The Jains of India', the children are introduced to the Jains, who are a religious sect in India. The Jains hold the belief that all life is sacred and are careful not to hurt any living thing.

The Jains of India

There are very many small creatures in our world. Many of them are so small that we cannot see them unless we use a magnifying glass or a microscope. Each has a different shape and size, and has a different way of living. Small creatures with six legs are called insects. Others with eight legs are called spiders. Some creatures are even smaller than insects and spiders.

Many small creatures live on land, but some live in streams, ponds or in the sea. Some creatures spend their early days in water and later live on land. These creatures may be small, but they can be clever too. Bees, wasps and ants have learnt how to live in big communities where they share the work and care for each other.

These creatures can be very useful in the world. Bees give us honey, and wasps take pollen from one flower to another to make new seeds.

In India there are some people called Jains and they are very careful that they do not harm any living creature, however small it may be. They know that the world needs all living creatures, even if they are tiny. Some Jains even wear masks over their faces, just like doctors do when they operate on people. They do this so that they will not swallow any tiny creature which may be flying about in the air.

The Jains also carry a soft broom to sweep the road before they walk on it so that they will not accidentally tread on a small creature. We do not wear masks or carry brooms but we know that small creatures have an important part to play in the world. They are our friends and we need to show them kindness.

The story of Mahagiri

Mahagiri was a big strong elephant. He worked in the forests of India where he used his trunk to lift great logs. The day of the Eid festival was near. Mahagiri's master always took Mahagiri to the town so that the children could have rides on the elephant on the day of the festival itself.

Mahagiri arrived in town the day before the festival. The people there wanted to put up a big flag-pole in the centre of the town. The people asked Mahagiri's master if his elephant could carry the big pole and put it into a deep hole. Mahagiri's master agreed and found a boy to ride the elephant and help him do the job properly.

With the boy on his back, Mahagiri slowly carried the pole in his big trunk to the middle of the town. The elephant boy then gave the sign for Mahagiri to put the pole into the hole.

At that moment, Mahagiri backed away

The elephant boy whipped him, lash! lash!, but Mahagiri tossed his head and again turned away giving a loud trumpeting noise. However much the boy rider hit him, Mahagiri would not put the pole into the hole.

Mahagiri's master could not understand why Mahagiri was not doing as he was told. He thought there must be something very wrong. Mahagiri had always been such a good, kind, obedient elephant. The master went forward and looked down the hole.

There at the bottom he saw a tiny little kitten. It had fallen down and no one knew it was there. As soon as the kitten was pulled to safety, Mahagiri put the pole into the hole. Mahagiri really was a good, kind elephant because even when he was being beaten he would not do anything that would hurt another creature.

Creepy crawly caterpillar

Creepy crawly caterpillar
Curled up in the lane
Creepy crawly caterpillar
Felt a drop of rain
Creepy crawly caterpillar
Closed her tired eyes
And creepy crawly caterpillar
Dreamed of butterflies.

More ideas

POEM
Here is the beehive, where are the bees? *(Sing a song 2, Nelson 1979)*

HYMN
For butterflies and bees *(Hymns and songs for children, National Society 1969)*

..Things to do............

Discussion

★ Name some small creatures. Discuss the differences between insects and spiders.

★ Discuss the usefulness of insects in pollinating plants, providing honey etc.

Library corner

★ The butterfly *(Macmillan 1971)*

★ Spider silk *(A&C Black 1973)*

★ Let's look at some insects *(Medici Society 1977)*

★ The fly *(CUP 1977)*

★ Ants; dragonflies *(Wayland 1978)*

★ The honey bee *(Ward Lock 1979)*

★ Spiders; the snail *(Macmillan 1979)*

★ Insects *(Macdonald 1979)*

Activities

★ Mathematics: look at the hexagonal shape of a honeycomb, and the symmetry of a butterfly's wings.

★ Science: sink a container into the ground so that the top is just below ground level. Place some damp leaves inside it and partially cover it with twigs. Leave for a week. Look through a magnifying glass at any small creatures that have fallen into the container.

To make caterpillars and butterflies

Materials
Wax crayons
Powder paint/paint brushes
Black activity paper
A large sheet of card or paper
Gummed paper circles

1 Arrange gummed circles in different ways to make caterpillars. Add antennae and a face to each.
2 Use a wax and water technique to get 'veined' paper. Cover paper with wax crayon. Press hard. Screw up the paper to break wax coating. Run it under a tap. Wash over with thin powder paint to give 'veined' effect. Cut symmetrical wings from 'veined' paper.
3 Cut a head and body from black activity paper. Add antennae.
4 Make colourful flowers from gummed paper. Stick these, and the butterflies and caterpillars, on to a large piece of card. Paint in stems and leaves.

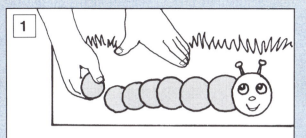

Cut circles and arrange them to make caterpillars

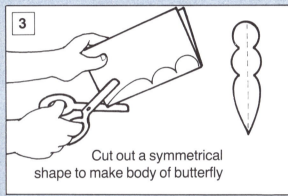

Cut out a symmetrical shape to make body of butterfly

Houses and Homes

Even the youngest child is familiar with houses and has some concept of what is meant by home. The aim of this topic is to introduce children to other types of home. 'A big house in a big city' is a story about people who care for homeless children. The story of 'The two builders' introduces the concept of building on firm foundations and showing care in the work we do.

A big house in a big city

Long ago in London there lived a little boy who people called 'Carrots'. They called him Carrots because he had orange-coloured hair. Carrots was a poor, unhappy boy. He had no mother or father and no home to live in. He had to beg for food during the day, and at night find a box or crate to sleep in. There were many children like Carrots in London.

At that time a young man named Thomas Barnardo lived in London. He was training to become a doctor and he heard the sad story of these children. He used to go out at night and offer some of the children a warm and comfortable place to sleep.

The little boy Carrots came and asked for a place but Thomas Barnardo had no more room. Sadly he had to turn Carrots away. That night Carrots went and slept inside a big crate behind the market-place. The next morning, when the men came to open the market, they found that poor Carrots had died during the wintry night.

When Thomas Barnardo heard what had happened he was very upset. He nailed a big notice to his front door which said "NO CHILD WILL EVER BE TURNED AWAY".

Even today there are big houses all over our country where homeless boys and girls can live happily. They are known as Dr Barnardo's Homes.

The two builders

Long ago there were two men who each decided to build a house to live in.

The first man gathered together all the things needed and started to build his house. The ground on which he decided to build his house was very sandy and so he found the digging quite easy. He worked very quickly and soon his house was finished.

The second man did not start to build straight away. He thought a great deal about the things he would need and where he should build his house. He carefully chose a place where the ground was very hard and very rocky. When he began to dig the foundations he found that it was very hard work and that it was taking him much longer than his friend. But, after a long time, the house was finished.

The two men moved into their homes. Soon the wind began to blow and the rain began to fall. The storm raged so fiercely that there was a flood. The water swirled around the two houses. The house which was built on the sand soon began to tilt. Before long it had crumbled and fallen down. But the house on the rocky land had been built with great care, and this house stood quite firm, despite the floods.

Five and twenty masons

Five and twenty masons
Went to build a house.
They knew no more about it
Than a little mouse.
They built up all the windows
And never left a door:
And when they reached the ceiling
They thought they'd do no more.
(from 'Third 60 songs for little children', OUP 1960).

A house upon a rock

(an action song)
The first man built his house upon the sand (×3)
And the rains came tumbling down.

The rains came down and the floods came up (×3)
And the house came tumbling down.

The wise man built his house upon a rock (×3)
And the rains came tumbling down.

The rains came down and the floods came up (×3)
But the house on the rock stood firm.

More ideas

SONG
The shiny little house *(Third 60 songs for little children, OUP 1960)*

HYMN
Thank you Lord for this new day *(Come and praise, BBC Publications 1960)*

..Things to do............

Discussion

★ How many different types of houses are there in our country? (bungalows, terraced houses, high-rise flats, semi-detached houses, thatched cottages etc.)

★ How many kinds of homes are there in the world? (tents, log cabins, caravans, boats, huts, caves, palaces etc.)

Library corner

★ Houses and homes *(Usborne 1978)*

★ Homes around the world *(Macdonald 1984)*

Activities

★ Make street friezes with box houses. Number the houses odd and even.

★ Make a 3D house for use in a model town (see instructions).

★ Draw a pictorial map of your journey from home to school.

★ Make a table display of building materials (bricks, flints, wood, cement). Display background pictures of homes in other lands, made from various materials.

★ Drama: ask the children to act as various members of a family. Instruct them that they are first to prepare a meal and then visitors will arrive. The visitors include a gas worker, the postman, a police officer and a good friend.

To make a 3D house

Materials
A sheet of card (A4 size)
Glue
Crayons
Paint/paint brushes
Scraps of gummed paper

1 Take the sheet of card. Fold it in half lengthwise. Fold again. Open out flat. Fold the sheet widthwise, and fold a second time. Open out. The card now has 16 rectangles showing.
2 Cut from edge of card to the first fold. Paint roof, door and windows.
3 Take hold of A and B. Gently pull one over another until the apex of the roof emerges. Glue or staple these together.
4 Pull C and D round and fasten them to the house shape and to each other. Insert a small box to make the shape more rigid.
5 To convert to a log cabin, cover the walls and roof with corrugated paper. Paint brown.

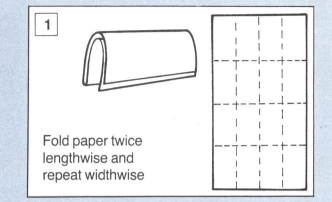

Fold paper twice lengthwise and repeat widthwise

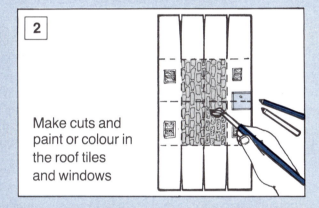

Make cuts and paint or colour in the roof tiles and windows

Raise the form and paste the flaps A over B and D over C

Families

It is within their own families that children first experience living with others. The aim of this topic is to help the children to recognize that everyone has a part to play within the family for the good of the whole. From there, concepts of cooperation, forgiveness, tolerance, sharing and caring for the needs of others — as in the story of 'The Chinese twins' — can be developed.

The Chinese twins

Ling and Ming were twins. As they grew up, they were always together. They loved each other very much and shared everything.

The twins were part of a big family who were rather poor. One day it was a special holiday so their mother started handing out coins to her children. But when it came to the turn of Ling and Ming, she had only one coin left. The boys said, "Do not worry, mother. We like to share our things with each other, so we will share this coin too."

The boys took the coin and went off to play in the woods. As they walked along among the tall trees they saw something shining on the ground. They picked it up and saw that it was a piece of gold as big as an acorn. Ling picked up the gold and gave it to Ming, but Ming wanted Ling to have it. Each boy wanted the other to be happy. So they passed the gold backwards and forwards until they began to quarrel for the first time in their lives. At this point they decided to leave the gold where they found it and go on happily together.

Soon afterwards the twins met an old beggar who asked if they would give him some money or food. As the boys only had one coin, they told him where he could find the gold.

Later that day, as they were on their way home, the old beggar man came towards them. "You two bad boys, you told me lies," he shouted. "I looked for the gold, but all that I found was a bad apple and I am still hungry."

The boys told the old beggar that they did not tell lies and, although he was so angry with them, they decided to give him their one coin. The beggar took this and hurried away.

The boys went back to look under the tall tree and they found not one piece of gold, but two. Ling picked up a piece and gave it to Ming, and Ming picked up a piece and gave it to Ling. The brothers took their pieces of gold home, and gave them to their mother as a present.

The clever sister

Long ago in Egypt there lived a family — father, mother, a boy named Aaron and a girl named Miriam. The family were very happy because a new baby boy had just been born. But soon their happiness changed to sadness because the Pharaoh made a rule that all baby boys were to be killed.

The family decided to hide the baby, but they were afraid that his cries would be heard. Then they had an idea. They put the baby into a floating cradle they had made. Then they hid the cradle in some rushes at the side of a stream which ran close to their house. Miriam hid behind some bushes and watched over the baby.

One day the Pharaoh's daughter, who was a princess, came down to the stream with her servants to bathe. Miriam was frightened that they would see the baby. As the princess was about to bathe, she said, "What is it that I see in the rushes?" The servants found the cradle and took it to her.

When the princess looked into the cradle, she saw two bright eyes staring at her and heard the happy gurglings of a tiny baby. Miriam heard the princess say that she would take the baby back to the palace and bring him up as her own son.

Miriam then ran forward and asked if the princess needed a nurse for the baby for she knew who would be glad to look after him. When the princess said that she would need a nurse, Miriam ran and brought her mother.

So the baby was not killed because Miriam had been so clever. Instead he went to live at the palace and his mother went to be his nurse. The baby was named Moses and when Moses grew up, he became a very great man.

More ideas

SONG
I'd like to build the world a home (Apusskidu songs for children, A&C Black 1975)

POEM
The finger family (Sing a song 2, Nelson 1978)

HYMN
Join with us (Come and praise, BBC Publications 1978)

..Things to do............

Discussion

★ Try to broaden the children's experience of families by talking about different types of family unit, the relationships within them, the roles played by the various members of the family and the idea of the extended family. Also discuss themes such as cooperation, sharing, earning and providing, young and old.

★ Discuss family festivals: baptism, wedding, coming of age, Mothering Sunday, Eid ul-Fitr, Raksha Bandhan.

Library corner

★ Families *(Macmillan 1981)*

★ One of the family *(Lion 1979)*

★ A day with Ling *(Hamish Hamilton 1982)*

Activities

★ Draw graphs to show the following information: the number of people in your family; which children have brothers, and how many; which children have sisters and how many.

★ Use the library corner to find out how families lived in the distant and recent past. How do their lives differ from ours today?

★ Make charts to show different relationships within families. Ask the children to write their names and fix them around the diagram which represents their own family group.

To make the Shape family

Materials
Gummed paper
Scissors
A large piece of paper

1 Make a shape house using a square, a triangle, two small squares and two rectangles.
2 Make shape people: Mr Shape, Mrs Shape, boy Shape, girl Shape and baby Shape. Use gummed paper of different shapes and colours.
3 Make a dog shape, a cat shape and a kennel shape.
3 Encourage the children to experiment making other suitable objects. Add details with a felt pen.

Cut the shapes shown and arrange to make a house

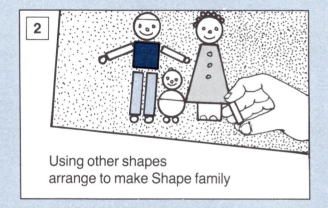

Using other shapes arrange to make Shape family

The aims of this topic are to develop self-awareness and a positive self-image. By helping children to become aware of their own physical characteristics, abilities, feelings, needs, likes and dislikes, we help them to become aware of the needs and feelings of others. The story 'A special job for everyone', stresses that each person has special gifts. The story of 'Aesop and his master' can be used to remind children that they have a choice whether to use these gifts well, or mis-use them.

A special job for everyone

In Africa there once lived a little girl named Marta. Marta lived with her grandfather. One evening, Marta's grandfather told her a story. He told her how the Great God had made all the world and all the creatures in it.

Marta's grandfather told Marta that the Great God had a special job for each person to do, whoever they were. Marta found this hard to believe, so she said, "I have never been to school and I cannot do anything special at all." Grandfather said, "Marta, you have ears, eyes, hands, feet and a tongue. All of these you can use to do something special."

Many years later, when Marta was grown up, there was a famine in Africa. The people and animals in Marta's village were starving. Some of them died.

Marta decided to move away. She took the few things she owned and went down the dusty road away from her village.

After she had walked for a little distance, she heard a faint cry. She used her ears to find out where the sound was coming from. Then she used her eyes to help her see what was making the noise. In the deep grasses she found a tiny baby.

Marta used her hands to lift him up and her tongue to speak words of comfort to him. She then walked on foot with him in her arms until she came to the next village. There, lorries had brought some food for the villagers.

Marta made her home in this village and looked after the little boy, whom she named Busha. Many times she thought about what her grandfather had said.

When Busha grew up Marta told him grandfather's story. Busha then asked, "Marta, what special job have you done?" What do you think Marta said?

Aesop and his master

Long ago in Greece there lived a slave called Aesop who was very clever. His master often asked him to do strange things.

One day the master asked Aesop to show him something which was very beautiful and good, and something which was ugly and bad. Aesop thought about this for a long time. Then he had an idea. He put the tongue of a sheep in one corner of the room and the tongue of a sheep in another corner of the room.

When the master returned, he said to Aesop, "Why have you put a tongue in two corners of the room?" Aesop replied, "Master, a tongue is a very beautiful thing when it tells the truth, makes promises which are kept and says beautiful words which help and comfort people. But a tongue is also an ugly, nasty and dangerous thing which can tell tales, speak words which hurt people, or make promises which are not kept."

Aesop's words made his master feel very ashamed because he had often said things which had hurt people and had often made promises which he had not kept.

Me

It's six whole years since I was born
Six years of being me
I wonder who I was before
And how it used to be?
I can't remember where I lived
Or what I used to wear
I don't remember wearing socks
Or ribbons in my hair
It must have been the strangest place
No dinner and no tea
Just years of being no years old
Just waiting to be me.

Me

(an action rhyme for younger children)
I have ten little fingers
I have ten little toes
I have two eyes
I have two ears
I have one little nose.

More ideas

HYMNS

He gave me eyes so I could see; hands to work and feet to run; I'm very glad of God *(Someone's singing Lord, A&C Black 1973)*

..Things to do.............

Discussion

★ Do all people look the same? What do you look like? What makes you different from other children?

★ What sort of activities do you enjoy? What are you able to do? Is everyone able to do what you can do?

★ Do you always feel the same? Why do you sometimes feel happy and content, and at other times sad and angry?

★ What sort of things do you need? Does everyone need the same as you? Are there certain things that every person needs?

Library corner

★ You and your body *(Macmillan 1979)*

★ Me and You *(Macdonald 1982)*

★ Eat, drink, grow; teeth; hair *(Macdonald 1983)*

Activities

★ Ask the children to bring photographs of themselves at different ages. Discuss how they have changed over the years.

★ Language work: make sentences beginning with "I am...", "I have...", "I like...", "I feel...", "I need..."

★ Listen to a recording of 'My Favourite Things' from 'The Sound of Music'. Paint pictures or write about favourite things.

To make a moving person

Materials
Card
Brass paper clips
A pencil
Scissors
A darning needle

1 Make templates of body parts.
2 The children draw round the templates to make the body parts: a head, a body, two upper arms, two forearms, two upper legs, two lower legs, two feet. Draw dots where the joints will be.
3 To help the children push the brass paper clips through the joints, make a small hole where the dots are, using a sharp needle.
4 Assemble in body form, using the brass clips.

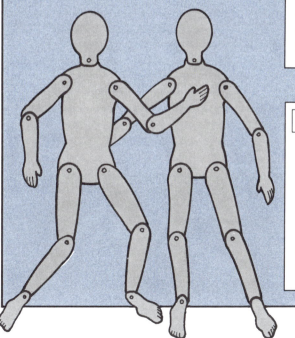

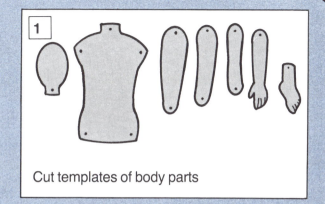

Cut templates of body parts

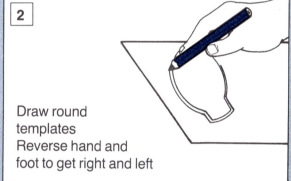

Draw round templates
Reverse hand and foot to get right and left

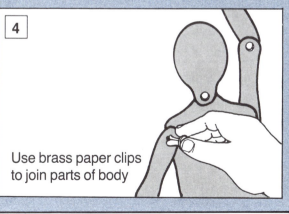

Use brass paper clips to join parts of body

Eyes

The aim of this topic is to stress the importance of the gift of sight, a faculty we often take for granted. The story of 'The blind man and the lame man' shows how two disabled people shared their gifts to help each other. The other two stories demonstrate how disabled people can achieve success and help other people.

The blind man and the lame man

One day a blind man and a lame man were travelling along a road together. Suddenly the road became very bumpy. The lame man found it very difficult to walk without falling. He asked the blind man to help him along but the blind man said that he could not see and would probably lead the lame man into danger. The men sat down together by the side of the road and the blind man had an idea.

The blind man told the lame man to get up on his shoulders and to look in front and tell him which way he should go. The blind man used his strength to carry the lame man, and the lame man used his eyes to guide the blind man. By using the gifts which each possessed they were able to help each other and carry on safely with their journey.

A blind boy who loves music

Jameel is a little boy who goes to a special school for children who are blind. He has never been able to see. All his life he has had to use his ears to listen and his fingers to touch things so that he could find out about the world around him. Jameel loves music and has learned how to play a trumpet. He cannot see the music like other children so he has to remember the notes in his head.

Some months ago a special children's orchestra was formed. Boys and girls from different schools were asked to take part. They practised hard until the orchestra could play very well and it was then decided to hold a concert.

On the night of the concert all the parents and many other important people came along to listen. The children began to play their instruments and at the end of each piece the audience clapped.

The children had started to play another piece of music when suddenly there was a power failure and all the lights went out. The children could not see the music and stopped playing. But Jameel played on because he did not know that the lights had gone out and his music was all in his memory. At the end of the piece the people stood up and clapped very loudly for Jameel, the little blind boy. Jameel gave a big bow.

Soon the power cables were mended. The lights came back on and all the children were able to see their music so the concert was able to carry on.

A blind boy who helped others

About two hundred years ago a little boy was born in France. His parents were Mr and Mrs Braille and they called their boy Louis. Louis was just like other babies at first, but he became blind when he was only three years old. The little boy could not see all the wonderful colours and beautiful things around him. At that time many people who were blind could not find any work to do, so they had to go out on the streets, begging for food and money.

When Louis grew up he always tried his best to help other people, although he was blind. He thought how wonderful it would be if blind people could read like anybody else. Louis thought about this for a long time and then an idea came to him.

He decided to make a special alphabet which people could feel rather than see. He worked hard and finally made an alphabet in which the letters were raised up above the surface of the paper. This alphabet is named 'Braille', after Louis Braille, the man who invented it.

Since then, many blind people have read books by touching raised dots with their fingers. Even though Louis was blind, he was able to help very many people.

Good night

"Tu-whitt, tu-whitt, tu-whoo, tu-whoo,
Good night to me, good night to you,"
Tis the old white owl in the ivy tree,
But I can't see him, and he can't see me!
(Book of a thousand poems, Evans 1959)

More ideas

HYMNS
He gave me eyes so I could see; I'm very glad of God; give to us eyes; praise to God for the things we see (*Someone's singing Lord*, A&C Black 1973)

..Things to do..............

Discussion

★ Ask the children to look up, look down and look around. What can they see? Ask them to cover their *eyes* and do the same.

★ Discuss the problems that blind people face. How can they be helped?

★ Talk about the *eyes* of animals. How, and why, are they different from our *eyes*?

Library corner

★ Johnny gets some glasses *(Hamish Hamilton 1978)*

★ Eyes *(Macdonald 1983)*

★ Sight *(Macdonald 1984)*

Activities

★ Take the children on a 'looking walk'. Ask them to record the things they see.

★ Use a magnifying glass and binoculars to look at various objects.

★ What colour are your eyes? Draw a graph showing the number of children who have blue eyes, brown eyes etc.

★ Contact the Royal National Institute for the Blind asking for posters, examples of Braille etc.

★ After close observation, ask the children to draw an *eye* showing the eyebrows, eyelids, eyelashes, pupil and iris.

Seeing double pictures

Materials
Coloured chalks
Thick black crayon
A sharp pencil
Activity paper
Plain white paper
Paper clips

1 Make stripes of coloured chalk on a sheet of activity paper. Press hard.
2 Colour over this with a black crayon. Make a thick coating.
3 Take a sheet of white paper and place on top of the crayon surface. Fasten with paper clips to hold firm. Make a drawing or pattern with a sharp pencil. Press on very hard.
4 Remove the top sheet and turn it over. You will see a picture in black. On the bottom sheet you have a multi-coloured picture where the coloured chalk shows through the wax crayon.

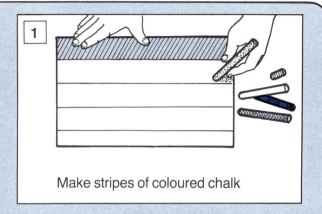

Make stripes of coloured chalk

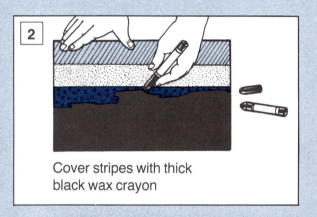

Cover stripes with thick black wax crayon

Place paper on crayon surface and draw a picture

Ears

The aims of this topic are to foster awareness of the importance of the sense of hearing, and to help the children to have a better understanding of those who suffer from a hearing or speech disability. The story of 'Susu Chatterbox' focuses attention on the patience and skill of those who care for the disabled. The story of 'When a little boy listened' is about hearing the voice of God.

When a little boy listened

Long ago there lived a lady whose name was Hannah. Hannah was very sad because she had no children. She went to the temple and prayed to God. She promised God that if He sent her a baby son she would take him back to work in the temple as soon as he was old enough.

Not long after, Hannah gave birth to a baby son. She named him Samuel. Hannah kept her promise to God. When Samuel was still very young, she took him to live in the temple. There, he helped the old priest, whose name was Eli.

Young Samuel did any little jobs which Eli asked him to do. One night, Samuel and Eli were in their beds when Samuel heard a sound. He thought that old Eli was calling for him. Samuel got up and went to Eli and asked him if he was calling.

The old priest said, "No, I did not call you, go back to bed Samuel." Samuel went back and lay down on his bed but the same thing happened again and again. When Samuel went to Eli, the old priest said, "If the voice comes again, listen very carefully because it may be God who wants to speak to you."

The voice came again and Samuel said, "Speak to me. I am listening, Lord!" God told Samuel that when the old priest Eli died, Samuel must be a leader of the people. Samuel then knew that he had some special work to do.

(for the full story of Samuel and Eli, read the first book of Samuel, chapter three, in the Bible)

Susu Chatterbox

Not long ago, a new baby was born. Everyone in the family was so happy. The baby was a little girl and was named Susu.

As the weeks passed, Susu's mother noticed that the baby did not seem to hear any sounds. When Susu's brother shook the rattle, Susu did not even look that way. So Susu's mother and father took the baby to see a doctor and came home looking very sad.

The doctor had told them that Susu could not hear because she was deaf. When the other babies began to talk, Susu did not because she could not hear or learn any sounds. Susu's mother took her to many clinics where she had hearing tests and where nurses and doctors spent a lot of time trying to help her.

When other children of her age went to school, Susu could not go with them. Instead she went to a special school for children who are deaf and dumb. At this school there were some clever teachers. They spent a great deal of time teaching Susu to hear sounds in a different way by feeling tiny movements round the throat. They taught Susu how to talk by making signs with her hands. Soon Susu could ask for the things she needed in sign language.

Susu was given a hearing aid and after a time she began to make strange noises. The teachers were very patient and full of praise, for they knew how hard Susu was trying. She tried very hard until she could talk to all the other children.

One day Susu's mother and father went to meet her and the teacher said to them, "I don't know what I'm going to do with Susu. She talks all day long. She is a real chatterbox!"

What a wonderful day that was. From that day, Susu's mother and father called her Susu Chatterbox.

Two

Two little ears to hear each sound
Two little eyes to look around
One little nose to smell things sweet
And one little mouth likes food to eat.

More ideas

SONGS
Old Macdonald had a farm; I went to visit a farm one day (Sing a song 1, Nelson 1978)

HYMNS
I can talk to God (Come and sing, Scripture Union 1971)
God always listens; little boy come (Hymns and songs for children, National Society 1969)
He made me (Come and praise, BBC Publications 1978)

..Things to do............

Discussion

★ Talk about the sounds we hear, and what they mean. Sirens (danger); laughter (happiness); crying (sadness) etc.

★ How do we make sounds using musical instruments? Striking, blowing, plucking, shaking etc. What instruments require these actions?

Library corner

★ *Hearing* (Studio Vista 1975)

★ *Sound and music* (Franklin Watts 1984)

★ *Hearing* (Macdonald 1985)

Activities

★ Take the children on a 'listening walk'. Take a cassette recorder and go for a short walk round the school. Once back in the classroom, play the cassette back and make a list of the recorded sounds.

★ Make musical instruments from coffee tins, yoghurt cartons, combs and paper, bottles filled to various levels etc. Make a rattle (see instructions). Form a class band.

★ Make a display of pictures of musical instruments from different parts of the world.

★ Make a list of animal noises. Write sentences that include an animal and the noise it makes, e.g. the lamb bleats, the dog barks etc.

To make a musical instrument

Materials
An empty squeezy container
Dried peas, or rice
A piece of dowel, 20cm long
Colourful wrapping paper
Floral ribbon
Glue/sellotape

1 Cut up the wrapping paper into small pieces. Stick these on to a squeezy container until it is completely covered.
2 Put some dried peas inside the container. Insert the dowel into the hole of the container. Pad tightly with newspaper if necessary. Use glue and sellotape to make a firm join.
3 Lie a piece of sellotape flat, sticky side up. Lay strips of floral ribbon on the sellotape, leaving 2cm at each end of the sellotape. Make two of these.
4 Wrap one round the top, and the other round the base, of the container. Now you have a rattle to shake.

Cut wrapping paper into small pieces and stick to container

Fill with peas and insert and fasten dowel

Make a fringe and wrap to cover joining

Hands and Feet

Hands and feet are useful parts of the body which we use in many different ways to carry out helpful and caring tasks. The story of 'The wise king' deals with a love of peace and a sense of fair play. The story of 'Krishna cuts his finger' deals with jealousy, love and self-sacrifice.

The wise king

This is the story of a king called Edward, who once ruled England. King Edward knew that the people in the towns often quarrelled when they were buying and selling cloth. Some people thought that they had not been given enough cloth for their money. They would shout out at the merchants and call them cheats and robbers. The merchants sometimes gave too much and sometimes they did not give enough, so the people were very unhappy.

King Edward did not like to hear his people quarrel. He wanted them to be happy and content. He also wanted them to be fair to each other and not give too little or too much. So he thought of a good plan. He sent for his servants and said, "Measure my foot, please."

The servants measured the king's foot. They did not know why the king wanted to have his foot measured and wondered what he was going to do next. "This is the length of my foot," said the king. "We will all make a copy of this and then we can all use the same measure when we buy and sell cloth."

From that day the people measured everything in feet, based on the length of King Edward's foot. A foot was always the same length and so the people felt that they were being fairly treated. Soon they stopped quarrelling about cloth and lived more peacefully together.

Krishna cuts his finger

A long time ago the boy Krishna lived on earth. He shared a house with two girls. One was his real sister named Subhadra. The other girl was called Draupadi. She was almost like a sister to Krishna.

Subhadra was jealous because she thought that Krishna loved Draupadi better than he loved her. Subhadra was always saying to Krishna, "I am your real sister. You must love me better than you love Draupadi. I love you so much that I would do anything that you asked me to do." To this Krishna replied, "I can love both of you the same."

One day Krishna cut his finger and it was bleeding very badly. He went to Subhadra and asked her to help him. Subhadra looked at the finger. She said that there was nothing she could do, but she would try to find a bandage.

At that moment, in came Draupadi. She was wearing a beautiful sari. It was one of her favourite pieces of clothing. When she saw Krishna's finger bleeding badly she did not worry about spoiling her sari. She immediately tore a strip from it so that she could bandage Krishna's hand.

To this day, Hindu people remember how Draupadi was a loving, helpful girl at a special festival which is called Raksha Bandhan. The girls tie a band on the right hand of their brothers, or adopted brothers. The boys then promise to protect and take care of their 'sisters' of all times.

For more about the festival of Raksha Bandhan, and the story of Krishna, see pages 146-147.

Feet

Big feet, black feet,
Going up and down the street;
Dull and shiny father's feet
Walk by me.

Nice feet, brown feet,
Going up and down the street;
Pretty, dainty, ladies' feet,
Trip by me.

Small feet, light feet,
Going up and down the street;
Little children's happy feet,
Run by me!
(Book of a thousand poems, Evans 1959)

More ideas

SONG
If you're happy and you know it (Apusskidu songs for children, A&C Black 1975)

HYMN
Hands to work and feet to run (Someone's singing Lord, A&C Black 1973)
Jesus's hands were kind hands (Hymns and songs for children, National Society 1969)
He made me (Come and praise, BBC Publications 1978)

..Things to do............

Discussion

★ Ask the children to look at their hands and to name the different parts. What can we do with our hands?

★ Ask the children to look at their feet and name the different parts. What can we do with our feet? Can you paint with your feet? Some people can.

★ Discuss different kinds of feet on animals and birds. How have they adapted to their environments?

Library corner

★ Touch and feel *(Wheaton 1981)*

★ I can touch *(World's Work 1982)*

★ Hands *(Macdonald 1983)*

★ Touch and feeling *(Macdonald 1985)*

Activities

★ To see how well your shoes fit, draw round your shoe, and round your foot. Cut these shapes out. Place your cut-out foot on to your cut-out shoe. How do they compare for size?

★ Physical education: explore movement using hands and feet, and without using hands and feet.

★ Measure your foot and compare it with a foot ruler. Draw round an adult's foot and compare it with a foot ruler.

To make a 'feely-box'

Materials
A large box
A small piece of material
Decorative paper
Wallpaper
Scissors
Glue
A selection of small articles of different shapes and sizes

1 Cover a box with decorative paper, leaving the top clear.
2 Cut a small circular hole a third of the way down the box.
3 The children cut hand shapes from coloured paper and stick them to the box, leaving the top open.
4 Cover the hole with a small piece of material, sellotaped on the inside. Make a slit for a child's hand to pass through.
5 Put the selection of small articles inside the box and then seal it.
6 Make a suitable notice inviting the children to feel the objects inside.

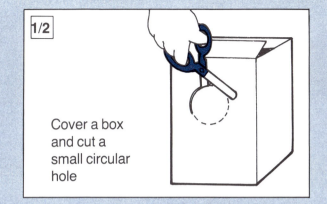

Cover a box and cut a small circular hole

Make hand prints and paste them to the box

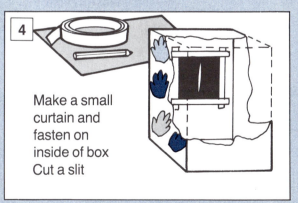

Make a small curtain and fasten on inside of box. Cut a slit

Air

The aims of this topic are to introduce the child to the concept of invisibility and to show the wonderful ways in which different living species have adapted to different environments and ways of life. The story of 'The sun and the wind' demonstrates that gentleness sometimes proves more effective than force. The story of 'Jesus and the storm' deals with faith and calmness in times of stress and trouble.

The sun and the wind

One day an old man was walking along a road. He wore a thick overcoat with a large collar. "It is very cold," he said to himself. At that moment the sun peeped from behind a cloud. The warm rays shone down on to the earth below. The wind was already very cross and was puffing hard. But when the wind saw the sun it was more cross than ever and started to quarrel. "Why do you need to come along and show your shining face?" the wind said rudely. "I am stronger than you. Today it is my turn to blow my icy blasts upon the earth."

The sun said to the wind, "My rays are very gentle today but I can also be very strong." The sun and the wind decided to test themselves. They saw the old man walking along and agreed that they should each try to get him out of his coat.

The wind wanted to be first to try its strength. The wind blew and the coat flapped about. The old man shivered, but as the wind blew stronger, the man pulled his coat more tightly around him.

Then came the sun's turn. The sun sent down its warmest beams on to the path where the old man was walking. Soon the old man unfastened his coat. Finally, the old man took off his coat and carried it over one arm. As the old man did this he said, "The wind was very cold, but the sun is very strong today." "Did you hear that," said the sun to the wind. "Yes, I suppose you have won our contest," said the wind. "Your warm sunbeams are gentle but they have more strength than my icy blasts."

Jesus and the storm

Fishermen go out to sea in all kinds of weather to bring us our food. When there are very strong winds the sea is rough and dangerous. Long ago many fishermen lived on the shores of Lake Galilee. They fished from little boats and they knew that storms could come very suddenly. Some of these fishermen were special friends of Jesus.

One day Jesus was with the fishermen out on the lake. All was calm and peaceful. The little boat was gliding along and all was set for a good day's fishing.

But then the wind started to blow. Little waves began to break against the side of the little boat. Very soon a great storm was raging. The fishermen were tossed about in their boat and they all became very frightened. They knew that they were in great danger and that their little boat could easily sink.

Just then, Jesus stood up in the boat and said quietly, "Peace, be still". Soon the wind began to blow more gently. The great waves became small waves and then ripples again. The storm was over and the little boat sailed on once more on a calm sea and came safely back to the shore.

Even today the wind can be very dangerous and cause disasters in many parts of our world. Sometimes houses are destroyed and people are left homeless. At these times the people need our help.

The wind

*What can be the matter
With Mr Wind today?
He calls for me so loudly,
Through the keyhole, "Come and play."*

*I'll put my warm, red jacket on
And pull my hat on tight,
He'll never get it off, although
He tries with all his might.*

*I'll stand so firm upon my legs,
I'm strong, what do I care?
Now, Mr Wind, just come along
And blow me if you dare.*
(Book of a thousand poems, Evans 1959)

More ideas

SONG
Windmill in old Amsterdam (*Apusskidu songs for children, A&C Black 1975*)

HYMNS
I love the sun (*Someone's singing Lord, A&C Black 1973*)
Dear God who made the world so fair; for butterflies and bees (*Hymns and songs for children, National Society 1969*)

..Things to do............

Discussion

★ A riddle: what is it that is all around us but we cannot see? Clue: blow on your hand.

★ Talk about how all living things need air. Discuss the different ways that animals, plants and fishes take in air.

★ People use moving air to help them. Can you think of some examples? (e.g. windmills, sailing boats, fan heaters, drinking straws etc.).

★ When can moving air be dangerous? Can you think of examples? (e.g. storms, tornadoes, damage to crops and buildings).

Library corner

★ Things that go *(Usborne 1981)*

★ Wind power *(Wayland 1981)*

★ Breathing *(Franklin Watts 1984)*

★ Huff, puff, blow! *(Macdonald 1983)*

Activities

★ Make kites and suspend as mobiles.

★ Blow up balloons and let them go. Blow bubbles with soap liquid.

★ Obtain a pair of lungs from a butcher. Show the lungs to the children and explain how they work. Obtain a large fish head from a fish market. Show the children the gills and explain how they work.

To make bubble patterns

Materials
Several empty margarine tubs
Powder paint
Liquid soap
Straws
Paper
Scissors

1 Mix different coloured powder paint in the tubs. Add one tablespoon of liquid soap to each tub.
2 Using a straw, blow into the tub to make bubbles. Allow the solution to come over the rim of the tub.
3 Place a piece of paper over the rim to create bubble patterns. Make patterns of different colours using all the tubs.
4 Cut the bubble patterns out to make a class picture of children or clowns blowing bubbles.

Mix powder paint and add liquid soap

Blow into mixture until bubbles appear

Take a print from circumference of margarine tub

Clothes

The aim of this topic is to promote understanding of the reasons why people wear different types of clothing. The story of 'Mr Singh's turban' demonstrates that children may make fun of people who dress differently until they are taught to understand the reasons for the differences. 'Hargobind's cloak' is an old Sikh story which demonstrates unselfishness and thought for others for Hargobind will not accept freedom for himself while others remain captive.

Hargobind's cloak

A long time ago in India there lived a man named Hargobind. He was a clever man and friendly to everyone. Although he was a Sikh he became a friend of the emperor, who was a Muslim. At that time there were quarrels between the Muslims and the Sikhs. But the emperor often visited Hargobind and they would eat a meal together.

One day the emperor fell ill. Some people blamed Hargobind for the emperor's illness. They invited him to the emperor's palace. When Hargobind arrived, they arrested him and threw him into jail, although he had done nothing wrong.

Inside the jail, Hargobind found that there were more than fifty other prisoners. Many weeks passed and then the prisoners heard that the emperor was getting better. The emperor was angry when he found out that Hargobind was in prison and ordered that he should be set free immediately. When Hargobind heard the news he said, "I will not go free unless all the other prisoners are freed also." The emperor then said that Hargobind could take as many of the prisoners with him as could hold his cloak as he passed through a narrow gateway.

Hargobind had an idea. He asked the guards to bring him a cloak with long tassels on the end of it. He then told each of the other prisoners to hold on to a tassel. In this way they were able to walk through the gateway. So all the prisoners were freed because of Hargobind's clever idea. Today, the Sikhs call him Guru Hargobind because he was so wise.

Mr Singh's turban

Amjit and his mother and father had just moved house so Amjit had to go to a new school. On the first morning Amjit's father, called Mr Singh, went into the classroom with him to meet the teacher. Mr Singh is a Sikh and wears a turban on his head. When the other children saw him, they all began to stare at the turban and some began to laugh.

Amjit had long hair, like his father, which his mother combed into a tight knot and covered with a little piece of cloth. The children stared at him too and later in the day some of them began to tease him. At his last school, the girls and boys had all been friendly and kind: they knew that Amjit wore his hair like this because he was a Sikh.

When Amjit went home that night he was very sad. He told his mother how the children had been teasing him and said he did not like the school at all. When the teacher heard about this she decided that the boys and girls should learn more about the clothes people wear, but first of all she told them that Amjit and his family were Sikhs.

Sikhs do not cut their hair. They call their uncut hair, kesh. The boys wear a little top-knot to keep the hair tidy but the fathers wear a turban made from a long strip of material. Sikhs also wear a comb, called a kanga, in their turban. The kanga is used to keep the hair tidy. Shorts are always worn. The Sikhs call these shorts, kaccha.

On special occasions, Sikhs wear a sword, called a kirpan, but on normal days they usually wear a little brooch like a sword. Every male Sikh always wears a steel bracelet on his right wrist and this is called a kara.

The teacher then explained that the five K's are symbols that remind Amjit's father, and all Sikhs, of things that happened long ago.

Wash day

This is the way we wash our clothes,
Rub-a-dub-dub, rub-a-dub-dub
Watch them getting clean and white,
Rub-a-dub-dub, rub-a-dub-dub.
This is the way we hang them out
Flippity-flap, flippity-flap
See them blowing in the wind,
Flippity-flap, flippity-flap.
This is the way we iron them
Smooth as smooth can be
Soon our wash day will be done,
Then we can all have tea.
(Book of a thousand poems, Evans 1959)

More ideas

POEM
Little Polly Flinders *(a nursery rhyme)*

..Things to do...........

Discussion

★ What are you wearing today? Name the different types of clothing and discuss the different materials from which they are made. Think about the different people who helped to make them and how they came into the shops for us to buy them.

★ Have you clothes that you only wear on special occasions? Are there any jobs which require people to wear special clothes? (e.g. the police, the army)

Library corner

★ Clothes *(Macdonald 1971)*

★ Clothes *(Nelson 1978)*

★ Thank you for a woolly jumper *(Lion 1983)*

Activities

★ Cut out pictures from old catalogues and magazines and make wall charts of winter clothes, summer clothes, day clothes, night clothes and special clothes.

★ Soak samples of various materials in water. Which dries fastest when hung out to dry?

★ Dressing-up box activity: children dress up and tell the others about the clothes they are wearing.

★ Make simple outline shapes of people in card. Let the children use all kinds of collage materials to dress the shapes.

To tie and dye

Materials
Strips of white, or pastel, material
Small pebbles
String
A cold water dye (bought)

1 Follow the instructions on the container to make a cold water dye.
2 Take strips of material and:
  a Make knots
  b Tie at intervals
  c Wrap small pebbles in the material and tie tightly.
3 Place the material in the dye until the dye begins to 'take'. Pull the material out, untie it and allow it to dry.

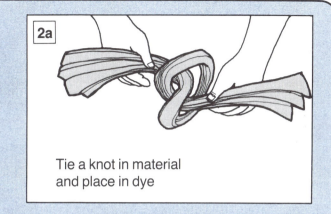

Tie a knot in material and place in dye

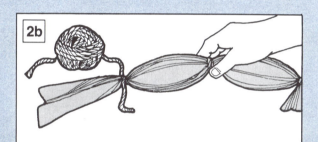

Tie material with string at intervals and place in dye

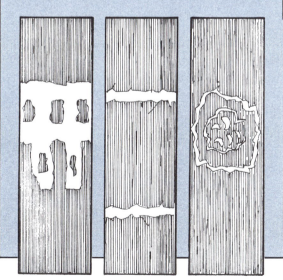

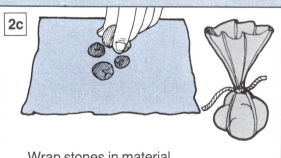

Wrap stones in material
Tie and place in dye

Summertime

The aim of this topic is to help children appreciate beauty in the world around them. Throughout the ages, people have enjoyed the long, warm summer days and have held Midsummer celebrations. Today, many people go on holidays in the summer. The stories of 'Little Pedro' and 'Ayesha finds a friend' are about holidays but can lead to discussions on friendship and generosity.

Little Pedro

Little Pedro lived by the sea on the island of Madeira. He lived with his uncle because he had no parents. Pedro's uncle had once owned a fishing boat, but this had been damaged and there was no money to repair it.

Many people go to Madeira for their summer holidays. These visitors used to throw pennies over the side of their boats. Pedro earned his living by diving into the blue water to find them.

Little Pedro liked his work. At the end of the day, Pedro would share his money with his uncle. Sometimes there was not enough to buy food and Pedro and his uncle would go to bed without eating.

Pedro wished that he could earn enough money to buy a boat for his uncle. Then they could row visitors round the island, and make enough money to have supper every night.

One day something unusual happened. Instead of diving for pennies, Pedro dived into a rough sea and saved a small boy who had fallen from a boat. Pedro handed him safely back to his parents.

The next day the father handed Pedro a bag and a note which said, "Thank you for saving our son." In the bag was lots of money. "Thank you very much!" said Pedro. Pedro gave the money to his uncle who bought a lovely new boat. Every summer, Pedro and his uncle take visitors on a sail around the island. Now they earn enough money to eat a good meal every night.

Ayesha finds a friend

Ayesha's father had been offered a new job. This meant that the family had to move house. They were going to live in a house which was near to the sea. Ayesha thought that it was very exciting but she did not want to leave all her friends.

The day for the move arrived. All the furniture was put into a large van and off they went to their new home. It was summertime, and all the children were on holiday so Ayesha could not go to school. She was very lonely and thought about all the friends she had left behind.

One day, she went to the beach with her mother. While she was there, the tide came in. Floating on top of the waves was a bottle which soon came to rest on the sand. Ayesha's mother had an idea. She said to Ayesha, "If you want a friend, we will put a little note inside the bottle with your name and address on it. Then we will throw the bottle back into the sea and probably some girl or boy in a land across the sea will find it and write to you." So Ayesha did this.

Two days later, a knock came on their door. When Ayesha opened the door, she saw a little girl standing there with her father. "Are you Ayesha?" the little girl's father said. "We live only half a mile away. We were on the beach this morning and found your note in the bottle. We moved here just a week ago. My daughter Susan is very lonely and she would like a friend."

The bottle had not travelled very far but it did not matter. The two little girls became great friends and at the end of the holiday they went to their new school together.

Hay time

Come out, come out, this sunny day,
The fields are sweet with new-mown hay,
The birds are singing loud and clear,
For summertime once more is here;
So bring your rakes and come and play,
And toss and tumble in the hay.
The sweet wild roses softly blow,
All pink and white the roses grow,
The nodding daisies in the grass
Lift up their heads to hear you pass
Upon this happy, sunny day,
When you come out to make the hay.
(Book of a thousand poems, Evans 1959)

More ideas

HYMN
It fell upon a summer's day *(Someone's singing Lord, A&C Black 1973)*

POEM
Summer morning *(Tinder-box assembly book, A&C Black 1982)*

SONG
Swinging *(Third 60 songs for little children, OUP 1960)*

..Things to do............

Discussion

★ Where do you go for your summer holidays? What sort of holiday do you prefer? Do you go to the seaside? Have you ever been abroad? Would you like to go on a holiday abroad?

Library corner

★ *Sunshine and shadow (A&C Black 1971)*

★ *Seaside treasures (Mills & Boon 1971)*

★ *A day by the sea (Hamish Hamilton 1978)*

★ *Summer (Evans 1979)*

★ *The four seasons (Franklin Watts 1983)*

★ *Sun calendar (A&C Black 1983)*

Activities

★ Arrange a trip to the seaside. Collect shells and pebbles. Have a competition for who can find the smallest shell or prettiest pebble.

★ Visit a farm. Ask the farmer what special tasks he has to do during the summer. Collect a variety of different grasses.

★ Make a display of 'things from the seaside.' Include shells, pebbles, seaweed, pictures of fishing boats and sea birds.

★ Make a frieze of 'under the sea'. Include brightly-coloured fish, an octopus, shells, seaweed, coral, a diver and a wreck.

To make a maypole

Materials
Clothes pegs
Floral ribbon/pieces of material
Card
Crêpe paper/card
Pipe cleaners/cotton wool
A piece of dowel, 1cm x 30cm
Plasticine

1 Wrap the rounded end of a clothes peg in a thin layer of cotton wool. Tie a 5cm square of white material to it.
2 Make arms by tying a pipe cleaner round the neck of the clothes peg. Use crêpe paper or material to make a long dress. Add face, hair, and shoes.
3 Cover the dowel by winding a strip of crêpe paper around it. At the top, add a circle of card already decorated with tiny pieces of coloured paper. Put dowel in plasticine base.
4 Tear the floral ribbon into fine strips. Attach the doll to the maypole.

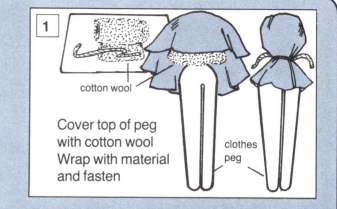

1 Cover top of peg with cotton wool. Wrap with material and fasten

2 Wrap material round peg for dress
Wrap pipe cleaner around for arms
Draw face

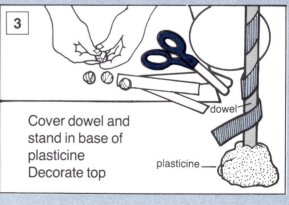

3 Cover dowel and stand in base of plasticine
Decorate top

Flowers

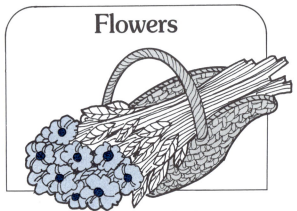

The aims of this topic are to develop observational skills; to increase an awareness of order and beauty; and to show how flowers are useful in the production of fruits and seeds.

Flowers

People in lands all over the world love flowers because of their colours and scents. But flowers not only look pretty and smell lovely. They are very useful too, for without flowers we would have no fruit, or seeds to plant the following year.

People who grow the fruit we eat are pleased when their trees blossom. Banana farmers in Jamaica and orange growers in Spain watch their trees carefully for the first signs of white flowers. They know that if there are no flowers there will be no fruit.

Long ago in Europe, people thought that there was a special goddess called Flora who looked after the flowers and made them grow. The people of China had a festival for the goddess of flowers. At this special festival all the children made head-dresses which they decorated with colourful paper flowers.

In Holland, many people make their living by growing flowers. The people grow flowers in order to get new bulbs. They sell the bulbs to countries in different parts of the world in exchange for other things.

Special festivals are held in Holland in the spring and summer. There are great processions with floats decorated with flowers. In spring, many people visit the fields in Holland. They see strips of bright colour because all the daffodils and tulips are in bloom.

The people of Japan love flowers. They have a special way of arranging flowers that they call Ikebana. They have many flower festivals. Flower festivals are held in our country too. At some, money is collected which is given to people who are in some kind of need. After the festival, the flowers are taken to poor, sick or lonely old people.

The first snowdrop

In a tiny cottage at the end of the wood lived a little old lady and a little old man. They both hated the winter for it was very cold and the days were very short. When the weather was bad they could not leave their home. Their legs were no longer young and strong and they were always afraid that they might slip and fall.

One winter had been very harsh. There had been much snow and the little old man told the old lady that the logs in their store were almost finished. He was worried that if the winter lasted much longer they would have no fuel for their fire.

"That giant called Winter is never going to leave the earth and go back to his icy palace," said the old man. The little old lady said, "Don't worry. I have known many winters. Spring always comes after Old Man Winter, bringing warm winds to blow upon our earth to waken the plants and bulbs. She sends her messengers first, the dainty snowdrops that shake their heads in the breeze. You will see them before very long."

That night the old man went to bed. But he hardly slept because he was worrying whether the logs would last until the weather was good enough for him to go to the forest and chop some more.

The next morning the old man got up early and looked out of the window. There, just beside the path that led to his front door, he saw a dainty little snowdrop waving its head in the breeze. He called to his wife, "What do you think I can see from the window?" The little old woman called out "One of Spring's messengers. Ever since the world began, warm Spring has always been able to chase away Old Man Winter. Very soon now Old Man Winter will return to his icy palace and the birds will sing and the flowers will bloom once more."

Snowdrops

I like to think
That, long ago,
There fell to earth
Some flakes of snow
Which loved this cold,
Grey world of ours
So much, they stayed
As snowdrop flowers.
(Book of a thousand poems, Evans 1959)

More ideas

HYMNS
The flowers that grow in the garden; all the flowers are waking; I love the sun (*Someone's singing Lord*, A&C Black 1973)

POEM
My garden (*Sing a new song*, REP 1969)

..Things to do.............

Discussion

★ How do flowers grow? What do they need? Where do they grow? What are the differences between garden flowers and wild flowers? Do we need flowers?

★ Have you seen any flowers recently? Name them. What colour were they? What did they look like?

★ Why do flowers have such bright colours and strong scents?

Library corner

★ Flowers *(Longman 1977)*

★ Garden flowers; the wayside; bulbs *(Evans 1979)*

★ Plants *(Macmillan 1978)*

Activities

★ Observe different parts of a flower using a magnifying glass.

★ Press some flowers by placing them in tissues and between boards. Add a weight and leave for several days. Mount the pressed flowers on to a piece of coloured card.

★ Plant sunflower seeds and record their growth on a chart. Hold a 'tallest sunflower' competition.

★ Make a flower frieze using yoghurt cartons (see instructions).

To make flowers

Materials
Yoghurt cartons
Gummed paper circles
Green tissue, or crêpe, paper
Paint/paint brushes
A roll of frieze paper
Scissors

1 Mark a clean yoghurt carton at 1cm intervals around the rim.
2 Cut down from each mark to within ½cm of the bottom of the carton so that a fringe is formed. Bend each strip back. Stick a circle of gummed paper on the bottom of the carton to represent the centre of the flower.
3 Arrange many flowers on to the frieze paper. Paint in the stems and add leaves from crêpe, or tissue, paper.

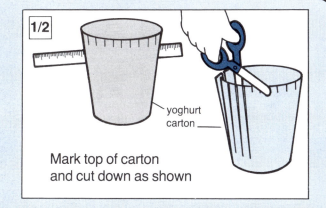

Mark top of carton and cut down as shown

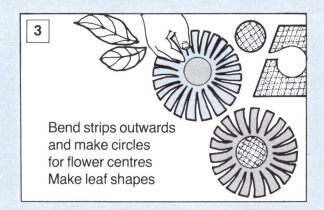

Bend strips outwards and make circles for flower centres
Make leaf shapes

People Who Help Us

Every day there are numerous people who help us whom we may never see. The aim of this topic is to help the children to a realization that no one is completely self-sufficient. We depend on others, and there are times when we should give, and times when we should receive.

Bernard the helper

In a village at the foot of some very tall mountains lived a little boy named Bernard. The mountains were very dangerous and were covered in snow. Often, travellers who came over the mountains knocked on the door of his house and asked for help. Sometimes they were hurt or injured. At other times they needed food and warmth because they were very tired.

When Bernard was older, he set out with some friends to build a shelter up in the mountains so that the travellers would have a place to rest. Bernard and his friends had big dogs to help them. The dogs were very strong and used their noses to sniff out travellers who had fallen and had become covered with snow.

When the dog found a traveller it barked and Bernard and his friends then knew that someone needed help. The men would then help the poor traveller. They took him back to the little shelter and looked after him until he was fit to go on his way.

All this happened a long time ago, but every day there are people who need special help from others. Each one of us has someone who helps us every day.

Helpful people

Travellers on the roads today are helped by the police, the AA (Automobile Association) and the RAC (Royal Automobile Club). When accidents occur, ambulance crews and sometimes firemen go to help. When we travel by bus, train, ship or aeroplane, we rely on many people who work on these different forms of transport.

People who are sick need the help of doctors and nurses. They also depend on the many other people who work in the hospitals, like cooks and laundry workers, people who take X-rays, and pharmacists who make pills and medicines.

When a new baby arrives in a family, health visitors and district nurses visit the parents and help them to look after the new baby. When the babies grow older they are taken to school where teachers help them to learn many interesting things.

Old people often need help. Sometimes they need people to help them clean their homes and home helps visit them, while other people take them a good, hot meal at lunchtime. Have you ever heard of 'Meals on Wheels'? Old people are often very lonely and their visitors cheer them up by talking to them and caring for them.

Many people have worked hard so that we have plenty of food to eat. Some of these people work in our own country, and some work in other lands.

Most of these people will be unknown to us. But there are people whom we do know. We may have met the people who deliver our milk, and our post, in the morning. Sometimes, when things go wrong in our homes, people come round and help us to mend them. Have you ever thought where the rubbish goes? It is taken away by refuse collectors. All these people help us in lots of different ways.

We meet lots of helpful people in our school too. There are cleaners, caretakers, secretaries, cooks, welfare workers, and, of course, your teachers. They make sure that you are well looked after and that you learn lots of interesting things.

And then there are your parents. They help you in lots of ways. Can you think of some of the ways in which your parents help you?

The postman

Rat-a-tat-tat, rat-a-tat-tat,
Rat-a-tat-tat tattoo!
That's the way the postman goes
Rat-a-tat-tat tattoo!
Every morning at half-past eight
You hear a bang at the garden gate
And rat-a-tat-tat, rat-a-tat-tat
Rat-a-tat-tat tattoo.
(Book of a thousand poems, Evans 1959)

More ideas

SONGS
Here comes the policeman; Jackie the sailor (*Sing a song 2, Nelson 1979*)
The fireman (*Apusskidu songs for children, A&C Black 1975*)
Down at the station (*Sing a song 1, Nelson 1978*)

..Things to do..............

Discussion

★ Talk about people who help us at school, e.g. caretakers, cleaners, cooks, teachers, welfare workers, secretaries.

★ Who visits us at home? Postal staff, refuse collectors, doctors.

★ Talk about people who help us in an emergency, and agencies that help people who are poor, hungry and lonely in this country and in other parts of the world.

Library corner

★ *What people do* (Macmillan 1979)

★ *Working around the world* (Macmillan 1981)

★ *Let's go to the shops; the fire station; the police station* (Franklin Watts 1981)

Activities

★ Arrange a visit to a police or fire station.

★ Make a scrapbook entitled 'people at work'. Use pictures from magazines and newspapers as well as the children's own paintings and drawings.

★ Vary the usual home corner by setting up corners within the classroom which reflect the jobs done by different people in the community: e.g. a post office, a hospital, a baker's shop, a pharmacy, a school. Act out situations showing how different people help us.

To make bendy figures

Materials
Activity, or cartridge, paper
Pencils
Scissors
Crayons
Paint, or gummed paper

1 Make a template of an all-purpose body shape (slight modifications may be necessary). Place template on to a fold on the paper and draw the outline. Cut this out.
2 Decide on an occupation and draw the appropriate clothing on to this basic shape.
3 Once the shape has been coloured, fold it along its original crease from the waist downwards, and make alternate cuts from fold and from edge. These should almost go across the width of the figure. Open out.
4 Stick the figures on to the frieze and bend slightly to right or left.

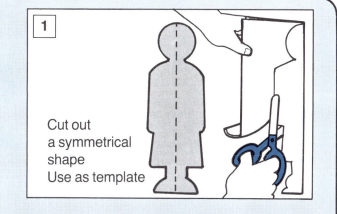

Cut out a symmetrical shape
Use as template

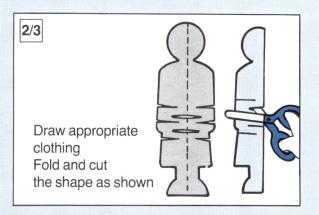

Draw appropriate clothing
Fold and cut the shape as shown

Children of Many Lands

The aims of this topic are to help the children to see themselves as part of one big world family and to give every child the opportunity to form a good self-image. The material in 'Children of the world' can be used by selecting and discussing a small section each day.

Children of the world
In every country of the world there are many children. Some children live in very hot lands, some in warm lands, some in cool lands and some in very cold lands. In some countries there is too much rain while in others there are times when there is not enough rain.

Where do children live?
There are children who live up in the mountains, children who live in towns and cities, some who live in the countryside and some who live by the sea.

In some ways we are all alike:
All children are alike in some ways. We all have heads, arms, legs, eyes, ears, noses. Each one of us has a skeleton inside us. We have the same needs because we all need homes, food, and clothes. We have the same feelings too because we can all feel happy, sad or angry. And we all need and depend on other people.

In some ways we are different:
In some ways we are different from each other. Some children are tall and some are short, some fat and some thin. Our hair may be blonde, reddish, brown or black. Some children have curly hair while others have straight hair. Some wear their hair short and others let it grow long.

Children have different coloured eyes. Our skins are different colours too. Some children have pink skins, some yellow, some brown and some black. Children have different names too.

Our homes and families:
Children usually belong to a family. Some have big families with lots of brothers and sisters while some children have no brothers and sisters. Families live in either houses, flats, tents, caravans, huts, caves or boats.

Homes in different parts of our world are made from different materials: stones, bricks, cloth, wood, grasses, sticks or mud can all be used to make a home. Some Eskimo children used to live in little rounded snow houses called igloos. Igloos were made from snow and ice, but today Eskimos use other materials to build their homes.

People build their homes using the materials which they can get hold of easily. In countries where the weather is cold, strong houses made of bricks or stones are needed. But in some lands people do not need such thick walls. The shapes of our homes vary too, depending on where we live.

Our clothes:
It would be very silly if we wore scarves and gloves on a very hot day. Children in our country wear different clothes in winter than they wear in summer. Children in hot lands do not need warm clothes. They usually wear loose clothes to keep them cool. People use materials which they can get easily, to make into clothes. Most people in our world wear some kind of clothes.

Our feelings:
All children have feelings. We can feel excited, angry, sad, frightened, happy, or lonely. We all need friends and people to help us feel happy. Some children from other countries come to live in this country. They are sometimes lonely because they speak a different language. They need us to help them, to talk to them and make them feel welcome. They will feel happy if we let them join in our games.

Many children in the world are sad, afraid and unhappy. Some live in poorer lands. People from richer countries go to the poorer countries to take medicine for sick children and to take food when the harvest fails. Machinery, such as tractors and ploughs, and fertilizers are taken to help the farmers to grow better crops.

The world family:
All people in the world are like one big family. They need to work together and learn how to share all the wonderful things in the world so that no one is hungry or sad or lonely, and everyone can have a share of happiness.

More ideas

STORY
The little boy and his house *(Stories for five year olds, Faber and Faber 1973)*

SONGS
Thank you for my friends; ten little men in a flying saucer *(Sing a song 1, Nelson 1978)*

..Things to do..............

Discussion

★ Talk about how the lives of children differ in various parts of the world: the different food, climate, shelter, clothes etc.

Library corner

★ Peoples of the world *(Usborne 1978)*

★ All the things we share *(Lion 1979)*

★ Peoples and customs *(Macmillan 1979)*

★ Children around the world *(Macmillan 1982)*

★ Different peoples *(Macdonald 1982)*

★ Maps of many lands *(Macdonald 1983)*

Activities

★ Look at a globe and find hot lands, cold lands and temperate lands.

★ Find recipes from different lands. Try the recipes and sample the dishes.

★ Collect and display dolls in traditional dress from different lands.

★ Collect things from other lands, e.g. postcards from holidays abroad and presents brought back from abroad.

★ Make a collection of things made in other lands e.g. cotton goods from Taiwan, a cassette recorder from Japan, small toys from Hong Kong, etc.

To make a ring around the world

Materials
Card
Frieze paper
Paint/paint brushes
Collage materials
Ribbon
Glue
Scissors

1 Cut out a large circle to represent the world. Draw the land formations and paint in the land and sea.
2 Cut out several simple outlines of children. Distribute these to different classes. Each class paints the basic shape and then dresses it, using collage materials, to represent a child from a particular country.
3 Display the global shape and place the children from different lands around it. Join them together using a bright ribbon to form a ring around the world.

Cut and paint a circle to represent world

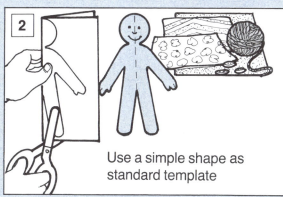

Use a simple shape as standard template

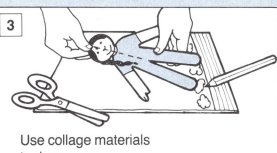

Use collage materials to dress
Draw faces

Introduction

Why we celebrate festivals

All over the world, people enjoy celebrating festivals. Throughout a wide variety of religions and cultures, people have felt it was important to put aside certain days of the year to stop work and enjoy themselves. In doing so, they experience the feeling of 'togetherness', based on a shared culture and history.

Themes

Many celebrations share themes. This is not very surprising when we remember that people all over the world have the same basic needs wherever they live. Certain times of the year are celebrated in almost all countries and cultures. These include the beginning of the year, the time when the seeds for the food crop are sown, and the harvest, whether it is wheat, yams, apples, lemons, wild berries, or even fish.

Symbols are often common throughout different cultures: green leaves and burning candles symbolize life, for example. The giving of gifts, telling of stories and eating of special foods are common to many festivals too.

The festivals are listed under theme headings, to emphasize the common elements of the various festivals, as well as the differences in culture and history that make each festival especially interesting. The fact that they appear as they do, instead of according to a calendar of the solar year, does not mean that they should be celebrated at any time other than the proper one. The theme headings are simply to suggest one of a number of possible ideas for an approach.

When festivals happen

To find out when each festival occurs, it is a good idea to consult a calendar of religious festivals, such as the *Shap Calendar of Religious Festivals*, published by the Commission for Racial Equality. This gives the actual dates on which festivals fall, plus a brief outline of their significance. The calendar includes many more festivals than are covered here, and dates (for a specific year) the moveable feasts found in many faiths.

About this section

Twenty-four festivals are described in the following pages. At the beginning of each description, there is a short section explaining what the festival celebrates and when it happens. This is followed by a description of the ways in which it is celebrated. Very often, there is a traditional story attached to a festival, and this will either be told in words suitable for reading aloud, or written as a short play which children can use as a basis or inspiration for one of their own. Following this, there may be a few extra ideas for celebrating in school with suggestions for things to do, make, or cook. Finally, ideas for books, poems, songs and music are given.

About the poems

The following books have been used to provide sources for the poems recommended:
Seeing and doing, anthology of songs and poems, compiled by Rosalind Farrimond, *Thames/Methuen 1982*
Rhyme time, poems collected by Barbara Ireson, *Hamlyn Beaver 1977*
Wheel around the world, compiled by Chris Searle, *Macdonald 1983*
The young Puffin book of verse, compiled by Barbara Ireson, *Puffin 1970*.

Delights and warnings, anthology of poems selected by John and Gillian Beer, *Macdonald 1979*
The Oxford book of Christmas poems, edited by Michael Harrison and Christopher Stuart-Clark, *OUP 1983*
The Tinder-box assembly book, compiled by Sylvia Barratt, *A & C Black 1982*

About the songs

The songs suggested come from the following books:
The Puffin colony song book, *Puffin*
Love, work and hope, songs for a new generation, *Oak Publishing*
Granny's yard, *Bell and Hyman*
Tinderbox, *A & C Black*
Flying a round, *A & C Black*
Alleluya, *A & C Black*
Celebration songs, *Oliver and Boyd*
Festivals, books 1 and 2, compiled by Jean Gilbert, *OUP*
Faith, folk and nativity, *Galliard*
Faith, folk and charity, *Galliard*
Look away, *World Around Songs*
African songs, Lynn Rohbough, *Delaware* (Ohio, USA)

About the music

The following are ideas for recorded music, short sections of which might be suitable for assemblies:
Missa Luba, a Congolese mass (LYRI/LLST 757)
Missa Criolla, South American folk setting of the mass (PHI/SBL 7684)
Indian street music (NON/H7Z035) (libraries only)
Music from the Himalayas (ARG/2FB 40) (libraries only)
Planet Suite, Gustav Holst (especially Jupiter)

Enigma Variations, Edward Elgar
(especially *Nimrod*)
Ninth Symphony, Ludwig van Beethoven
(especially the last movement with its Ode to Joy)
St. Nicholas, Noyyes Fludde, Spring Symphony, all by Benjamin Britten
Tom Paxton's children's song book
(BRADM/601)
Beatles songs (especially *Eleanor Rigby, Nowhere Man* and *Let there be Peace*)

In the suggested pieces for each festival, all recordings were available at the time of publication.

Listening to recorded music

Children should always be settled and ready for any listening activity. Let them listen to the music at least once before discussing it. With young children, always prepare the listening material carefully and keep the extracts short.

Can they identify any instruments? Was the music loud/quiet, slow/fast? Sometimes it helps them concentrate if they close their eyes while they listen. Try giving them a visual stimulus after they have heard the music – either a picture of the instruments being played, or better still, the instruments themselves, or something else which will help set the mood, or the scene, of the music.

Involving parents

Many of the festivals here involve religions and cultures with which teachers may be unfamiliar. Even if this is not the case, it is a good idea to involve the members of the community whose festival you are celebrating, as they will be able to give a lively, first-hand account of what happens. Try to get parents or local religious leaders to help out.

Contents

THEME: BEGINNINGS
These four festivals are just some of the many that celebrate beginnings and the chance of a new start that comes with each new year. Several of the other festivals in this book are also appropriate to celebrate as 'beginnings', as well as a number that are not covered here.

Christmas	**106**
Hogmanay	**108**
The Chinese New Year	**110**
The Islamic New Year	**112**

THEME: SPRING AND SUMMER
Spring festivals are times when we think about the new life and new growth we see about us, as the days get warmer and the summer draws near.

Crops are sown and begin to grow, young animals are born, and the days grow longer.

In every way there is promise of good things to come. The arrival of summer is also a cause for celebration. Many of the festivities for both seasons can be traced back to ancient times.

Passover	**114**
Easter	**116**
Holi	**118**
May Day	**120**
Pentecost and Whitsun	**122**

HARVEST
Harvest festivals have always been times for special thanksgiving, and opportunities to pray for success in the future too.

Sukkot	**124**
Yam Harvest	**126**

LIGHT AND DARKNESS
Light is a powerful symbol in many cultures.

It stands for knowledge and life, while the lack of it symbolizes the opposite.

Diwali	**128**
Hanukah	**130**

FEASTS AND FASTS
Fasting is common to many religions. It is a way of trying to concentrate on spiritual things by avoiding the material comforts of life.

Quite often there is a feast either before or after a fast, so the two form closely connected events. Feasting is a popular and widespread way of celebrating, and is not limited to these times.

Ramadan	**132**
Shrove Tuesday	**134**
Purim	**136**

SPECIAL PEOPLE
Any number of festivals can be related to important individuals who either founded or contributed to religions, or taught ways of living.

The Buddha's Birthday	**138**
Baisakhi	**140**
St. Patrick's and St. David's Day	**142**

FAMILY AND FRIENDS
These are perhaps the most special people we are ever likely to meet, and celebrating friendship and love is important all over the world.

Mothers' Day	**144**
Raksha Bandhan	**146**
Weddings	**148**
Birthdays	**150**

And finally, the important theme of worldwide friendship between peoples of different colour, culture and faith:

One World	**152**

Christmas

About Christmas

Christmas is celebrated all over the Christian world, usually on December 25. It marks the birth of Jesus Christ, the founder of the Christian religion, who Christians believe was the Son of God. Some early Christians chose this date for the festival of Christ's birth because it was already a well-established pre-Christian festival, marking the beginning of the new year.

Celebrating Christmas

For practising Christians, this is a time for worship, in prayer and song, and for retelling the story of the birth of Jesus. It is also a time for parties and feasting – though what is actually eaten varies considerably from country to country.

In Britain, and many other countries, a turkey is the main dish at Christmas lunch. This has supplanted the more traditional goose. Mince pies and plum pudding have a long history. In many countries it was the custom to fatten a pig for Christmas, and to serve a boar's head at the Christmas feast.

In Poland, the important meal of the season is on Christmas Eve. Fish is eaten rather than meat, along with pickles, soups, special dumplings and poppy-seed cake.

The evergreens, that are such an important part of Christmas decorations, all originate from the ancient pre-Christian festival. In Christian tradition they symbolize eternal life.

Lights – also a symbol of life – are important at Christmas. People light candles in churches, and often decorate their Christmas tree either with lighted candles or with electric 'fairy lights'. In the days when open hearths were common, people burned

a 'yule log' – the biggest log they could find – for several days over the festival.

For children the presents are the most important part of Christmas! But in many countries these do not come on Christmas Day at all. In Germany and the Netherlands, they arrive on December 6, brought by St. Nicholas. St. Nicholas was a bishop who lived many hundreds of years ago. He is known as Santa Claus and is remembered as the patron saint of children.

In Spain, among other countries, presents arrive on January 6, the festival of the Epiphany. This marks the visit of the 'wise men from the East', who brought gifts to the baby Jesus. Spanish children put out their shoes for the kings to leave their gifts in.

Christians of the Eastern Orthodox faith, in the Soviet Union and some other parts of Eastern Europe, celebrate Christmas on January 7. This is because they use an older version of the calendar than the one we use, and so there are several days' difference. In the Soviet Union, children are brought gifts by an old woman known as 'Baboushka' ('Granny'). There, the story goes that Baboushka once tried to make her own way to Bethlehem to take a gift to the baby Jesus.

The Christmas Story

One of the most ancient ways of telling the Christmas story is by means of the Nativity play. The following is only an outline. Children can use it to work out their own ideas once they are familiar with the story. Ad-libbing is essential!

CHARACTERS

Essential characters are Mary, Joseph, the innkeeper, the shepherds, angels, the three wise men and, in this version, at least one Roman soldier. 'Extras' can include the

innkeeper's family, more Romans, King Herod, guests at the inn, and various animals.

Before the curtain goes up, enter Roman soldier:

Hullo! My name's Marcus. I want to tell you about what happened a long time ago, when I was stationed in Judea, the land of the Jews. We had a tough time there because nobody liked us Romans. One of the things that annoyed the Jews most of all was when our emperor insisted he wanted everyone to travel to their home town and be registered. He wanted to see how many people there were in his empire. Goodness knows why! The Jews kept going on about how one day this saviour would turn up. They called him the Messiah. They thought he would save them all from us Romans.

SCENE 1:

The kitchen of the inn. Everyone is busy cooking, serving meals, arranging sleeping quarters and so on. Enter Marcus.

Marcus: *Hullo everyone!*

Innkeeper: *Oh, you again! I'm not handing out any free meals tonight. You had your share last night. You Romans, you think you own the place. I haven't got a minute to spare because of you lot and this stupid head count your emperor is forcing us to do. Look at this! I'm going to have people sleeping on the kitchen table tonight!*

Marcus: *That's a pity. I've just found a couple of people who really need a place to stay. Can't you find a corner for them? They've come all the way from Nazareth ...*

Enter Joseph and Mary.

Innkeeper: *Look, I'm sorry. There just isn't anywhere. Yes dear, I can see the problem. When's the baby due?*

Mary: *Any time now.*

Innkeeper: *Well, I don't know. I'll try and get rid of some of these people tomorrow, but tonight's just impossible ... unless you want to sleep in the stable.*
Marcus: *That's a good idea! I've had a snooze or two myself there some nights, when I'm supposed to be on patrol.*
Marcus leads Mary and Joseph to the stable.

SCENE 2
The shepherds sitting round a fire. Marcus's voice comes from off-stage.
Marcus: *Now, while all this was happening in Bethlehem, there were these shepherds, looking after their sheep ...*
Shepherd 1: *Listen! Can you hear singing?*
Shepherd 2: *It's all those people in Bethlehem, having a party.*
Shepherd 3: *No it isn't! Look!*
Enter angels. The shepherds are terrified and try to hide under their cloaks.
An angel: *Don't be afraid! We've brought you wonderful news. The Messiah you've all been waiting for has been born at last. You'll find him wrapped in swaddling clothes, lying in a manger. He's only a tiny baby, and you are the first to know he's been born.*
The Angels sing a carol, and then leave.

Shepherd 1: *Let's go and see him!*
Exit shepherds

SCENE 3
Enter Marcus: *Now about this time, three wise men turned up in Jerusalem. They said they were looking for a new king. They brought with them expensive gifts of gold, frankincense and myrrh. They headed straight for the palace of the king in Jerusalem. He was called Herod. Herod didn't like the idea of there being a second king in Judea. So he asked his fortune-tellers to find out where the baby king was. They told him that the baby was in Bethlehem. He then sent the wise men on their way. He told them to drop in on their way back and tell him all about the baby, so he could go along and see him. Actually, he wanted to get rid of him. He didn't succeed, but that's another story ...*

SCENE 4
In the stable. One by one the characters approach Joseph, Mary and baby Jesus in the stable, bearing gifts (see picture).
The wise men come in last. This scene can either be mimed, or the children can be encouraged to write their own dialogue.

POEMS
Carol of the brown king, Langston Hughes, **Rhyme time**. *Christmas pudding*, Jean Chapman; *Christmas stocking*, Eleanor Farjeon; *Lullaby carol*, Gerard Benson, all in **Seeing and doing**.
SONGS
Standing in the rain, **Faith, folk and nativity**
Oh have you nowhere? **Celebration songs**
MUSIC
Amhal and the night visitors Menotti

Hogmanay

About Hogmanay

Hogmanay is the Scottish name for New Year's Eve, December 31. All over the world, people of different religions and cultures celebrate a variety of New Year festivals, at different times of the year. Almost all of them, however, keep to the European/American system of a 365-day year, starting on January 1, in addition to whatever local calendar is used.

In some places, the change from the old year to the new is marked with very little celebration, but in most places it is at least an occasion for a party. In Scotland, and among Scottish people wherever they are, it is much more than that.

Celebrating Hogmanay

Hogmanay, and most other new year festivities, are folk festivals, with customs dating back thousand of years. Festivities start with a party which begins on New Year's Eve and goes on until at least the early hours of New Year's Day. The highpoint of the celebration is at midnight because it is the exact time when the old year ends and the new year begins.

It is an important tradition that the first person to come into the house at the beginning of the year must be a man who is, preferably, tall and dark. He must be carrying certain things. These are usually a piece of coal (see picture), and sometimes bread, salt and a piece of mistletoe. He may carry money, or even a herring! He is supposed to be a stranger, but people are often so anxious to make sure he is the right sort of person, that they arrange for someone to arrive just after midnight. Quite often, the man has been at the party all along, and has been sent out especially in order to come back in again.

The way he enters the house is important. Everyone waits for the clock to strike midnight. At the last stroke, there is a loud knock on the door. The door then opens and the 'stranger' walks in. He puts the coal on the fire and the mistletoe on the mantlepiece. The host gives him a drink and everyone wishes everyone else a happy new year.

The custom of visiting a house at the turn of the year is called 'first-footing'. The stranger probably represents the new year, which is why he must be welcomed and cannot be turned away. When everyone is gathered together, they all sing the famous song *Auld Lang Syne*.

Other new year customs

Scotland is not the only place where the new year is welcomed with special celebrations. Similar customs exist over much of the north of England, and there are a whole variety of different traditions in Britain, as well as in other countries.

In many places, particularly in the north of England, a special cake is baked for the new year. It is cooked using the same recipe as the Christmas cake, but without the marzipan.

Other customs include ringing out the old year with muffled church bells. These sound very soft and feeble. At the turn of the year, the bells are rung out loud and clear. Crowds gather in public places in cities to celebrate together.

In many places, children used to spend the morning of New Year's Day going from house to house, visiting neighbours. This custom still survives in some places. It used to be common for children to sing, as they do when they go Christmas carolling. In return they might be given mince pies, cake, oranges or money and perhaps a small glass of sherry. All this had to be done before noon. If the children visited old people who had not had the chance to go to a New Year's Eve party, the children actually took the place of the 'first-footer', being the first people over the threshold in the new year. In parts of Wales it used to be the custom for the children to bring water into each house they visited and sprinkle it around, using a green branch to do so. They too would be rewarded with food or money.

In Mexico it is the custom to spend the last five days of the old year in a mood of sorrow, with a festival of rejoicing once the new year begins. Elsewhere on the American continent, some American Indians keep an ancient custom of putting out all fires before the new year begins and lighting new fires once it has started.

New Year's Day in Japan

New Year's Day in Japan is the most important festival of the year. It goes on for six days, starting on January 1. But everyone starts getting ready from December 13 onwards.

To begin with, people make sure their homes are spotlessly clean. They must decorate them too, using special symbols which they believe will bring them good luck in the year to come. They use small pine trees, which are symbols of long life; straight bamboo stems, which stand for straightness of character; and ferns, oranges and ropes of straw for good fortune. Lobsters are cooked too: their crooked backs are a sign that people honour old age.

Everyone begins New Year's Day itself with a drink of fresh well water. There are special foods for the occasion, too. These are chosen because their Japanese names sound like the Japanese words for things everyone wants. So people eat a special kind of seaweed, which has a name that sounds like the word for 'happiness', and black beans, which have a name that sounds like 'good health'. They eat herring roe, because its name sounds like 'lots of children', and chestnuts, whose name sounds like 'strength'.

The second day of the festival is especially important for traders. They decorate their trucks and carts and load them up with the goods they sell. Then the drivers, dressed in their best new clothes, drive them through the streets, past a big crowd of onlookers.

On the last day of the six-day festival, everyone takes the decorations down, and the year begins in earnest.

A poem for new year
This traditional song might well have been sung by children as they went from house to house on the morning of New Year's Day.

The new year
*Here we bring new water
From the well so clear,
For to worship God with,
This happy new year.
Sing ley-dew, sing ley-dew,
The water and the wine;
The seven bright gold wires
And the bugles they do shine.*

*Sing reign of fair maid,
With gold upon her toe –
Open you the west door,
And turn the old year go:
Sing reign of fair maid,
With gold upon her chin –
Open you the east door,
And let the new year in.*
(Traditional)

Activities for the new year
1 Act out a dialogue between the old year and the new. The old year should give advice, and point out some of the important things it has done over the past year. The new one will suggest plans of its own.
2 Work out some dance or movement ideas around the idea of the old and new years. The old year could move very slowly, stiffly and in a tired fashion. The new year will skip and dance very enthusiastically.
3 Make some 'bells', using bottles with different amounts of water in them. Tapped gently, these will produce a variety of notes.

Ask the children to see if they can compose or play simple tunes once they have made bells that will play a scale.

POEMS
The old year, John Clare, **The Oxford book of Christmas poems**;
The months, Sara Coleridge, **Seeing and doing**
SONGS
The twelve days of Christmas, traditional carol
Auld Lang Syne, traditional, words by Robert Burns

109

Chinese New Year

About the Chinese new year

The Chinese new year is a two-week long festival that takes place in January or February. In the Chinese calendar, it starts on the 23rd day of the 12th moon. This is usually some time between January 21 and February 19. Throughout the world, Chinese communities celebrate with festivities both at home and out in the streets.

Celebrating the new year

Before the new year celebrations begin, Chinese people make sure their houses are cleaned and swept. People like to greet the new year with all the business from the old one finished, so account books are brought up to date. It is a time for wearing new clothes, and making a fresh start.

Tradition has it that at new year, Tsao Chun, the kitchen god, goes to Heaven to report on the families among whom he lives. In the ancient Chinese religion there were many gods, but only one God of Heaven, to whom all the others were answerable.

At the end of the year, the family tries to make sure Tsao Chun will say good things about them when he goes to Heaven. So they offer him sweets and wine, and smear his lips with honey so that he will say sweet things about them. Then, right at the end of the year, his picture is burned. This symbolizes his journey to Heaven.

On New Year's Eve, the family writes mottoes on lucky red paper and fixes these around the doors of their homes. These are to wish everyone good luck in the year to come. Pictures of fierce warriors are pasted to the doorposts, to keep out anything evil.

In the evening, the family seals all the doors of the house with red paper and everyone sits down together for a special meal. There is no meat at this feast, out of respect to the animals. Only vegetables are served, along with oranges and tangerines. These are symbols of long life. There are also special pastries filled with nuts. At the end of the meal everyone wishes everyone else a happy new year.

The next day the doors are unsealed, and a new picture of Tsao Chun is pasted to the wall. He has come back from Heaven once more, and can now start watching the family for another year. Everyone stays quietly at home on this first day of the new year – the celebrations begin in earnest on the second day, when people start to visit friends and relations. It is the custom to give children gifts of money at this time. These are sealed in lucky red envelopes.

Celebrations continue for two weeks, with firecrackers to frighten off anything evil, and dancing. On the third day of the new year there is a celebration called the Feast of the Lanterns. Decorated lanterns are hung from the trees, and in the streets there is the magnificent Lion Dance.

The 'lion' is an unusual-looking animal, made of bamboo and covered with highly decorated silk and paper. It is constructed so that people can move inside it. The 'lion' dances through the streets (see picture), opening and closing its mouth, and collecting presents of money in lucky red envelopes, which are hung outside the shops it passes.

Years of the animals

The gods chose twelve animals to name the years after, but the animals disagreed about whose name should be given to the first year. Each animal thought he was more important than the others, and should come first, and they had a terrible argument.

The gods decided to settle things by making the animals have a swimming race across a wide river. The animal that got across first would give its name to the first year, the second to the second year, and so on.

"That's not fair," said the smaller animals – the rat, the hare, the snake and the cockerel. "Everyone knows that the big animals like the horse and the ox will get there first."

"You'll just have to see how well you do," said the gods.

So the animals lined up along the bank. One … two … three … GO! They were off.

It was really surprising to see how well some of the animals could swim. The ox was soon in the lead, for he was a strong swimmer, but the hare and the snake were not far behind, at least at the beginning of the race. The worst swimmer was the poor pig, who was a bit out of condition.

"Grunt! Grunt!" he muttered. "I'm cold and wet and I don't care if they never name a year after me!"

But the rat cared, and he was determined to get there first. As soon as the race began, he jumped on the ox's back and held on tight until the ox had very nearly reached the other side. Then he jumped off onto the dry land, just ahead of the ox.

"Hee! Hee! I'm the winner!" the rat shouted, dancing a little jig.

The ox had to settle for being second, followed by the tiger, the hare, the dragon, the snake, the horse, the ram, the monkey, the cockerel and the dog. Oh yes, and the pig. He was last, by quite a long way. But he was happier than anyone to see the other side!

The story of Tsao Chun

Tsao Chun, the kitchen god, was once a man. He was a poor stonemason, who lived long ago in China. He was poor, not because he was a bad stonemason, but because he was so slow and careful in the way he worked that he just couldn't make as much money as the faster, more careless workers.

Soon Tsao Chun was so poor that he and his wife thought they would starve. A rich man wanted to marry Tsao Chun's wife. Tsao Chun agreed to let this man marry his wife to save their lives. Tsao Chun missed his wife dreadfully. She missed him too, and so she decided to help. She persuaded her new husband to give Tsao Chun some work. Then, as he was working, she came to watch him. He saw her, but she looked so rich and fine he didn't even recognize her.

As Tsao Chun worked at the stone, his wife went into the kitchen and asked the servants there to make some little cakes.

"I want to give them to that poor mason," she explained. "He looks so tired and hungry."

Before she gave the cakes to Tsao Chun, she slipped a gold coin into each one.

"Now at least he will have some money," she thought.

But poor Tsao Chun never had any luck. On his way home, he stopped to buy a cup of tea. He sat down next to a stranger, and offered him a cake to eat with his tea.

"Thank you," said the stranger, and bit into a cake. At once, his teeth met the hard coin! When he saw the gold, he immediately offered to buy all the cakes. Tsao Chun sold all the cakes for a few small coins.

The next day, the kitchen servants told Tsao Chun who the beautiful woman he had seen was, and what had been in the cakes. He was heartbroken. He had not even recognized his wife, whom he missed so much, and he had given away the only riches he had ever had.

He decided to kill himself, for life didn't seem worth living. But just before he did so, the God of Heaven snatched him up and made him a god. Now he sits in everyone's kitchen, making sure they behave themselves.

Activities for the Chinese new year

1 Talk about the stories. What do the children think of the rat's tactics, or of the man who didn't mention the gold coins in the cakes?

2 Make a lion for the lion dance. Try making a light framework for the head using card strips. Cover the head with crêpe paper, and make a body using light cloth, decorated with paints or dyes. Look at pictures for ideas. If the children are to dance under the lion, it must be both robust and lightweight. Children might like to make more elaborate collage lions, or lion heads, using a variety of materials.

POEMS
The green spring, Shan Mei; *Spring song*, William Blake, both in **Seeing and doing**
SONGS
Chinese new year; *Lantern song*, both in **Festivals book 2**
MUSIC
Chinese drums and gongs **Lyrichord label** (LYRI/LIST 7102);
Chinese music – 11 Folk songs **Decca label** (DEC/ECS 2123) (library resource)

Islamic New Year

Islam in School

Teaching children about other people's religion is always going to be difficult, and Islam may seem to present special problems, not least because it has suffered from centuries of misrepresentation and misunderstanding. (For more on this subject, see **Religion in the multi-faith school** by Owen Cole, published by *Hulton*)

Teachers should avoid causing offence, and be aware that if they do so they may lead the children to repeat such mistakes. It is not, after all, what appears to the non-member of a faith to be offensive or not offensive that is the point – it is the effect on the members of the faith themselves.

As with most religions, it helps if you can get assistance from a member of the religion, perhaps an understanding parent. Children can be helpful, but they may be too shy, or too afraid of causing offence themselves, to point out errors.

Before tackling any Islamic festival, or indeed before covering the subject at all, one rule above all others must be remembered. This is that the Prophet Muhammad must *never* appear in a picture or a drama. It isn't just a question of not expecting Muslim children to do this. They will be upset to see anyone else doing it, so it must be impressed upon the whole class that this is not acceptable.

Festivals in Islam

Muslim festivals are not celebrated in the way that many other religious festivals are. They are times for prayer and thanksgiving rather than rowdy celebrations. This means that keeping a festival in school should reflect this

more serious approach, and be very different from celebrations for festivals such as Holi or Shrove Tuesday. An Islamic festival is essentially a solemn occasion, though there is room for joy too.

Islam has few festivals compared with other religions. The two major ones are Eid-ul-Fitr, which falls at the end of Ramadan (see pages 132 and 133), and Eid-ul-Adha, which takes place on the 10th of Dhul Hijja.

Ramadan and Dhul Hijja are the names of Islamic months. There is no equivalent in the solar year, since the Islamic year is a lunar one, and calculated on a different basis. Although many religious calendars are based on lunar months, and festivals are celebrated on the occasion, say, of a full or a new moon, most of them fit the lunar months into the overall framework of a solar year, which is marked by the changing seasons. The Islamic year is based on the twelve lunar months alone, which make the year about ten or eleven days shorter than the solar year. This means that, in terms of the Western calendar, Islamic festivals appear to occur a little earlier each year.

To make things even more complicated for the lay person, the actual day of the festival is often determined by the *sighting* of the moon. It is no good just knowing that a new moon is due – it must be seen before a festival such as Eid-ul-Fitr can take place. This means that it is possible that people will not know that a festival is about to begin until only hours beforehand. This can make a festival especially exciting, for the joy of the celebration is made more intense by suddenly finding out that it is Eid the next day!

The new year

The Islamic year starts on the first day of the month of Muharram. The occasion marks the

flight of the Prophet from his home town of Makkah (Mecca) to al-Madina (Medina). The prophet was forced to leave because the people of the city were determined to stop him preaching his religion. They had been very angry with him for telling them they must give up their wicked life-styles, stop praying to idols and worship only Allah, the one God. Leaving was a difficult process. The leaders of the city wanted to capture the Prophet and it would not have been advisable for him simply to walk out of the city gates in broad daylight, so he had to flee by night.

A story for al-Hijrah

The Prophet Muhammad was in great danger. He had been teaching the people of Makkah that they should give up worshipping idols, and worship only the one God, Allah. But they did not want to change their ways as he had told them to. They did not want to have to start caring for truth and justice, looking after the poor and needy, being kind to their neighbours, respecting their parents and elders, and loving children.

Life in the city became very difficult for the Prophet and his followers. They knew they would have to leave, or they would be killed. The people of al-Madina had asked the Prophet to come and stay with them, and he had already asked his followers to travel there ahead of him. But al-Madina was a long way off across the desert. How could he get there without being seen by the people who wanted to kill him? It seemed that the Prophet was trapped in the city.

In the end, the Prophet and his friend, Abu Bakr, managed to slip out of the city by night. But that was far from the end of their troubles. Getting to al-Madina was difficult because they could not follow the usual route and ride out openly on camels. They had to scramble across the hills towards a cave outside the city. There they could hide and rest until it was safe to go on.

The sun was high as they made their way to the cave. They were soon hot, dusty, tired and thirsty. At last they reached the cave and crept inside. It was cool and dark. They prayed, and then lay down to rest.

Then they heard the sound of galloping hooves, drawing nearer and nearer. Abu Bakr sat up, tense and afraid. The horsemen were soon so close it seemed he could hear them breathing.

"I can't see any sign of them," said a voice.

"Yet I'm sure they came this way..."

"They must be in this cave," said another voice. Abu Bakr heard footsteps so close they seemed to be almost in the cave with him. He kept very still, and so did the Prophet.

"Well, they're not in this one," said the first voice from right outside their cave. "They can't be. Look – there are spiders' webs all over the mouth, and bushes almost blocking the entrance. There's even a bird nesting here!" And they went away.

Abu Bakr wondered what they had been talking about. The entrance of the cave had been quite clear when they went in, with neither a spider nor a bird in sight.

Then he saw. Instead of the bare rock, the entrance of the cave was a mass of spiders' webs and thick undergrowth. A dove had built its nest among the branches, and was cooing gently.

"Messenger of God, what has happened?" asked Abu Bakr. But the Prophet just smiled, and the dove cooed.

They stayed hidden in the cave for several days. Abu Bakr's little daughter came to them every night, bringing them food and water. And every morning, a herdsman drove his animals close to the cave – so that no tracks could be seen. After three nights they learned it was safe to travel on to al-Madina. So they set out, mounted on camels, across the desert.

Activities for al-Hijrah

1 Using pins and coloured thread, weave patterns of spiders' webs.
2 Make vegetable printing blocks and work on the ideas of symmetry and repeating patterns that occur in Islamic art. (Note: do not allow the children to draw the Prophet)
3 Make a display about life in the desert.

BOOKS
Muslim nursery rhymes, Mustafa Yusuf McDermott; **Islam for younger people**, Ghulam Sarwar; **Love at home**, Khurram Murad; **Love your neighbour**, Khurram Murad; **Marvellous stories from the life of Muhammad**, Mardijah Aldrich Tarantino; **A great friend of children**, M S Kayani, all from *The Islamic Foundation* (223 London Road, Leicester).

MUSIC
Folk music of Iran, songs and instrumental music
Lyrichord label (LLST 7261),
A Persian heritage (H 72060)

Passover

About Passover

Passover is the most important festival of the Jewish year, and is probably the most ancient. It falls in late March or early April. Some parts of the Passover celebrations probably date back to very early times, but for centuries it has been celebrated as a time to remember how the Jewish people were delivered out of Egypt, where they had been forced to work as slaves.

Celebrating Passover

The way in which the Passover is celebrated is closely linked to the story of the way in which the Israelites left Egypt, and made their journey to the 'promised land' that was eventually to become Israel.

The Israelites had originally settled in Egypt because of famine in their homeland, and had been forced to work as slaves for the Pharaohs (rulers) of Egypt. Eventually Moses resolved to lead his people to freedom. He had heard the voice of God coming from a bush burning in the desert where he was looking after sheep, and this inspired him.

Together with his brother Aaron, Moses went to Egypt to challenge the Pharaoh to release the people. He did this only after God had sent a series of plagues to terrify the Egyptians, culminating in the deaths of all the eldest sons of every family, except those of the Israelites. At last, the people were allowed to leave. They had to prepare themselves very quickly, and travel fast, in case the Pharaoh should change his mind.

It is thought that Passover is based on two separate festivals that were celebrated long before the flight from Egypt. One was celebrated by nomadic shepherds who offered their first lambs as a sacrifice to God. The other was the Feast of Unleavened Bread, celebrated by the inhabitants of the land of Canaan (the ancient name for Israel) at the time of their spring barley harvest.

Today, the most important part of the Passover celebration is a special meal (see picture). This includes a service, held in the home around the table. The meal and the service are called the Seder, which means 'order', i.e. the order in which the food is eaten and the prayers are said.

Before the meal is prepared, the house is cleaned and the night before the Passover, all ordinary bread is destroyed. For the meal itself, there is a special kind of unleavened bread called matzah. Matzah is eaten to remind the Jewish people how they had to leave Egypt in a hurry, so that there was no time for their bread to rise.

At the beginning of the Seder, parsley, or watercress, is dipped in salt water and eaten. A shank bone of lamb, in memory of the lamb that used to be offered at the Temple, is also on the table. A roasted egg symbolizes another offering in the Temple and is also a symbol of spring. There is a dish of bitter herbs which symbolizes the bitterness of slavery.

Also on the table is a food called haroset. This is made of nuts, apple and wine, mixed together. This is to remind the people of the mortar they had to mix to make bricks when they were slaves in Egypt. A bowl of salt water reminds them of the tears they shed at that time.

During the Seder, everyone drinks four cups of wine to symbolize the joy of freedom, and for the same reason the actual meal will be big and lavish, like a feast.

Children play a special part in the Seder. Quite early on in the meal, four traditional questions have to be asked, and it is the youngest child who asks them. These questions are about the symbols at the Passover meal. The answers tell the story of how the people of Israel escaped from slavery in Egypt. There are many songs and riddles throughout, and one piece of matzah is always hidden for the children to find at the end of the meal.

Throughout the meal, one place remains empty. This is for the prophet Elijah who is expected to announce the time when everyone will be saved from oppression and injustice, and all the people can live in freedom. After the meal is over, his cup is filled and the door of the house is opened.

The Passover story

Once, long ago, the people of Israel were slaves in Egypt. They had to work very hard, and the Egyptian rulers treated them very badly. The kings of Egypt at that time were called Pharaohs. They were powerful rulers who wanted huge and magnificent buildings made for themselves, and the Israelites had to make the bricks.

One king was particularly cruel. He decided to have all the baby boys in Israelite families killed. One mother tried to save her child by hiding him among the rushes by the side of the River Nile. The Pharaoh's daughter found the baby, and brought him up as her own. His name was Moses.

Moses grew up as a prince, but he never forgot the people of Israel, and promised he would do all he could to help them. But while he was still quite young he was forced to leave Egypt because he killed a man who had been treating an Israelite slave badly. He lived in the desert for many years, among the people of the desert.

Then, one day he saw a strange sight. It

was a bush that seemed to be burning but yet did not burn up. He realized it was a sign from God. God told him that he must go back to Egypt and ask the Pharaoh to let the Israelites go. Moses set off, with his brother Aaron.

Of course, the Pharaoh would not let the people go. "Just because you asked," he said. "I'll make them work even harder." And he did. The people were not at all pleased with Moses, since he seemed to have made things worse for them. But he went on asking for their freedom, and the Pharaoh went on saying "No."

But God was determined that his people would be free, so he made some strange things happen. The River Nile turned to blood. There were plagues of frogs, insects and diseases. The Egyptians were in despair. But the Pharaoh still insisted that the Israelites stay.

Then God told Moses: "I am going to send one last plague. At midnight the Angel of Death will pass through this land. Every one of you must kill a lamb and smear the doorposts of your homes with the blood. When the Angel sees this, he will pass by your homes. But everywhere else, the eldest son of the family will be killed."

And that is what happened. The eldest son in every Egyptian family was killed, but the people of Israel were saved. After this, the Pharaoh agreed to free the Israelites. In fact, he said they must go at once! They hardly had time to prepare for their journey. They had to pack up so quickly that their bread did not have time to rise, which is why the flat, matzah bread is eaten at the Passover meal to this day. The people set off, with Moses as their leader, and made their way towards the land that was to become Israel.

Activities for Passover

1 Act out the story of how Moses asked for his people's freedom, and how the Pharaoh refused. You need three main actors – Moses, Aaron and the Pharaoh. Let Moses ask for the people's freedom and then when the Pharaoh refuses, everyone can join in and mime the plagues that befell the people. These include frogs, flies, cattle disease, giant hailstones that ruined most of the crops, a plague of locusts that ate the few remaining crops, three days of darkness and the final plague when the Angel of Death came. Pick the plagues you think make the best drama! Or you could make this a theme for movement work.

2 Make collage pictures of the story of the flight from Egypt.

3 Set a table as for the Seder, and show the children each of the symbolic items.

POEMS
Spring song, William Blake: *A spring song*, Mary Howitt, both in **Seeing and doing**

SONGS
Who's that yonder dressed in red? Spiritual *Agada* **Alleluya**; *Go down Moses*, **Look away**

115

Easter

About Easter

Easter is the most important festival in the Christian year, though it is less popular than the celebration of Christmas. Easter Sunday is the first Sunday after the spring full moon. This means it falls in March or, more usually, April, around about the same time as the Jewish Passover. In fact, there is a relationship between the two festivals, as the events leading up to the first Easter took place during the Passover festival.

Easter itself is a single Sunday, but the whole of the previous week is important in the Christian calendar. It is called Holy Week, and during this time Christians remember the story of how Jesus arrived in Jerusalem for the last time, was crucified, and rose from the dead.

Celebrating Easter

Christians celebrate Easter and Holy Week by attending church and re-telling the story of the Crucifixion and Resurrection. The Resurrection is seen as a sign that God is powerful enough to defeat death itself, and as a promise of a new life for everyone.

Just as Christmas retains elements of a much earlier festival, so Easter has many customs attached to it that are related to a tradition more ancient than Christianity. Even the name 'Easter' comes from an ancient European spring goddess, Eostre. The idea of using an egg to symbolize the new life that spring brings is also very old. Before chocolate eggs were created, people used to paint ordinary hard-boiled eggs, and among members of the Eastern Orthodox Church this is still very popular.

In Germany, and a number of other countries, it is the custom for parents to hide Easter eggs around the house or garden. On the morning of Easter Sunday, children hunt for the eggs. Tradition has it that they are left in their hiding places by the Easter Hare, which is also an ancient symbol of spring.

Easter eggs are not only eaten but are also used in a variety of games in different parts of the world. One of the most popular involves rolling hard-boiled eggs down a grassy slope.

An old English tradition is 'pace-egging' — when children went from house to house like carol-singers at Christmas, and hoped to be given decorated eggs as a reward for a song.

Other Easter customs include baking special cakes (especially in Greece and Italy), throwing water over people (in Eastern Europe) and, very commonly in Britain, a variety of rowdy football matches. These often involve just about anyone in a village or town who wants to join in.

But the more serious side of the Easter festivities takes place in church. The Sunday before Easter, called Palm Sunday, is really the beginning of the festival, when it is the custom to hand the people small crosses made of palm leaves. This ceremony recalls the story of how Jesus rode into Jerusalem on a donkey the week before he died, and the people welcomed him by carpeting the road he took with branches from a palm tree.

As the week progresses, the final days of Jesus's life are recalled, culminating in the story of how, after eating the Passover meal with his friends, he was arrested, tried and crucified. Jesus's death is remembered on the Friday of the week, and this is known as Good Friday. Churches are decorated solemnly, as if in mourning. In people's homes, hot-cross buns are eaten. These are fruit buns, marked with a cross. The cross is said to stand for the wooden cross on which Jesus was brutally crucified.

Finally, there is Easter Sunday itself, when churches are decorated with flowers and there are services to celebrate the resurrection of Jesus.

In many parts of the world, the Easter celebrations spread from the churches out into the streets. In some Spanish towns it is the custom to hold a procession every night of Holy Week. The men of the town carry huge platforms through the streets, and on the platforms there are statues of Jesus and his mother Mary.

In Jerusalem, there is a huge procession on Palm Sunday, when Jesus's last ride into Jerusalem is re-enacted. On Good Friday there is another procession, this time along the road Jesus took to be executed. People take the parts of Jesus carrying the cross, the men who were executed at the same time as Jesus, and the soldiers.

The celebrations for Easter Sunday itself are especially dramatic in the Eastern Orthodox Church. Easter in the Orthodox calendar usually falls later than in Western churches. On the night of Easter Saturday, worshippers gather in the darkened church. At midnight, the priest acts out a search for the body of Christ. Then he cries out that Christ is risen, and everyone holds up a lighted candle, so that the church is ablaze with light (see picture). The church bells ring, and Easter celebrations begin, with singing and processions.

The Easter Story

Jesus lived nearly two thousand years ago in the country we now call Israel. At that time, it was a part of the great Roman empire, but there were local rulers and religious leaders who remained quite powerful.

Jesus taught a new kind of religion, and the

leaders of the old religion were afraid he would start a revolution. They were particularly worried one Sunday when Jesus rode into the city of Jerusalem on a donkey, and crowds lined the road to cheer. They were angry when Jesus went into the Temple, which was the most important place of worship in the city, and chased out all the traders and money lenders who had set up their stalls there to make money from the pilgrims and worshippers.

Jesus's enemies plotted to kill him. They managed to get one of his followers, called Judas, to help them catch him. It was the night of the Jewish festival at Passover. Jesus had eaten the Passover meal with his followers and he went out into a garden to pray. While Jesus was there, Judas led his enemies to him. Jesus was arrested, and tried in a religious court. He was accused of calling himself the Son of God, and of breaking God's laws. The punishment was death.

But no one was allowed to have anyone put to death without permission from the Romans, so Jesus had to be tried again by the Roman governor, who was called Pontius Pilate. Pilate did not want to upset the religious leaders, and he let them go ahead.

Jesus was killed by being nailed to a large wooden cross. This was the way that robbers and murderers were killed in those days, though Jesus was neither of these things. Two robbers were killed with him and his friends stood nearby and helplessly watched him die. When he was dead, a man named Joseph asked if the body could be put in a tomb in his garden. Jesus's friends laid the body in the tomb, which was like a small cave in a rock, and they rolled a stone in front of the entrance.

A few days later, two women, who were friends of Jesus, came to visit the tomb. When they arrived in the garden, they found the huge stone had been rolled away, and the body was gone. Two angels were there who told them that Jesus had risen from the dead.

Activities for Easter
1 Make Easter cards. Traditionally these featured rabbits or hares. Velvet or fur fabric would be ideal for a textured effect.
2 Decorate the hall or classroom with patterns of eggs, rabbits and spring flowers.
3 Decorate eggs by dyeing them with vegetable dyes or food colouring. Boil the eggs in the coloured water until they have picked up some of the dye. Take them out, let them cool and polish them up by rubbing them with cooking oil.

SONGS
Spring alleluia, **Celebration songs** *The angel rolled the stone away*, **Faith, folk and charity**

MUSIC
Pace-egging song from *Frost and fire*, a calendar of ceremonial folk songs by the Watersons **Topic** records (RT/136)

117

Holi

About Holi

Holi is a Hindu festival which falls at the time of the full moon in the Indian month of Phalgun. It usually takes place around the end of February or the beginning of March. Like many Hindu festivals, it is celebrated in different ways in different parts of India, and even the number of days over which the festival is held varies from place to place. It is usually at least three days long.

Celebrating Holi

Holi is the sort of festival that gives everyone a chance to let off steam. Holi, a spring festival, is a harvest festival too, since it celebrates the ripening of the first wheat and barley crops. It is also a fire festival.

It often begins with a procession through the streets, sometimes with a man, dressed as a bridegroom, riding a donkey past a crowd of cheering onlookers. There may be carnival characters too, with funny names.

Because Holi is a fire festival, bonfires are important in the celebrations. Some people light a small bonfire at home, and there is usually a big community one too. Sometimes an image of a character named Holika is burned on the fire.

In the past, it was the custom for young boys to burn just about everything they could find on the Holi fires, so the people had to be careful about what they left lying around, or that might be the end of it! The idea of burning last year's rubbish and starting anew, is an important aspect of Holi.

In some places, it is the custom to walk around the fire a number of times, often holding a coconut as a sign of fertility. It is the custom too in many places to eat roasted coconut, and sometimes some of the new barley crop, also roasted.

The second day of Holi, which is also known as the Festival of Colour, is particularly boisterous. One of the traditional customs is the practice of throwing coloured powder at passers-by (see picture). In fact, it usually gets a lot wilder than that. People throw water, squirt dye and throw paint or even mud at each other. Part of the tradition is that you are allowed to throw things at, and be rude to, people who you are usually supposed to treat with respect. So students throw things at their teachers, and workers can insult their bosses. Any apparently respectable member of the community has to be very careful indeed at Holi time! By mid-afternoon, most people are very wet and dirty, and go home for a bath.

Visiting friends and relatives is another part of the celebrations. People go freely in and out of each other's houses and are offered sweets to eat. Despite the freedom to be rude to your 'betters', Holi is also a time for making up quarrels and being friendly.

The story of Holi

Once there was a wicked king, named Hiranyakasipu, who lived a long time ago in India. He thought he was so special and important that he decided that all the people in his kingdom should give up worshipping any other gods and worship him instead.

The people were very frightened of Hiranyakasipu, so most of them obeyed him, whether they wanted to or not. The truth was, none of them wanted to at all. But one person did decide to disobey Hiranyakasipu, and that was his own son, Prahlada.

Prahlada worshipped the great god Vishnu, and he believed it would be wrong to give him up and worship his father instead.

So he carried on with his prayers and hymns to Vishnu, right inside the palace, under his father's roof. Of course, Hiranyakasipu soon heard about it, and he was very angry.

"What do you think you're doing?" he stormed. "You know my orders! I said the only person who should be worshipped is me! What sort of example do you think you're setting for my subjects? Soon they'll all be disobeying me!"

"I do what I think is right," replied Prahlada. "And I hope the people do follow my example. I worship Vishnu. I cannot worship you, because you are not a god."

Of course, this made the king angrier than ever. He made sure his son was punished over and over again. He was beaten, attacked by poisonous snakes and thrown into dungeons. But he always survived because he was protected by Vishnu. And as soon as Prahlada was let out of the dungeon, he began to sing hymns to Vishnu again.

So Hiranyakasipu decided to kill his son. He knew this would be difficult, since Prahlada seemed to be able to live through anything. The king realized that he would have to use magic. He asked his daughter Holika to help him. She had been given a rare gift by the god of fire. She was protected from flames and could not be burned.

Holika arranged for a big pile of wood to be built. When it was all ready to be set alight, she sat on top of it.

"Come and sit next to me, dear brother," she said. "I want to talk to you."

Prahlada climbed to the top of the pile of wood, and at once Hiranyakasipu ordered his servants to set it alight. The flames shot up so high that they seemed to reach the clouds. They were so hot that Holika's magic could not save her, and she was burned to death. But the god Vishnu protected Prahlada, and when the flames had died down he scrambled down from the fire, completely unhurt.

But Hiranyakasipu was still determined to get rid of his son. He thought of nothing else. He had him thrown into a dungeon at once. After a few days he went to see him.

"I don't understand you," he said. "How can you worship a god you can't even see?"

"I may not be able to see him," said Prahlada. "But I know he's here."

"What do you mean, here?" stormed Hiranyakasipu. "How can he be here? Do you mean he's inside this pillar?"

He hit the pillar with his sword, and at once the god Vishnu appeared as a lion, roaring and sounding very fierce. So, as you can imagine, that was the end of Hiranyakasipu!

Another story for Holi

During the Holi festival, people remember stories of the god Krishna. Krishna came to earth as a baby boy and grew up to be a young man. He was so handsome that all the young women admired him, and he enjoyed teasing them.

One night he went into the forest and played his flute so beautifully that all the village girls went into the forest to dance. It was a magical dance. For although Krishna danced with only one of the girls, it seemed to each girl that he had danced with her alone.

It seemed too that each dance had gone on for months. And yet when they got home, their parents had not even noticed that they had been out, because they had been gone for such a short time.

Activities for Holi

1 The story of Krishna and the village girls makes a good basis for a dance-drama. Children might enjoy telling the story and putting on a show for the rest of the school.
2 Make a large picture of a bonfire. There is plenty of scope for mixing fire colours and making glowing embers and flames from cellophane and crêpe paper. The sky area above the bonfire could be filled with sparks, made by trailing drops of glue over it and sprinkling on powder paint. Shake off the excess paint when the glue is dry. Children could make self-portraits, cut them out and stick them around the fire.

A POEM
Extremely naughty children, Elizabeth Gobley **The young Puffin book of verse**
SONGS
Stick Dance; *Music for a Holi stick dance*, both in **Festivals, book 2**
MUSIC
Middle caste religious music from India, a collection of Hindu and Muslim religious songs and dances, **Lyrichord** label (LLST/7223)
Religions of India, a collection of Hindu, Buddhist and Sikh music and chants (ARG/ZFB 55) (library resource)
Songs of Krishna (ARG/ZFB 52) (library resource)

May Day

About May Day

May Day is the first day of the month of May. It is a public holiday in many countries, but in Britain the day off work comes on the first Monday of the month instead.

May Day is an ancient folk festival in Europe, probably dating back to a Roman celebration in honour of Flora, goddess of flowers. As well as being a folk festival, May is an important time for many Christians, especially Roman Catholics. They honour Mary, the mother of Jesus, at this time.

Celebrating May Day

The best-known May Day tradition is the dance around the maypole, so popular in rural primary schools. The maypole is a tall post, with coloured ribbons hanging from the top. Children taking part in the dance each hold the end of a ribbon and dance around the pole, weaving in and out in a carefully planned pattern (see picture). As they do so, a plaited pattern of ribbons forms at the top of the pole. Then, the dancers turn around and retrace their steps so that the pattern is undone. It takes a lot of practice to get it right!

May Day processions were popular in the past, and involved people parading through the village streets, carrying branches of sycamore or hawthorn (which is also known as 'may'). Sometimes a young tree was carried in this procession, with all its branches stripped from it, except those at the very top. The tree was decorated with flowers, such as cowslips, and wild birds' eggs that were 'blown' and then hung from the tree.

Today's processions sometimes involve a May Queen who might be a pupil at the school where the maypole dance takes place.

The parade may be on quite a grand scale, with the May Queen on a throne decorated with flowers being carried along on a decorated float.

Traditional dancing is not limited to the maypole. Morris dancing is popular all over the country, and May dances often include the traditional figure of the hobby horse, which is a man dressed as a horse.

On May 8 a very famous dance takes place at Helston in Cornwall. This is known as the Furry dance (no one quite knows why) and probably grew out of the old traditions of May Day. It is certainly very old.

Celebrations start early in the morning. The people of the town go out into the fields and gather wild flowers and greenery, which they bring back into the town. There are a number of dances through the town during the day, but the most important is called the 'noon dance'. All the most important people in the town take part, dressed in their best clothes and either wearing or carrying flowers. The doors of shops and houses are left open so that the dancers can pass right through them, because it is believed that they bring good luck.

In the USA there is a May Day tradition which has survived from the time when the first settlers arrived there. The founders of this new settlement were Puritans who disapproved of the rowdy celebrations that went on back in England. But the tradition of holding a festival at this time was too strong for them to stamp it out completely. Today there is a custom among children of making decorated 'May baskets' to give to parents or friends. Children use something like a small box or a paper cup as a basis for the basket, adding handles and decorating the whole thing with colourful fringes of tissue and crêpe paper.

A story for May Day

"Why has Susan next door got bits of cloth in her hair?" asked Tim.

"I don't know," said mum, who was busy driving the car. "Has she?"

"We saw her last night," said Tim.

They were going into town to do the Saturday shopping. They had to be quick, because it was May Day and the children were going to join in the dance around the maypole that afternoon. They had been practising for weeks. Susan, who lived next door, was the oldest girl in the school, so it was her turn to be Queen of the May.

"She'll look funny with her crown on, with all those bits of cloth," said Jane.

They hurried with the shopping, and did not even stop for a cup of tea, as they usually did on Saturdays. As soon as they had finished, they went back to the car.

But disaster struck! The car just wouldn't start. Every time mum turned the key — nothing happened! She got out and looked under the bonnet.

"Well," she said. "I think I can see what the trouble is. Let's go to the garage and ask Mr Smith to come and tow it in. I don't suppose he'll be able to do it till after lunch, though."

"But what about the maypole dance?" asked Jane.

"I don't know," said mum. "You'll have to miss it, I suppose."

"But we can't!" wailed Tim. Jane and Tim were both nearly crying. "We've been practising for weeks!"

"We missed it last year, too," said Jane. "We couldn't do it because of the rain."

"You did dance last year!" said mum. "It was the year before that it rained."

Soon they were at the garage. There was a man already talking to Mr Smith, so they had to wait.

"Hullo," said the man, when he saw mum. "You're in my evening class, aren't you?"

"Yes I am," said mum. "You're Mike Brown, the photographer from 'The Post'".

"That's right," said Mike Brown. "Funny I should meet you today. I'm coming to your village this afternoon to take pictures of the dancing."

"We won't be there," Jane told him. "The car's broken down and we can't get home. There's no bus any more, and a taxi's too expensive."

"I can give you all a lift," said Mike Brown. "Just sort out what to do about your car, and I'll come and pick you up in about ten minutes. Then I can bring you back later on to pick up your car."

They got back just in time for the dancing. Susan was already sitting on her throne. It was all decorated with flowers, and she was wearing a crown of flowers too. But that wasn't the only thing they noticed about her head. It was her hair that looked especially amazing. It was in huge, thick curls like sausages. She looked like a princess in a book of fairy-stories.

"They're called ringlets," she told them. "You make them by screwing your hair up in rags the night before you want them."

"I know," said Tim. "We saw you with them in."

Thanks to Mike Brown, Jane and Tim were able to join in the dancing round the maypole. They really enjoyed the May Day celebrations.

Activities for May Day

1 The most ambitious project you could work on is the maypole dance itself. This would require a lot of research and should be done in consultation with local folklore experts. In the absence of a maypole, children could use this festival as an opportunity to learn some simple country dances (such as 'Strip the willow') and perhaps put on a display for parents and the rest of the school.

2 Decorating with flowers is a traditional part of May Day celebrations. The May Queen's throne would have been decorated with blossoms. In Derbyshire, where an ancient custom survives at this time of year, flowers are used to make elaborate decorations around local wells.

3 Work on different and simple ways of making paper flowers to decorate the classroom.

POEMS
Here we come gathering nuts in May; *On May Day we dance*; *Round and round the maypole*, all traditional, in **Seeing and doing**

SONGS
Gardens **Tinderbox**
May song **Granny's yard**

MUSIC
Hal-an-tow from *Frost and fire*, a calendar of ceremonial songs by the Watersons **Topic** records (RT/136)

121

Pentecost and Whitsun

About Pentecost and Whitsun

Pentecost is the Greek name for a Jewish festival which is also known as Shavout, or the Feast of Weeks. The word Pentecost means 'fifty days', and the festival is given this name because it falls fifty days after the Passover.

In the Christian faith, the festival is important because it marks the day on which God came to Jesus's disciples in the form of the Holy Spirit. This story is told in the Acts of the Apostles in the Bible. The Christian celebration is more commonly known as Whitsunday, or Whitsun.

Celebrating Pentecost

The Jewish festival of Shavout is a harvest festival, when synagogues are decorated with fruit and flowers. It is the time when the Jewish people remember the story of how Moses climbed Mount Sinai, where God gave him ten important rules for the people of Israel to obey. These rules are known as the Ten Commandments. One of the readings in synagogues at this time is the story of Ruth.

Whitsun

In the early days of the Christian Church, Pentecost was the day on which new converts to the religion were baptized. These new Christians would wear white for the ceremony which is how the festival came to be known as 'Whit' or 'White' Sunday.

Whitsun is a very important festival in the Christian year. It ranks almost with Christmas and Easter in terms of religious significance, but it is hardly celebrated at all outside churches. At one time, the day after Whitsun, known as Whit Monday, was a public holiday, but even that is no longer the case.

It used to be common for a Whitsun procession to take place after a morning church service. The priest would lead his congregation along the boundaries of the parish, in order to re-enact the story of how Jesus's disciples went all through the city of Jerusalem after they had been visited by the Holy Spirit. Processions the following day were once quite common and Whit walks still take place in some cities (see picture).

Whitsun was once a favourite time for performing 'miracle plays'. These were plays about events described in the Bible. They were for the benefit of those who could not read and therefore had no access to the Bible story. Miracle plays still survive in some cities today and are important tourist attractions.

The story of Ruth

The story of Ruth begins with the story of another woman, called Naomi. Naomi came from Israel, but many years before the story begins she had moved with her husband to a land called Moab. They had been forced to leave their home because of a famine.

Naomi and her husband had come from Bethlehem, and they always meant to return there. But as the years passed, they became more and more settled in Moab. Their two sons, Mahlon and Chilion, married women from Moab, called Orpah and Ruth.

Then something very sad happened. First, Naomi's husband died. Then her two sons died, leaving Naomi all alone, and far from home. Naomi went to see Orpah and Ruth.

"I am going home to Bethlehem now," she told them. "There is nothing left for me here."

"Of course there's something left!" cried Ruth. "You still have us!"

"No," said Naomi. "You must stay here. This is your home. You are both young and you will marry again."

Orpah agreed to let her leave, though she wept as she did so. But Ruth had made up her mind to stay with Naomi.

So she went with Naomi to Bethlehem. They were very poor, and by the time they reached the town they had almost nothing to eat. But it was harvest time, and they hoped that someone would help them. In the fields around Bethlehem, the reapers were cutting the barley.

Ruth went to see a rich man named Boaz, who lived nearby. She asked if she could follow the reapers around the field, and pick up the grain they left behind.

Boaz was very kind, and agreed to let Ruth pick up as much barley as she wanted. He even told the reapers to be a bit careless, and drop quite a lot for her to collect. And when the reapers had a party after the harvest, Ruth was invited. Boaz had fallen in love with her and he soon asked her to marry him.

So before long Naomi had a new family to look after her in her old age. As for Ruth, she and Boaz had children, and when they grew up they had children themselves, and Ruth became a grandmother. One of her grandsons was David, who became King of Israel.

The story of the first Whitsun

It was the Feast of Pentecost. Jerusalem was full of pilgrims who had come to worship at the Temple. They came from many different lands, and although they were all Jewish, they spoke many different languages, and could not always understand each other.

But while everyone else enjoyed the festival, the disciples of Jesus were feeling very sad. They had had some strange experiences since Jesus, their leader, had been tried and crucified. They had hardly got used to the idea that he was dead before they began to hear stories that he had actually risen from the dead! They had even seen him for themselves. But it had not been the same as the time before he had been killed. For he seemed only to be with them sometimes, appearing when they were not expecting to see him at all.

Then, a few days before Pentecost, he had taken them to the Mount of Olives, just outside Jerusalem, and disappeared from their sight for ever. They knew he had gone to be with God in Heaven. But what, they wondered, was supposed to happen now? Jesus had told them that they would be filled with the Holy Spirit of God, but they were not at all sure what that meant.

So there they were, all together in a room on the day of Pentecost, feeling rather sad, when another strange thing happened to them. They heard a sound like a rushing wind. It seemed to be blowing very hard, yet none of the lamps in their darkened room flickered. Then it seemed as if flames of fire were burning above their heads, yet none of them was burned.

Suddenly, they felt very happy. They knew that the Holy Spirit had come to them, and that God wanted them to go out into the city and start telling everyone about Jesus, and baptize them in his name.

As they spoke to the people, they realized that a miracle was happening. For although the people they were speaking to all spoke different languages, and should not have understood what they were saying, it seemed that everyone heard the message in their own language!

Many of them had never heard the story of Jesus, and they were outraged when they heard that he had been killed. Thousands of them were baptized that day. They were the first members of the Christian Church.

Activities for Pentecost and Whitsun

1 Following up the tradition of decorating synagogues with fruit and flowers, get the children to make pictures using pressed flowers, as well as seeds and pulses.
2 Act out the story of Ruth.
3 Perform a miracle play based on a popular Bible story. Explain to the children that the idea of the play is to pretend that the events in it are happening in modern times and not long ago as the Bible story describes.

A POEM
The plough, Victor Jara, **Wheel around the world**
A SONG
Dona Dona **Alleluya**
MUSIC
Dance of the raven and the dove from *Noyye's Fludde* by Benjamin Britten

Sukkot

About Sukkot

Sukkot is a harvest festival that is celebrated for eight days during September or October. Sukkah is a Hebrew word meaning 'huts', and describes the huts made of branches, leaves and fruit made for the festival. It is the time when the Jewish people remember how they lived in tents and huts in the desert after they had escaped from Egypt.

Celebrating Sukkot

The harvest is the time when food crops are gathered in. It is a special time in rural communities, where a good crop is needed to survive through the winter. But people in towns and cities also depend on a good crop, so the ancient tradition of holding a special service of thanksgiving for the harvest applies to urban areas as well.

During Sukkot, the Jewish people remember the story of how God looked after his people, providing food when it seemed that none would appear. In many households it is traditional at this time to build a hut, or 'tabernacle', called a sukkah, in the garden and eat there (see picture). Sometimes people even sleep in their sukkah for eight days.

Another symbol connected with Sukkot is the lulav. This is made from branches of palm, myrtle and willow held together with a fruit like a lemon, called an etrog. When these are shaken, they sound like rainfall. This is done to express the hope that the coming year will be a good one for the new crops yet to be planted.

Long ago this festival was one of the occasions on which people made a pilgrimage to Jerusalem. The connection between the memory of hardship in the desert, God's mercy in providing food, and prayers for a good harvest, is easy to see.

The Sukkot story

PART 1: CROSSING THE RED SEA

You probably remember the story of how the people of Israel worked as slaves, making bricks for the powerful Pharaohs of Egypt. They had to work terribly hard, and they were treated very cruelly. In the end, God sent Moses to rescue them.

Moses asked the Pharaoh to let the people go but the Pharaoh refused. Because of this, God made some strange and terrible things happen in Egypt. The land was overrun with insects and frogs, and the eldest son of every household died. At last, the Pharaoh decided that the people of Israel could leave Egypt. They left the next day, taking their sheep and cattle with them.

But no sooner were they out of sight, than the wicked Pharaoh changed his mind. He decided he wouldn't be able to do without his slaves, so he made up his mind to get them back. He called his generals, the leaders of his army of horsemen and charioteers.

"Gather your troops together at once!" he commanded. "Go out into the desert and bring those people back."

So the generals gathered their horsemen and charioteers. The Pharaoh too climbed into his golden chariot, and the mighty army galloped out into the desert.

Meanwhile, Moses and the people of Israel had made their way across the desert to the Red Sea. They camped on its shores, wondering how they were going to cross the wide expanse of water. In the morning they woke to see the great army on the horizon, pounding across the sand towards them.

They were terrified. What could they do? The soldiers were closing in on all sides, driving them into the sea. Moses went to the edge of the water and looked out across the waves. As he did so, the strangest thing happened.

A wind began to blow. It grew stronger and stronger. Soon it was a terrible gale which blew back the waves of the Red Sea, leaving a pathway of shallow water down its middle.

The Israelites set out at once to cross the sea, with Moses leading them. Soon they reached the other side safely. The charioteers stood on the shores of the sea and watched amazed.

"After them!" screamed the Pharaoh. "Don't let them escape!"

The horses kicked and bucked and refused to move. So the Pharaoh himself whipped his own horse and charged into the gap in the sea. Hundreds of charioteers followed ... and as they did so, the wind dropped and the waves closed over their heads. That was the end of the Pharaoh and his great army.

PART TWO: FOOD IN THE WILDERNESS

Now that they had escaped from the Pharaoh, the people of Israel thought that the rest of their long journey to the land that God had promised them would be easy. But they were wrong. They had to travel for many days through a harsh desert. They were hungry. But worse than that, they were very thirsty. They began to complain to Moses.

"What was the point of rescuing us?" they asked. "We're just going to die out here. At least we had food and water in Egypt."

But once again, God came to their rescue. Soon they came to a place called Marah, where there was a great pool of water. They were so happy to find it that some of them began to drink at once.

124

"Ugh!" they cried. "It tastes horrible! It's impossible to drink!"

You see, the word Marah means bitter, which was how the water tasted.

"What are we going to do?" asked the people. "It's all your fault, for bringing us here," they complained to Moses.

So God told Moses to take a branch from a special tree that was growing nearby, and to throw it into the water. Gradually, the water changed. It stopped being bitter and became sweet and clear.

They went on into the desert. The people had stopped complaining for a while, but soon they began again. For there was still almost nothing to eat.

"What shall I do?" Moses asked God.

God answered that he was not to worry. There would be meat every evening, and bread in the morning.

That very night, a flock of quails arrived. They were migrating across the desert and had been flying for days. They were very tired, and once they had landed on the ground, they seemed unable to move at all. The people caught them easily, and that night they had a feast of roasted birds.

The next morning they woke up and came out of their tents. The strangest sight met their eyes! All around them, the ground was covered with white flakes.

They picked up a few and tasted them... they were sweet and sticky! They had no idea what they were, so they called them 'manna' meaning, 'what is it?'

God had kept his promise. He had given them meat in the evening and bread in the morning. The people knew now that he would look after them and guide them on their long journey through the desert. They wandered on for forty years – and had many more adventures – before they came to the land God had promised them. It was called Canaan, but they renamed it Israel. (It is appropriate at this time to tell the story of Joshua and the crossing into the Promised Land – see the Book of Joshua in the Bible.)

Activities for Sukkot

1 Build a small tabernacle of twigs and branches and use it as the basis of a harvest display of fruit and other crops.
2 Decorate the room with palm leaves made from green crêpe paper.
3 Talk about harvests in general, especially in the context of a display of produce. Ask parents to contribute foods which are important in their families. Talk about the most important foods for people in different parts of the world and try to display as many of these as you can.

SONGS
Happy festival, Yom tou lanu, **Festivals book 1** *Zum gali gali gali; Hineh mah tou*, both from the **The Puffin colony song book** *Shalom* **Alleluya**

MUSIC
Songs and dances of the Jews, from Bukhara, Uzbekistan and Cochin (WES 9805) (library resource); *Music from Israel, sacred and secular* (ARG/ZFB 50)

125

Yam Harvest

About the yam harvest

Yams are a kind of sweet potato which are grown and eaten by people in many parts of the world, especially in tropical climates. In some areas, such as parts of West Africa, people more or less depend on yams for their food. A food that people rely on in this way is called a staple crop. With such a food, it is especially important that the harvest is good, as the alternative may well be starvation.

Cassava is another staple crop grown in West Africa, but people do not like it as much. Cassava is eaten after the old yams have been finished. Everyone looks forward to the time when they can give it up and have yams again instead.

The new yams in West Africa are harvested in August or September, at the end of the rainy season. This is a very important occasion. In fact yams were so important in the past that anyone who could grow enough to have a large store of them was considered very wealthy. Even today, when there are other sources of wealth, the yam harvest is a very special time of thanksgiving and celebration.

Celebrating the harvest of the new yam

The harvest is celebrated in many areas of West Africa, often in slightly different ways. But the idea of thanksgiving and prayer for a prosperous future is important everywhere.

Christians and Muslims alike have special services of thanksgiving at harvest time, but the idea of celebrating the first of the new yam crop goes back to a time long before either religion spread to West Africa. The festival arises from a much older tradition, in which part of the new crop had to be offered to the god believed to be responsible for making sure it grew well. This god is often actually called the God of the Yam, but may be described as God of Good Yield, or some other name. In parts of Nigeria, Ogun, the traditional God of Iron, is associated with the yam festival, and music made with iron instruments features in the celebrations.

It is very important that all the parts of the festival, including the preparation, are carried out in the proper way, or, maybe next year's crop might be a disaster. Although details vary, celebrations usually run something like this:

First, people offer sacrifices to the gods of the land and ask for their protection during the festival. Without this, tradition says, evil spirits might upset things during the festival, and spoil the happy atmosphere.

Next, the yam god's shrine has to be cleaned up and painted. After that, the people make sure that the pots the yams were cooked in the year before are especially clean. Families then group together and go to offer yams to the yam god, through the priest.

Next they visit their family shrines, where they offer yams to their ancestors and kill a cockerel as a sacrifice. The cockerel is cooked and eaten, with the yam. Lastly, there are songs and dances in praise of the yam god. Masked dancers play an important role in this part of the festival.

In some places, in parts of Ghana for example, the festival is especially important for children. Once the yam has been offered to the god, it is given to the children, who represent the new generation and the community of the future. A small group of children is chosen to be blessed by the priest and each child is given a small piece of yam. After this part of the ceremony, the people make offerings to their ancestors.

The yam harvest is such an important festival that everyone tries to get home to their village for it, even if they usually live and work miles away in a big city – and even if, for most of the year, they are practising Christians or Muslims. Children get a holiday from school, too, so that they can join in the festivities.

Memories of the yam festival

This is how the yam festival is remembered by a Nigerian named Dominic Effiom. "When I was a child, I lived in the Calabar region of eastern Nigeria. The night before the festival, everyone stayed at home to help with the cooking and other preparations. One of the reasons I enjoyed the festival so much was because of the food! If the festival fell on a school day, we were all given the time off so that we could join in.

Each farmer saved the best yam he had grown so that he could show it off to everyone else. And everyone took yams to the chief priest so that he could offer them to the gods. After that, the yams were boiled, pounded up (see picture) and then eaten, while the rest were put in a barn, stacked up ready to be planted later on. These yams were the beginning of the next year's crop.

During the festival, people performed plays, and there was plenty to eat and drink. We drank mainly palm wine, and we ate yams, of course. The food I liked best was made with yams, fish and crayfish, which are a bit like lobsters. It had palm oil and peppers in it too. People who did not live near the sea or a river where they could get fish, used to make this meal with chicken instead of fish. We all had to help with the cooking.

During the festival, we used to spend a lot of time visiting relatives and we used to make sure we saw a lot of our families and friends, just as people in Europe do at Christmas.

Dancing was important at the festival. We all got a chance to dance, as there were different dances for each age group. I didn't enjoy all the dances, though. There was one that frightened me because the dancers wore masks, and I didn't like that. One mask was especially frightening. It had three heads and it was made of red and black wood. There was lots of raffia hanging from it so you couldn't see who was wearing it.

The dance I liked best was called the Abang dance. It was for people who were between 14 and 19. The boys played the drums and the girls danced. They wore brightly coloured skirts and matching tops, and bands of coloured cloth around their arms. They wore lots of beads around their necks, too, and their hair often all coiled up like a crown, with strips of coloured cloth hanging down from it. They used to paint their faces with white paint. We would visit people's homes, and give them all presents."

Activities for Yam Harvest

1 Study pictures of African masks and use them as a basis for art and craft work.
2 If possible, buy and cook some yams, so that everyone gets a chance to taste some. It is usually boiled and then pounded in a pestle until it is soft. Recipes using yams can be found in West Indian cookery books.
3 Make rattles or similar percussion instruments to use in movement sessions with African music. Yoghurt pots and tins make good bases for these and different sizes of pulses or seeds inside them will make different noises. Decorate them on the outside by painting them in bright colours (mix glue with powder paint for a colour that will hold on to plastic) and sticking on beads and coloured string. Gourds hung with beads are sometimes used as percussion instruments in Africa. You can make these by pasting papier mâché over a balloon which has been smeared with petroleum jelly. When the papier mâché is quite dry, burst the balloon. The end result will be something like a gourd, both in shape and feel.

POEMS
Mango, little mango, anonymous; *Guinea corn*, anonymous; *Awo!*, anonymous, all poems on an African theme from **Wheel around the world**
SONGS
Dipidu, **Tinderbox**
Everybody loves Saturday night, **Tinderbox**
Asikarali, **Puffin colony song book**
MUSIC
Drums of West Africa, **Lyrichord** label (LLST/7223)
African rhythms and instruments, Volume 1, Music from Ghana and Nigeria, **Lyrichord** label (LLST/7328)

Diwali

About Diwali

Diwali, the Hindu festival of light, takes place at the end of the Indian monsoon season, when the farmers start to sow their winter crops. This means it usually falls in October or November.

The festival celebrates the return of Rama, a legendary god-king, to his kingdom. It is one of the most important festivals of the Hindu year, and follows the ten-day festival of Dussehra when, in some parts of India, it is the custom to act out the story of Rama and Sita (see below).

Celebrating Diwali

Everyone looks forward to Diwali, since it is a time for parties, dancing and giving presents. It is known mainly as a festival of light, but it is also a new year celebration when everyone wears new clothes and cleans their house, outside and in. People make sweets as gifts and visit friends and relations.

The most important part of the Diwali celebrations is the lighting of lamps. People place rows of lights along their doorsteps, balconies, courtyards – in fact, almost everywhere (see picture). The name 'Diwali' actually means 'a row of lights'. They may be any sort of light, from traditional clay lamps and candles to modern electric lights. They are lit to welcome Rama home from exile to his kingdom.

It is a time for setting off fireworks and it is traditional to decorate the floors of important rooms in the house, using chalks and coloured flour.

The celebration of Diwali is also a harvest festival, celebrating the summer crops. As well as that, it is a new year festival, held in honour of the goddess Lakshmi. She is the goddess of good fortune, so she is especially important to people in business.

Hindus make sure they have made up all their accounts for the year at this time, and carry out a puja (an act of worship) in honour of Lakshmi. They burn a candle in front of an image of her, and pray for good fortune in the coming year.

The story of Rama and Sita

Many stories are told at Diwali, but the most important one tells of Rama's return to his kingdom. We tell the whole story here, of how Rama lost his kingdom and how his wife Sita was stolen. But strictly speaking, it is only the last part that belongs with the Diwali festivities.

Long ago in India there lived a young king named Rama. At least, he should have been king, but he had been driven out of his kingdom and had been forced to hide in the forest with his young wife Sita, away from his enemies in the palace.

For a while, Rama and Sita lived happily in the forest, among the gentle animals that lived there. But danger was nearby. For the evil demon-king, Ravana, from the island of Lanka, had seen Sita. He decided he would like to have her as his wife, and he made up his mind to steal her from Rama.

Ravana was full of magic and trickery. He sent a beautiful deer into the forest. It was so lovely that Sita was enchanted by it as soon as she saw it. She begged Rama to capture it.

"It is so good, so beautiful," she said. "We could keep it with us, always."

Rama set off after the deer, which seemed quite tame. But as soon as he put out his hand to touch it, it skipped a little way off, and then stood quite still, almost as if it was laughing at him!

Rama went deeper and deeper into the forest, and all the time the deer skipped ahead of him, just out of reach. Soon he was out of sight, and Sita was left alone.

A minute later, the demon-king Ravana, with all his ten heads grinning, swooped from the sky in his chariot, and snatched Sita away. Poor Sita cried for help, and for a while it seemed that she might be rescued. For the king of the vultures heard her call, and tried to rescue her. But Ravana was too powerful for him, and the poor bird was soon badly wounded. He fell from the sky to the forest floor.

While Rama was still searching for the deer, he found the poor vulture, and tried to save him. There was nothing he could do. But before he died, the king of the vultures told Rama what had happened. Rama knew that he must go and look for Sita.

Rama travelled towards Lanka, where Ravana had his kingdom. On his journey, he met a monkey called Sugriva. He too had been a king once, and he too had been driven from his kingdom. Rama helped him win back his throne, and in return Sugriva sent a huge army of monkeys, led by their quick-witted general, Hanuman, to help Rama save Sita.

Hanuman had magical powers. He was able to fly to Lanka, where he found poor Sita. She had refused to marry the demon-king even though he had threatened to kill her. Hanuman decided he must speak to Ravana.

Ravana was not in the habit of talking to messengers, so Hanuman had to play a trick in order to see him. He ran around the garden, pulling up all the plants. The guards were very angry when they saw this. They caught Hanuman and brought him before their master. Before Ravana could do him any harm, Hanuman spoke.

"Mighty king," he said. "I am a messenger from the great king Rama. I know that you are a proper king and an honourable man, so you will not hurt the messenger of another king." And then he went on to say how wicked he thought Ravana was!

Of course, the demon-king was very angry.

"I may not be able to kill a messenger!" he shouted. "But I'll make you suffer!" And he ordered his guards to tie a burning rag to poor Hanuman's tail.

Hanuman leapt away from the demon-king and his guards, and ran out into Ravana's great capital city. He jumped across the rooftops, setting fire to every house he landed on. It wasn't long before half the city was a mass of flames. Then he flew back to Rama and the army of monkeys.

Rama and his army had built a huge bridge, right across the sea, from India to Lanka. Now they were able to cross over, and go into the burning city. There was a terrible battle and a great fight between Ravana and Rama. Rama managed to kill the demon-king with a burning spear.

At last, Rama and Sita were together again. The wicked people who had driven him from his kingdom were now dead, and Rama's brother had been ruling until Rama could come home. When Rama returned to his kingdom, all his subjects lined the streets on the way to the palace. Everyone cheered and waved as Rama and Sita rode past in their chariot on their way to a magnificent coronation ceremony. Rama was king again, at last.

Activities for Diwali

1 There is plenty of work that can be done on the theme of lights and candles. Older children can, with plenty of supervision, make candles, using dyes or melted-down wax crayons to give them colour. They can make model lamps, using clay, or paper lanterns to hang from the ceiling. Decorate the room with fairy lights.

2 Act out part of the story of Rama and Sita. Some of it is ideal for movement work, particularly the part where Hanuman leaps across the rooftops with a burning rag tied to his tail!

3 Using large sheets of paper fastened together, make 'floor paintings' with strong-coloured paints.

SONGS
Diwali, **Festivals book 1**
Diwali, **Tinderbox**
MUSIC
Religions of India, collection of Hindu, Buddist and Sikh music and chants (ARG/ZFB 55) (library resource)
Raga Rang, Indian classical instrumental music, **EMI** (ECSD 2773)
BOOKS
Hanuman, A. Ramachandran, *A & C Black*
The festival, Peter Bonnici, illustrated by Lisa Kopper, *Bell and Hyman*

Hanukah

About Hanukah

Hanukah is the Jewish festival of faith and light. It falls in December or January, and recalls the events of 163 BC when a small guerrilla army of Jewish people fought to free their country from foreign rule. This means that it is also a festival of freedom, which is something that the Jewish people value very highly, having been denied it so often and so brutally throughout their history. The fact that such a small army could win against a huge empire was seen as a great miracle, and this is reflected in the symbols and celebrations of the festival.

Hanukah is also a time for exchanging gifts and it is a special festival for children.

Celebrating Hanukah

The Hanukah celebrations last for eight days, and take place mainly in people's homes. It is a time for parties and giving presents. It is also marked by the use of a special kind of eight-branched candlestick, called a Menorah or Hanukiah.

The Menorah has a candle for each day of the eight-day festival and a new one is lit each evening. Thus, on the first day one candle burns, on the second, two, and so on. The Menorah also has an extra candle which is used to light the others. This is called the 'servant' candle. The Menorah is placed somewhere where passers-by can see it, usually in a window, to announce the miracle to all who pass.

Hanukah is a time when people play games. One in particular is connected with this festival. This is called 'spinning the dreidle'. The dreidle is a small top with four sides. On each side there is one of the first letters from the Hebrew words meaning 'a great miracle happened here'.

To play the game, you spin the dreidle. Depending on which way it falls, you may win sweets or nuts, or you may have to 'pay' some into a 'bank' so that someone else can win them next time the dreidle spins.

Tradition has it that this game is very old indeed, and dates right back to the time when King Antiochus of Syria ruled over Israel. It is his overthrow that is celebrated at Hanukah.

The story goes that the people used to play this game, or appear to do so, while they were studying. At the time, they were forbidden to study their religion. So if a soldier, or any person in authority, came by they would immediately start playing the game. They would simply say, if asked, that they were enjoying a game with their friends.

The Hanukah story

Long ago, the Jewish people were conquered by the Syrian ruler, King Antiochus. This king believed that the best of everything came from Greece, for Greece had long been a powerful and important influence in the ancient world.

Antiochus wanted people to wear Greek clothes, to have the same sorts of athletics competitions that the Greeks did, and, worst of all, to worship Greek gods.

He made sure statues of Greek gods were put in every town and village. He filled the Temple in Jerusalem with these statues, too, and forced the Jews on pain of death to make sacrifices to them.

The king was very powerful and many people were too frightened of him to disobey his orders. They began to pray to the new gods, to make sacrifices to them, and so they broke their ancient laws. But they were not happy about this. They knew they should pray only to God. There were some who simply refused to obey and were killed because of it.

In one village there was a priest named Mattathias. He was an important person in his village, so the king's soldiers knew that it was especially important to get him to obey the king's orders. If Mattathias would worship the Greek gods, they thought, the other people would do the same.

But instead, Mattathias killed the soldier who had given the order, and at once began to organize a rebellion against the Syrians. Mattathias had five sons. One of them, called Judas Maccabaeus, became the leader of the rebellion against the Syrian rulers.

There were only 6000 soldiers in Judas's army compared with the Syrian king's 50000. But the Jewish army fought cleverly and bravely, and were able to defeat the Syrians, even though they were outnumbered by nearly ten to one.

At last, the battles were over, and the brave Jewish soldiers had won back their holy city of Jerusalem.

The Jewish soldiers knew that the most important thing they had won was their freedom to worship in the Temple, and they planned to do that as soon as they could.

But they were horrified when they saw it! Not only was it filled with statues of the Greek gods, but there was also dirt and rubbish everywhere. It was impossible to worship there. Everyone agreed that their first job was to clean it up and re-dedicate it to God. Then they could pray there once more.

So they took away the statues and all the rubbish, mended everything that had been spoiled and broken, and cleaned the Temple from top to bottom. They planned a great service of thanksgiving once this was done, with oil lamps burning throughout the building. The people would sing hymns of praise and worship God once more in their most important building.

There is a famous story about what happened when they entered the Temple. They wanted to keep the flame of eternal light burning continuously as a symbol of God's presence. But they found only one pot of oil, enough to keep the flame burning for only one day. The nearest source of oil was four days' journey away, so it would take eight days before new oil arrived. How could the flame be kept alight?

It was then that a miracle happened. For although there was almost no oil left at all, the flame went on burning for the full eight days until the new oil came.

It then became a custom to commemorate the re-dedication of the Temple in an eight-day festival each year, and so it has been celebrated up to the present day.

Even today, the Jewish people remember Judas and his small army, who fought so bravely and against such a powerful enemy, and eventually won the freedom to worship God in the way they believed was right. The festival of re-dedication has become today's celebration of Hanukah.

Activities for Hanukah

1 Draw pictures of the Menorah, with its eight branches and the servant branch (see picture). A class picture could include children giving and receiving presents. Use plenty of glitter, fixed on with glue, or shiny paper to emphasize the theme of light and candles.

2 Make candles, or decorate them, as for Diwali (see page 129).

3 One of the special things about the gifts that are exchanged at Hanukah is the way they are wrapped. It is important to make sure they look as pretty as possible. Preferably, they should be done up in blue and white paper. Children could extend this theme by designing their own wrapping paper, using potato or other vegetable prints to make simple but attractive, evenly-spaced patterns. They could try using stencils for this instead. They could use this paper to wrap a small gift – perhaps some sweets that have been made in class, or something else they have made, of which they are particularly proud.

4 As part of a movement lesson, act out the process of cleaning the Temple, and end this with a mime of lighting the Menorah.

SONGS
Hanukah, traditional, **Seeing and doing**; *Hevenu shalom a'leychem*, **Alleluya** *Chanukah*; *Spinning top*; *Potato pancakes*, all from **Festivals, book 1**

MUSIC
Songs and dances from Israel **Arion** label (ARN/34296, ARN/4034296)
Selection of folk dances (INT EP 10) (library resource)

Ramadan

About Ramadan

Ramadan is the ninth month of the Islamic year, and a time when Muslims are expected to keep a fast. The Islamic year is a lunar one, usually about ten or eleven days shorter than the solar year, so it is not possible to give an accurate equivalent in terms of the more widely used calendar year (see page 112).

Because festivals are decided by the appearance of the moon, they cannot begin until the moon has actually been sighted. Sometimes people have to wait until the night before the festival before they can be sure of the day on which it will begin – they may not know until only hours beforehand whether they can celebrate or not.

The fast of Ramadan

Fasting during Ramadan is very important to Muslims, since it is one of the five 'pillars', or basic duties, demanded by the faith. The others are the declaration of the faith, giving to charity, saying the five daily prayers and, at least once in a lifetime, making a pilgrimage to Mecca in Saudi Arabia. Everyone over the age of ten, who is not sick, pregnant or travelling, must fast during Ramadan.

Throughout the month, Muslims are expected to pay special attention to all aspects of their faith. Prayer is important at all times, but is emphasized during Ramadan, and people are supposed to make a special effort not to be unkind, cruel or deceitful.

The fast itself begins at dawn, from the moment when it is possible to distinguish a white thread from a black one. From that time onwards, neither eating nor drinking is allowed, which can be very harsh in a hot country. In some countries, schools start and finish earlier in the day during Ramadan to make things easier for both children and teachers, who may be very tired by the afternoon.

When darkness comes, it is time to break the fast. People usually have a snack and then offer the evening prayer. Then they sit down to a proper meal, which often begins with dates.

Lailat-ul-Qadr

Lailat-ul-Qadr is the 27th night of Ramadan. It is especially important for Muslims who remember the story of the first occasion on which the angel Gabriel appeared to the Prophet Muhammad in a cave near Mecca. The angel asked the Prophet to repeat the first words of the Qur'an. Muslims believe that over several years, the whole Qur'an was revealed by God to the prophet, bit by bit, always through the angel Gabriel.

Since the occasion takes place during Ramadan, it cannot be celebrated with any kind of feasting. Instead, it is a time for prayer. The Qur'an is read right through the night, from the moment when the fast is over until first light, when the fast begins again.

Eid-ul-Fitr

Eid-ul-Fitr marks the end of Ramadan when Muslims enjoy themselves after the fast, but it is also a time for prayer.

Children especially look forward to Eid-ul-Fitr, when they are given presents (see picture). People wear new clothes and send cards with the greeting 'Eid Mubarik' (Blessed Festival) written on them. Gifts of sweets, often sugared almonds, may be exchanged. Heads of families make a special point of visiting other families. They exchange greetings and give money to children, who look forward to all this with great excitement.

In some countries, it is the occasion for a funfair, when the whole family can go out and enjoy themselves together.

A story for Eid-ul-Fitr

This is part of a short book written by a London girl named Nadia Bakhsh, when she was ten years old.

"On Friday, just before Eid, my parents and I shopped around for some nice material. We bought a piece that was red and had blue specks like raindrops. That same night we took the material to the tailor.

The next day I asked my mum, "Didn't we bring back some mehndi from Pakistan?"

Mehndi is made from a shrub called henna. The leaves are crushed to make a powder. We made this into a thick paste, with water. My mum painted a pattern on my hands with this paste, using a matchstick.

Two hours later I washed this paste off, which left a beautiful crimson pattern. That night I slept peacefully, thinking about Eid.

Sunday was a busy day, for we hoped that Eid would be the next day. We went to the tailor's house to collect my Eid suit made from the material we gave him on Friday. He didn't want to be paid.

"This is my Eidi to Nadia. It is free," the tailor said. Eidi is something given to an adult or a child as a gift.

When we got back home we began to wrap up Eid presents for our friends. At five o'clock in the evening we got ready to go visiting some friends.

First we went to my friend Huma's house and gave her family a card with some cash in it as an Eidi. Then we went to see a family who had a baby girl. We took the baby a blanket from Mothercare as an Eidi.

When we came home we looked for the

new moon to try to work out whether it was Eid or not the next day.

"Is it Eid tomorrow?" I asked anxiously.

"We don't know yet," my mum said.

The next day I woke up early and went downstairs to see if there were any Eid cards. There were a few, so I took them upstairs to my parents. My grandma sent me £5 as an Eidi. I displayed all the cards on the mantelpiece.

I asked, "Is it Eid today?"

"Yes. We checked with the Islamic Cultural Centre early this morning," said mum.

"Hooray!" I yelled with excitement.

We went to the mosque in the car. I have never seen such a crowd. We met some friends we hadn't seen for a long time.

Then my mum said, "It's nearly ten o'clock so we'd better go inside."

Inside we said our Namaz (prayer) before returning outside where a market was being held.

My dad bought us each a samosa. There were other kinds of food for sale too. Many stalls were open. Some were selling religious items, others just jewellery. It was surprising to see how many Muslims there were from different countries. There were European, African, Arab and Asian Muslims.

There were some men standing outside on a platform saying their Namaz. Some men were walking around telling all ladies and girls, including us, to put our dupattas (scarves) on our heads.

In the evening we went to the house of some friends. We had dinner. It was delicious. We had rice, cofta (meatballs), spinach, meat curry, yoghurt and a few other dishes too."

Activities for Eid-ul-Fitr

1 Study Islamic art and work on the ideas of pattern symmetry that can be seen in traditional styles of rugs and tiles. Get the children to make printing blocks from polystyrene tiles and use these to make patterns of 'tiles'.

2 On a larger scale, several children can work together to design a 'rug' with a pattern of flowers and repeating shapes. Use tiles again for this, printing on a large sheet of coloured paper. Display the rug on the wall.

3 Make Eid cards, with pictures of flowers.

BOOKS
Muslim nursery rhymes, Mustafa Yusuf McDermott; **Islam for younger people**, Ghulam Sarwar; **Love at home**, Khurram Murad; **Marvellous stories from the life of Muhammad**, Mardijah Aldrich Tarantino, all published by *The Islamic Foundation* (223 London Road, Leicester).

SONGS
A happy Eid, Khusir Idd; The Eid moon – Eider chand, both in **Festival book 2**

MUSIC
Folk music of India; Orissa. **Lyrichord** label (LLST/7271)

Middle caste religious music for India – a collection of Hindu and Muslim religious songs. **Lyrichord** label (LLST/7223)

Shrove Tuesday

About Shrove Tuesday

Shrove Tuesday is a Christian festival, and is the name given to the day before the traditional fast of Lent, which begins on Ash Wednesday.

Lent, and therefore Shrove Tuesday, falls at a slightly different time each year, since the actual date depends on when Easter falls. But Shrove Tuesday is almost always in February, and is one of the earliest spring festivals in the Christian calendar.

Celebrating Shrove Tuesday and keeping the fast of Lent

In the past, the season of Lent was kept by Christians as a very sombre time, during which no luxury foods were eaten. Often people survived on little more than bread and water. Christians used the time to remember the story of how Jesus himself fasted in the wilderness before setting out to teach, and how he was tempted to become a rich and powerful leader.

This season has become a time to concentrate on prayer, repentance and forgiveness. Ash Wednesday is the first day of the season. It used to be a time when Christians wore 'sackcloth and ashes', to show how sorry they were for the wrong things they had done over the past year. In the Roman Catholic Church, people still maintain something of this custom. The priest marks people's foreheads with the ashes of the palm crosses given out the year before.

Shrove Tuesday – the day before Lent – has always tended to be a time when people have a 'last fling' before the fast begins. This celebration takes a variety of forms in different parts of the world.

In Britain, Shrove Tuesday was a time for feasting and games. It is still quite common in many parts of the country for people to play a special kind of football at this time, in much the same way as at Easter. This dates from the days before football had any proper rules, when it was a free-for-all with whole villages joining in.

The custom of making pancakes on this day dates from the time when people wanted to use up all the cream, eggs and fat in the house, since they would not be needing them for the next forty days. In the Netherlands, people bake a special kind of meaty bread for the same sort of reason because people were not supposed to eat meat during Lent. There are different types of traditional foods in various parts of Europe, and celebrations take place on a fairly large scale in many countries. But the most dramatic festivities of all must be the carnivals of southern Europe and, especially, Latin America.

Carnival

One of the world's most famous carnivals takes place in Trinidad in the West Indies. The carnival was started in the nineteenth century and it is now one of the most important events in the year.

Fancy dress is an important part of the carnival. There is a big parade through the streets on the Monday as well as on Shrove Tuesday itself and there is keen competition over the costumes worn (see picture). People start planning their costumes at around Christmas time!

The celebrations begin at dawn on carnival Monday, with a fancy dress procession through the streets. People dress as devils, witches, cowboys and ghosts. There are figures from history too – Romans, Vikings, Aztecs and Egyptians. There are also some very dramatic costumes. There is a firebird with shimmering tail feathers, St. George, with a dragon as part of his costume, the king of the sea – and many more.

The parade passes through the streets to the sound of steel bands playing calypso music. In the evening, the costumes are judged and prizes given. There are fireworks, and the dancing goes on all night.

The next day is Shrove Tuesday itself. The procession is even more dramatic than the one the day before. The people wearing the winning costumes lead the parade. There is more music and dancing and the celebrations go on for hours.

Carnivals are held in several other countries too. One of the best known happens in Rio de Janeiro in Brazil, while another big celebration takes place in New Orleans in the USA.

The story of Lent

The story of Lent tells of how Jesus prepared to go out and teach the people, and how he struggled against the idea of making himself into a powerful world leader.

Jesus knew that soon he would have to leave his home in Nazareth, and travel throughout his country, Judea, preaching and teaching. He knew it was going to be difficult, and he needed some time alone to think.

At this time, hardly anyone had heard of Jesus. His cousin, John the Baptist, was much more famous. John spent his time preaching and baptizing people in the River Jordan. He told the people that another teacher was coming soon, one who would fill them with the Holy Spirit. The people knew he meant the Messiah whom they believed would come and save all people.

One day, Jesus came to John to be

baptized. John knew at once that Jesus was the Messiah. He said that he couldn't baptize Jesus because really it should be Jesus who baptized John. But Jesus insisted.

As Jesus stepped into the water, the people realized he was a very special kind of person. They heard the voice of God telling them, "this is my much-loved son."

After he had been baptized, Jesus went alone into the wilderness. This was a desert-like place, where there was almost nothing to eat or drink. Jesus stayed there for forty days, thinking about the work he was to do.

While Jesus was in the wilderness, the devil tried to tempt him. The devil said that the best way for Jesus to make people listen to him was to perform magical tricks.

"If you're so hungry," the devil said, "you could turn these stones into bread." But Jesus knew it would be wrong to use his great powers just to please himself.

"Another thing you could do," said the devil, "is throw yourself off a high tower." And it seemed to Jesus that he was on the highest tower of the Temple.

"If you jumped off this," the devil said, "God wouldn't let you get hurt, and the people would take a lot more notice of you."

But Jesus refused to listen to the devil.

"You shouldn't tempt God," he said.

And then the devil tempted Jesus to make himself into a very powerful ruler.

"Just worship me," the devil said. "I'll look after you. You'll rule the whole world."

But Jesus said, "Leave me alone. I worship only God."

After that, Jesus left the wilderness, and set out through the towns and villages, teaching the people about God.

Activities for Shrove Tuesday

1 Show slides and pictures of the carnival in Trinidad. Play calypso music and ask the children to draw pictures of the musicians and the people in the carnival in their fantastic costumes.

2 Make some carnival costumes. Children's costumes should be kept simple, easy to wear and light. But they should be lavishly decorated too. Use sequins, glitter, beads, shiny coloured paper trimmings from haberdashers or clothing manufacturers, gold and silver threads, and anything else you can find.

3 Organize a fancy dress dance with carnival costumes and a steel band to play calypso music.

POEMS
Pancake day, Shaun Fountain, **Rhyme time**
Carnival in Trinidad, Nydia Bruce-Solomon, **The Tinder-box assembly book**

SONGS
Junkanoo, **Flying a round**
Carnival night, **Tinderbox**; *Me stone is me stone, Ibo bo lay laz*; both from **Festivals, book 2**

MUSIC
Voodoo trance music, ritual drums from Haiti, **Lyrichord** label (LYRI/LLST 7279)

A BOOK
Nini at carnival, Errol Lloyd, *Bodley Head*

Purim

About Purim

Purim is a Jewish festival which falls in February or March. It follows the Fast of Esther. Both the fast and feast are related to the story of how Esther, the queen of Persia, stopped plans to kill all the Jewish people living in Persia (c. 500 BC).

Celebrating Purim

The most important part of the Purim celebrations is the story of Esther (see below). The story is read aloud in the synagogue the evening before the festival, and on the day itself. Teachers read it to their classes too (see picture). Every time the name of Haman, who plotted to murder the Jews, is mentioned, everyone is supposed to boo and wave rattles so that his name cannot be heard!

Purim has developed into a carnival in some places, and a huge model of Haman is carried through the streets. People boo and hiss at this, too, just as they do when his name is read out in the synagogue. It is a time for giving money to charity and sending gifts of food to friends, particularly a special kind of biscuit for Purim. It is called Haman-tashen and is three-cornered. It is supposed to look like Haman's hat (or possibly his ears!).

The story of the Fast of Esther and the Feast of Purim

The first part of the story is a narrative, and the second part is in the form of a play.

Esther was a young Jewish woman, who lived in Persia long ago. Although she was far from home, she was not alone, for there were many other Jewish people living in the land.

And although she was an orphan, there were good people to care for her.

One of these was her cousin, a wise man named Mordecai. He had looked after her when she was a child, so she loved him very much.

Esther grew up to be very beautiful. The king, whose name was Ahazareus, fell in love with Esther and asked her to marry him. Esther agreed because she liked the king very much, but Mordecai had a warning for her.

"Be careful," he said. "Wicked people are always plotting against the Jews. It might be best if you don't tell the king you're Jewish." So Esther took his advice, and did not tell the king who her people were. But she did not forget Mordecai. Each day, he waited at the palace gate and Esther would come out to talk to him and listen to stories about what was happening to her own people. And then, one day, as he waited, Mordecai heard two men plotting to kill the king.

Mordecai told Esther about this. Esther then went before the king and told him what Mordecai had heard, just in time to stop the evil men from carrying out their plot. The king was very pleased with Esther.

He also knew he should be grateful to Mordecai, and he made a note of it in his records. But then, perhaps because he was so busy, or perhaps because he was just careless, he forgot all about it.

At about this time, an evil man named Haman managed to make himself very important to the king. He became Chief Minister and decided that everyone should bow down to him whenever he passed by. But Mordecai would not obey his order.

"I bow to God, and God only," he said.

Haman was furious. He was not only furious with Mordecai, though. He decided to try and get rid of all the Jews. So he lied to

Ahazareus that the Jews were all plotting against him, and were refusing to keep the laws of the country.

In those days in Persia, it was the custom for people to decide when it was the right time to do something by casting lots. This was a bit like throwing a dice. Haman cast lots to see when it would be the best time to have all the Jews killed, and it seemed to him that the thirteenth of the month would be a good day. The festival of Purim is sometimes called the Feast of Lots because it takes place on the day when Haman cast lots.

A play for Purim
CHARACTERS

Esther, Mordecai, her cousin, King Ahazareus of Persia, Haman, his wicked adviser, servants and guards.

SCENE 1. BY THE PALACE GATE.

Enter Esther and Mordecai.

Esther: *Mordecai! I need your advice ... something terrible's going to happen! The king has agreed with Haman that all our people are to die. I'm going to pray and fast for three days, and I know that if we listen to God, he will tell us what to do.*

Mordecai: *You are right, Esther. We must pray and listen to God. I'm sure he will find a way to save us.*

SCENE 2. THREE DAYS LATER.

The king is sitting outside his palace, being attended to by servants and by Haman.

Enter Esther.

King: *Esther, my dear! How glad I am to see you. I was just telling Haman here how little I see my wife – and how he overworks me! I hardly get a minute of spare time any more.*

Esther: *I'm sure Haman knows that I'd like to see more of you, great king. That's why I've*

136

arranged a special banquet for you tomorrow, and I'm going to insist that you take an evening off from affairs of state to come and enjoy yourself. Haman, you're invited too, of course.
King: *We'd both like to come, wouldn't we Haman? Everyone knows your banquets are the best in Persia!*
Esther bows to the king, and leaves.

SCENE 3. LATER THAT DAY.
The king is at one side of the stage, looking at his court records. It is late at night, but he can't sleep. Haman is a little way off, behind a screen, hammering. He is building a gallows.
King: *Goodness! I forgot all about this! Mordecai the Jew saved my life, and I never rewarded him! Haman!*
Enter Haman, carrying a hammer.
Haman: *Sire?*
King: *Haman, what do you think I should do for a man who has saved my life?*
Haman (aside): *He means me! I'm saving his life by killing off all the Jews.* He turns to the king. *Sire, I think you should give the man a crown, and beautiful clothes and have a parade through the streets for him, so that everyone can cheer.*
King: *What a good idea! Arrange that for Mordecai the Jew!*
Haman (to the audience): *Mordecai! But I'm in the middle of building a gallows for him!* He runs off.

SCENE 4. AFTER THE BANQUET.
King: *Esther, my dear, that was the best banquet I've ever been to. I must reward you. Choose anything and I will give it to you.*
Esther: *Oh great king! May I ask for the lives of the Jewish people? I know that Haman wants to kill them. But they are good people, and they do not deserve to die.*
King: *Of course I shall grant your wish. But why do you care so much for the Jews?*
Esther: *Because they are my people! I am Jewish! It was my cousin Mordecai who saved your life. Haman is jealous of him. He's lied to you and tricked you, and he only wants you to kill the Jews because he hates Mordecai!*
Haman makes a run for it.
King: *After him! Guards! Put him in prison! And when you've done that, bring Mordecai the Jew here. I have to thank him for saving my life!*

Activities for Purim
1 Tell the story of Esther and ask the children to act it out.
2 As an alternative to acting out the story in a conventional way, make puppets and perform the whole thing as a puppet drama.
3 Using a Jewish cookery book, or advice from a helpful parent, make Purim cakes.

MUSIC
Songs and dances from Israel, **Arion** label (ARN/34296, ARN/4034296)

A BOOK
I am David, Anne Holm, *Magnet books*

137

The Buddha's Birthday

About Wesak

Wesak is a Buddhist festival, which is also known as Visakha Puja. It takes place on the day of the full moon in the month of Visakha, which is usually in May or June. It is the time when the Theravadan Buddhists celebrate the birth, enlightenment and death of the Buddha.

Celebrating the Buddha's birth

There are two main groups of Buddhists. Each celebrates the birth of the Buddha on a different day. Buddhists in China, Japan, Korea, Tibet, Vietnam and Kampuchea mostly belong to the Mahayanan school. They celebrate the three most important points in the Buddha's life, his birth, his enlightenment, and his death, on three different dates. His birthday is celebrated some time in March or April. Buddhists of the Theravadan school live mainly in Burma, Thailand and Sri Lanka. They celebrate all three events on the same day.

Wesak is, most importantly, a time for worship. People decorate their temples and their homes with flowers and lanterns. They carry burning incense sticks and candles around the temple and they put offerings of flowers in front of statues of the Buddha. All through the year it is important to Buddhists that they should be generous to Buddhist monks. The people are especially generous at Wesak. In some countries people give them gifts of food at this time. It is also a time to remember the Buddha's teachings about kindness to all living things. To symbolize this, people set free captive animals such as turtles and birds.

The story of the Buddha

The word Buddha means 'enlightened one', which is the same as saying 'the one who has seen the light'. By 'light', Buddhists mean the truth about life.

The Buddha was not always called the Buddha, for he was not always enlightened. He lived for many years before he saw the truth about the world. But he was always a very special person.

His name was Siddhartha Gotama. He was a prince, the son of a wealthy king and queen in India. There are many legends about what happened when he was born. Some say that the world was flooded with light and the blind could see and the lame could walk again. There is also a legend that the baby Siddhartha could walk as soon as he was born, and that wherever he stepped, lotus flowers grew.

Whether or not any of these things actually happened, the king and queen knew that their baby son was very special because the fortune-tellers had told them so. In those days it was the custom for fortune-tellers to predict what sort of life was in store for a child. Many people in India still keep this custom today. When the fortune-tellers saw the young Siddhartha, and had worked out what sort of person he was likely to be, they announced that he was going to be a great man. He could choose to value material things and become a powerful emperor. Or, they said, he might be a monk, and learn the deepest truths about life. But he would only follow this life if he saw four things: an old man, a sick man, a dead man, and a monk.

The king did not want his son to be a monk, however great he might be. He much preferred the idea that Siddhartha would be a powerful emperor. So he decided to keep his son inside the palace grounds, and make sure

he did not see any of the sights that the fortune-tellers had spoken of.

He built several palaces for his son, and made sure that he had everything he wanted. When the prince grew up, the king found him a young wife. They lived happily together in the beautiful palaces and lovely gardens, never stepping outside even for a minute.

But Siddhartha was not happy. He felt there was something missing in his life of luxury, and he longed to see what life was like outside the palace grounds. So, one afternoon, he persuaded the king's chariot driver to take him out into the world outside.

One of the first things he saw was a man with grey hair and wrinkled skin, shuffling along, using a stick to help him walk.

"What a strange man!" cried Siddhartha. "What makes him walk like that?"

"He is old, your Highness," the chariot driver told him. And Siddhartha learned for the first time that we must all grow old.

Next, they saw a pale, thin man, lying by the roadside. Siddhartha learned that he was sick and that sickness may come to us all, rich and poor.

After that, he saw people carrying a man who seemed quite still and stiff. The chariot driver told him that he was dead.

"And we must all die in the end," he said.

Siddhartha did not want to see any more, and he urged the chariot driver to take him back to the palace. But on the way he saw the last of the four sights – a monk. And it seemed to him that everything he had seen so far was a puzzle. Why must we suffer, grow old and die? Perhaps the monk knew.

He decided that he could no longer live in the luxury of the palace, away from the real world. He would become a monk, and seek the meaning of life.

So that is what he did. He became a monk,

138

and gave up all his belongings, his luxurious life, even his exotic food. He ate only one grain of rice a day, and he was soon as thin as a skeleton.

He hoped that by fasting he would learn to think clearly but he found that instead he just felt ill and confused. But although he decided to give up fasting he refused to go back to his old life. He chose a middle way, being neither too hungry nor too wealthy. And he would sit in the forest, under a tree, and think of answers to all the many questions that puzzled him.

There is a story that, as he sat in the forest, a wicked demon called Mara tried his best to stop Siddhartha learning the truth about life. He threw thunderbolts at him, but they simply turned to flowers in the air.

As for Siddhartha, as he sat under the tree (see picture), he saw the light. He saw that people suffer because they are greedy and selfish, because they want to take things and keep them, when really they should not have them at all. And from that moment on, he became the Buddha, the enlightened one.

He spent the rest of his life teaching and travelling about India. He taught that people should be unselfish, kind, and that they should hurt no living thing. They should not struggle for the things they cannot have. They should try to live in harmony with nature.

The Buddha lived until he was 80 years old, and when he died he left behind many followers. Today there are Buddhists all over the world.

Activities for Wesak

1 Make garlands of flowers, either real or artificial to decorate the room. This is also an occasion for making candles (see page 129).
2 Act out the story of how Siddhartha first realized that people become old or sick and die.
3 Since Wesak is a time for giving to charity, it might be an appropriate occasion for fund-raising activities, for famine relief or a local charity.
4 Since the Buddha taught that we should be kind to animals, encourage children to make zig-zag books and collect pictures about animals, perhaps with conservation as a theme. Contact the local RSPCA branch for educational material.

POEMS
I went to the wood of flowers, James Stephens, **Seeing and doing**
My House, anonymous (Cuba); *Family*, Carl Sandburg, both from **Wheel around the world.**
Hurt no living thing, Christina Rosetti, **The young Puffin book of verse**

SONGS
Majá Pade, **Tinderbox**
Flowers of peace; *O had I a golden thread*, both from **Love, work and hope**
Magic penny, **Alleluya**

MUSIC
Religions of India, a collection of Hindu, Buddhist and Sikh music and chants (ARG/ZFB 55) (library resource)

Baisakhi

About Baisakhi Day

Baisakhi is the name of the first month in the Indian year. Baisakhi Day is the first day of that month, so it is really a new year's day. It falls in April or May. Baisakhi Day is celebrated all over India, but it is especially important to Sikhs. For on this day they remember how, on Baisakhi Day in 1699, Guru Gobind Singh formed the brotherhood of the Khalsa. This was the day that the Sikhs became a strong, military brotherhood who swore to be loyal to their faith and to defend the weak. It marked the beginning of a new phase in the Sikh religion.

Celebrating Baisakhi Day

The Sikh religion was founded by Guru Nanak, who lived from 1469 to 1539. He was the first of ten Gurus (teachers). The last human one was Guru Gobind Singh, who told his followers that at his death there were to be no more human Gurus. Instead, the Sikh sacred book, the Adi Granth, was to be their teacher, and would henceforth be known as the Guru Granth Sahib. During the three-day festival of Baisakhi, Guru Granth Sahib is read aloud, from beginning to end. In the streets, the men dance special dances (see picture).

This is also the time when people who want to join the Sikh religion go through the ceremony which brings them into it. This ceremony involves drinking a special kind of sweetened water called amrit, and accepting the symbols of the brotherhood of the Khalsa. These symbols are known as the 'five Ks' (see page 92).

After the ceremony, people eat a vegetarian meal in the special kitchen attached to each temple. It is the tradition in Sikh temples that there is a kitchen to provide food for anyone who needs it.

The Baisakhi Day story

On Baisakhi Day in 1699, Guru Gobind Singh called the members of the Sikh religion to a town named Anandpur. Since Guru Gobind Singh was their leader, thousands of Sikhs came to hear him teach. When they had all met, the Guru did the strangest thing. He asked them a question.

"Who will give up his head for the Guru?"

At first, no one moved. They didn't really know what he meant, and they didn't like the look of the sword he was holding! Quite a lot of them thought their Guru had gone mad, and they decided to leave the meeting.

The Guru asked the question three times. After the third time, one man nervously came forward. The Guru took him into a tent, and the crowd heard a horrible swishing sound. The Guru came out of the tent, and it seemed there was blood on his sword.

Once again he asked: "Who will give up his head for the Guru?"

Again, one man came forward, and the same thing happened. In all, five men gave themselves up to the Guru, and one by one it seemed that they all died.

Then the Guru stood before the crowd of Sikhs again and was joined by the five men whose heads everyone thought had been cut off! It seemed like a miracle! No one was ever sure what had happened. But one thing was certain – these five had shown a very special kind of loyalty and bravery. From that time onwards they were known as the Five Beloved Ones (Panj Pyare).

The Guru told the other Sikhs that the five were an example of how Sikhs should be brave and willing to die for their faith. He went on to say that all Sikhs should form a brotherhood of this kind. This is the Khalsa, in which everyone is equal and shares the same bowl. From that time onwards, Sikhs took up their custom of all sharing the same name as a sign of equality. This is why all Sikh men are called Singh, which means 'lion', and all women are called Kaur, which means 'princess'. The story goes that over 20 000 Sikhs joined the Khalsa that first day.

A story about Guru Nanak

Once, there was a weaver named Daud, who was a great admirer of Guru Nanak, the first Sikh Guru. He wanted to show the Guru what a special person he thought he was. So he decided to give him a present.

Now, Daud was not a rich man, and he was not at all sure how he could give the Guru a present that was special enough.

"A gift is a way of showing love and friendship," he thought. "It must be the best thing I can give to show how much I love and admire the Guru. Let me think …"

All this time he was working, weaving a beautiful rug for a rich man. He always did his best and he was a very good weaver.

Then Daud had an idea.

"I'll weave the Guru a rug!" he thought.

And he set about weaving the best rug he had ever made. It wasn't very big. It was just about the right size for the Guru to sit on. But it was certainly the best woven and most beautiful rug that Daud had ever made.

When it was finished, he took it to the Guru, and the Guru admired it very much. He thanked Daud, most politely. But he did not put it on the ground, as Daud had expected him to.

"This is a lovely rug," said the Guru. "But you know, I never use such things. I would rather sit on the grass because it smells so sweet. But this rug is a sign of kindness and thoughtfulness, and that is how it will be used. Do you see that dog over there?"

The weaver looked at the dog. She was a thin poor animal, shivering in the cold wind. Close beside her huddled four tiny puppies.

"Cover them with the rug," said the Guru. "And then get them something to eat. That way, you will have saved their lives."

A story about Guru Gobind Singh

Today it is the custom for all Sikh temples to have a kitchen where everyone can eat together. This idea was started by Guru Gobind Singh, who said that all Sikhs should have an open kitchen to give food to anyone who needed it, especially travellers. One day he decided to see if the Sikhs of Anandpur were keeping to this rule.

He got up very early one morning and dressed as a traveller. He began to knock on the doors of the houses along the main street of the town, but no one answered. And then, after a while, he got a few replies, but not very polite ones!

"Go away!" cried the people. "We aren't even up yet! You can't possibly expect us to start cooking so early!"

But at last he came to the house of a man named Bhai Nandlal. Bhai Nandlal invited the Guru into his home and asked him to sit down and rest for a while. He went into his kitchen and the Guru could hear the sound of someone hard at work. Soon Bhai Nandlal came out with a tray of steaming food. There was rice, vegetables, and bread... but none of it was more than half cooked!

"It isn't quite cooked yet," he said. "If you can wait a bit longer, it'll be done soon. If you're really starving after your long journey, you might like to eat it now."

So that was how Guru Gobind Singh learned that there was one real Sikh kitchen in the city of Anandpur, and a real Sikh who was ready to offer food to someone who needed it at any time of day.

Activities for Baisakhi

1 Make parathas, which are a kind of Indian flat bread often eaten with curries. You should be able to find a recipe in most Indian cookery books.

2 Act out the story of Guru Gobind Singh looking for a real Sikh kitchen. He can knock on as many doors as you like and receive a wide variety of replies, so that any number of children can be involved.

3 Draw pictures of the dog and the rug. Children could make a large class collage picture illustrating this story.

SONGS
Kaigul-Hands; Thank you for my friends, both from **Tinderbox**
Make new friends, **Flying a round**

MUSIC
Religions of India, a collection of Hindu, Buddhist and Sikh music and chants (ARG/ZFB 55) (library resource)

St. Patrick's and St. David's Day

About saints

The various branches of the Christian Church honour a number of figures from the past as having special importance.

Different branches of the Christian Church revere saints to a greater or lesser extent according to their tradition. The Eastern Orthodox Church and the Roman Catholic Church honour many more saints than the Protestant Church, for example.

Many saints are almost mythical figures, about whom we know very little for certain, others have better-documented lives. Some are believed to take a special interest in certain situations, things, places or people, and these are known as 'patron' saints. St. Christopher, for example, is the patron saint of all travellers.

St. David and St. Patrick are both patron saints of countries. St. David is the patron saint of Wales, St. Patrick of Ireland. Although we know little of either of them for certain, we do know that they were both very concerned with the countries in which they lived and worked as Christian missionaries and ministers. In this respect they are different from the more mythical figure of St. George, the patron saint of England, who lived in the Middle East.

St. David's Day

St. David's Day, the national day of Wales, falls on March 1. It is a time when Welsh people make a special point of thinking about their own history and identity.

St. David

St. David was a bishop in Wales in about the sixth century. As a priest, he worked outside his own country for a while, travelling both in England and further afield. He founded a number of monasteries in Wales, including one in Dyfed in a place that is known in English as St. David's. He eventually became archbishop of Wales.

Celebrating St. David's Day

St. David's Day is very much a festival of Welsh culture which, in Wales, means it is a time for singing. It is also the custom for people to wear the emblem of Wales on this day. Strictly speaking this is a leek, but a daffodil is often worn instead.

A story about St. David

St. David was a saintly man, who cared little for riches and material things. He lived most of his life very simply, in a monastery in Wales.

Wherever he went, he heard people arguing about whether Jesus was an ordinary person, or some sort of spirit or ghost. The people of Wales were very worried about this. They wanted to be sure they were good Christians, but they did not know what to believe. Many Welsh people went to a meeting to hear the leaders of the Welsh Church discuss the question.

When it was St. David's turn to speak, it was very hard for anyone to see him, for he was a very short man! But he spoke very powerfully and clearly, so that they could all hear and understand him. He explained to the great crowd of people that Christians believe that Jesus was a real person, as well as being God.

The story goes that as he spoke, it seemed to the people who were listening that the ground under him rose up to form a little hill so that everyone could see him as he spoke.

Activities for St. David's Day

1 Make daffodil decorations using the real flowers (planted in pots earlier in the year to ensure that they bloom in time), paper flowers or pictures.
2 Learn simple greetings in Welsh.
3 Make a big red dragon collage. The dragon is the symbol of Wales.

St. Patrick's Day

St. Patrick is the patron saint of Ireland, and he is remembered on March 17. Irish people all over the world celebrate this festival which has become a celebration of Irish culture, and the occasion for lively parties!

St. Patrick

St. Patrick lived much earlier than St. David, in about the third century AD. He was probably born in Wales, though there is also a theory that he came from Scotland. As a boy, he was captured and sold as a slave, first to a sea-captain and then to an Irish chieftain. Ireland was still a pagan country at the time, and St. Patrick resolved that one day he would bring Christianity to the country. This is exactly what he did.

St. Patrick escaped from captivity and went to France, where he became a priest. He returned to Ireland when he was an old man, and spent the rest of his life there preaching Christianity to the Irish people.

Celebrating St. Patrick's Day

St. Patrick's Day is celebrated wherever there are Irish people. In New York, in the USA, there is a big procession, and everyone who is even the smallest part Irish tries to wear green, the national colour of Ireland. It is a time for celebrating and for playing Irish music. There is an old tradition in Ireland that this is the day on which you should plant your crop of potatoes.

A story about St. Patrick

When St. Patrick arrived in Ireland, he was determined to teach the people there to be Christians. He thought the best way to do this would be to teach the king of Ireland. If he became a Christian, the people would probably follow him.

Now, it was about the time of an important spring festival called Beltane. It was the tradition at Beltane for all the fires in the country to be put out, except for one special sacred fire.

At the moment when all the fires were supposed to be out, when all was darkness, the king looked out across the hills.

"What's that?" he called out in horror. "A fire!" And sure enough, a single fire flickered in the darkness.

"Arrest whoever is burning that fire!" ordered the king.

Soon an old man was brought to him. It was St. Patrick for it was he who had been burning the fire. The king was shocked at the sight of an old man in chains so he was quite gentle when he spoke to him.

"Why did you do it?" he asked. "It will bring us bad luck..."

"Your fires mean nothing," St. Patrick told him. "I have come to light a new fire."

And he began to tell the king the Christian story. Soon the king decided he would become a Christian, and he allowed St. Patrick to preach his message all over Ireland.

There are many other stories about St. Patrick. One of the best known is certainly not strictly true, but it has always been very popular. It tells of how St. Patrick managed to get rid of all the snakes in Ireland. The story goes that once there were a great many snakes in the country, and the people were very frightened of them. So St. Patrick used all his powers to make the snakes follow him to the top of a high hill. Then he drove them down to the other side and into the sea (see picture). After that, no snakes have been seen in Ireland to this day.

Activities for St. Patrick's Day

1 Act out the story of St. Patrick driving the snakes out of Ireland. Make snake costumes using sheeting, suitably coloured, perhaps with scales stuck on.

2 St. Patrick used the three-leaved plant, the shamrock, to explain how the Christian idea of God is of three beings and one at the same time. Use this motif for decorations working on ideas of symmetry and repeated patterns.

POEMS
Spring, Aileen Fisher, **Seeing and doing**
The fiddler of Dooney, W.B. Yeats, **Delights and warnings**
MUSIC
Irish ceilidh dance time (HPE/678)
Irish folk favourites (HPE/653)
Welsh mixed voices (BM 53)

Mothers' Day

About Mothers' Day

Mothers' Day falls on two different dates, depending on whether you are in the USA or Britain. In the USA, Mothers' Day falls on the second Sunday in May. It is quite a new festival, going back only to the beginning of this century. But in Britain, the festival of Mothering Sunday (which is its proper name) goes back several centuries. It is celebrated on the fourth Sunday in Lent, which usually means it happens some time in March. It is also called Refreshment Sunday, for it was the day on which people had a rest from the fast of Lent and refreshed themselves by eating ordinary food for just one day.

Celebrating Mothers' Day

A long time ago, the Christian Church had a rule that on the fourth Sunday of Lent, everyone should visit their 'mother' church. This referred to the most important church in their area. This soon became a time when families could meet and enjoy each other's company. And so, as well as being a time when people paid special attention to their 'mother' church, they also made it a special day for mothers.

By the 1700s, it had become a special holiday for young servants and apprentices. They were allowed to go home and visit their mothers on this day. It might be the only day of the year on which they could do so. This was especially hard for the younger ones, because it was quite common for children as young as ten years old to be sent to work away from home. It's not hard to imagine how very excited the young servants and apprentices were on Mothering Sunday and how much they enjoyed carrying home

flowers and special cakes (see picture). These cakes, baked especially for Mothering Sunday, were called Simnel cakes and were made with fine flour and spices.

Young boys who worked in towns as apprentices might scrape together their savings to buy their mother a brooch, or some other trinket, to mark this very special day.

Mothering Sunday had almost died out by the Second World War, when thousands of American soldiers and servicemen arrived in Britain. They told the British about their own special Mothers' Day, celebrated in May. They explained how they gave Mothers' Day cards and presents. The custom of celebrating Mothering Sunday in Britain was revived after this.

Today it is a festival when children make a special fuss of their mothers, perhaps doing extra housework, giving her flowers and a card, and generally making a point of showing how much they appreciate her. The traditional Simnel cake – or, to be exact, cakes, since there are several kinds – is still made by some people. It is a particularly important festival in primary schools.

Many children in different parts of the country spend their time in the days before Mothering Sunday making their own special card for their mothers.

The story of the Simnel cake

There is a special sort of cake for Mothering Sunday, which is called a Simnel cake. This is a story of how the first one was made.

Once there was an old woman named Nell, whose husband was called Simon. They both loved to cook, which was a pity really, for neither of them was very good at it. And what made it worse, was that they were always

quarrelling. Each one had very firm ideas about what to put in each dish, and how to cook it and each always thought the other was wrong!

One day they mixed a cake to eat for tea on Mothering Sunday. They had mixed in spices and fruit, eggs and flour when they began to quarrel.

"Let's boil it, like a pudding," said Simon.

"You silly man," said Nell. "Whoever heard of boiling a cake? We must bake it."

"Well, I'd like a boiled cake for a change," said Simon. And so the argument went on.

In the end, they agreed to do both. They would boil the cake for a little while first and then they would bake it.

It was delicious! They had never made anything so good. They decided to call this new kind of cake after themselves, so they called it Sim-Nell. And that is how the Simnel cake got its name.

A story for Mothering Sunday

This is a story about a time long ago, when children had to leave home and go to work when they were still very young. And because there were few good roads, and no cars or even trains, it was very hard for them to get home very often. Sometimes, they only saw their parents once a year, on Mothering Sunday. This story is about a girl called Mary, on her way home to see her mother.

Mary's heart was beating so fast that she thought it would jump right out of her chest. She didn't think she'd ever been so excited in her life. It had been nearly a year since she'd last walked down this little, overgrown lane. Now here she was again, and it seemed that she recognized every tree, every blade of grass and every pebble on the ground. She was on her way home again!

She was practising what she would say to her mother. She was only eleven, but she'd been working for long enough to feel she should behave like a grown-up. Her mother would expect that, surely. She couldn't rush into the house shouting like a little girl. She would have to knock politely on the door, and say "How do you do?" when her mother opened it.

Then she'd tell the family all about life on the farm where she worked. She would tell them the good things. She'd miss out stories like the one about the time when she'd forgotten to clean out the churns, so that the next lot of cream that went into them was sour. But she would tell them that Mrs. Hardy, who she worked for, had said she was a good little dairymaid, and how she could have three days off at Mothering Sunday time. Mrs. Hardy had also told Mary that she could bake a special cake to take home, all wrapped in a linen cloth, and that she could have a ride almost all the way home in the farm cart.

She stood still for a minute, trying to calm herself. And then she remembered something.

"Flowers!" she said aloud. "I must pick some flowers for Mothering Sunday!" And she began to pick a little posy of primroses as she walked along.

Soon she came to a bend in the road. There was the little cottage, in among the trees by the roadside. And there was her mother, standing by the garden gate!

"Now, try to be grown up and don't run," she said to herself, but it was no good. Her legs just wouldn't listen – they went faster and faster. Soon she was racing along the lane, tripping over her skirt, clutching the poor primroses so tightly that their stems were all squashed up in her hand, and the cake swinging like a pendulum in its linen cloth …

"Mother!" she shouted. "I'm home!"

And she threw herself into her mother's arms, while all her little brothers and sisters came tumbling out of the house to greet her.

Activites for Mothers' Day

1 Plant snowdrops in yoghurt pots in time for them to be in bloom on Mothering Sunday. Ask the children to decorate their pots. Cover them with coloured paper, cut-out flowers or sections of doilies, or simply paint them using powder paint mixed with glue.

2 Make cards for Mothering Sunday and ask the children to write a simple poem for the inside.

3 Make cakes for Mothering Sunday, with an M marked on each one in icing or marzipan.

POEMS
Mum'll be coming home today, Michael Rosen, **The Tinder-box assembly book**
The factory worker, Anthony Parker, **Wheel around the world**
SONGS
Supermum, **Tinderbox**
Jump Shamador, **Granny's yard**

Raksha Bandhan

About Raksha Bandhan

Raksha Bandhan is a Hindu festival that takes place at the end of the monsoon season in India, around July or August. It is a festival in which sisters honour their brothers, who in turn offer them protection. Although Raksha Bandhan itself will certainly fall in the holidays, its theme could easily be used in school at a later date.

It might be appropriate, at the beginning of the school year, to think about how older children can look after and help younger brothers and sisters who have come to school for the first time.

Celebrating Raksha Bandhan

Raksha Bandhan means 'ties of protection'. It is the custom at this time for sisters to tie a band of threads around their brothers' wrists (see picture), and to ask for protection in return.

The band itself is called a rhaki. The sister ties this around her brother's wrist, and marks his forehead with red dye. In return, as well as the promise of protection, he will give her a present of sweets.

A girl may in fact choose to honour someone who is not her brother in this way, making him, in effect, an honorary brother.

Another Hindu festival also falls on this date. This is the Day of the Coconuts. To celebrate this, people in some parts of India throw coconuts into rivers or the sea, in honour of Varuna, god of the sea.

The story of Raksha Bandhan

The story of this festival tells how Indra, king of the lesser gods, was beaten by a demon named Bali.

Indra could not protect himself from Bali, but his wife, Indrana, decided that she would get help. She went to see the powerful god Vishnu, to ask him what should be done.

Of course, she was afraid when she entered the great god's palace – but she remembered the danger her husband was in, and gathered up all her courage.

When Vishnu heard her story, he felt sorry for both Indrana and her husband. He gave Indrana a powerful thread to tie around Indra's wrist. This thread protected Indra, and he was able to drive the demon away.

A story of Krishna

The god Vishnu was once born on earth as a human being. He was called Krishna and he was very handsome, clever and kind. Everyone loved him, but some loved him more than others.

Krishna had a sister, named Subhadra, and an adopted sister named Draupadi. Sad to say, Subhadra was not really a very nice person. She wasn't very helpful or kind, though she still wanted people to be kind and helpful to her.

Subhadra really didn't like Draupadi, mainly because she knew Krishna liked her a lot, and she was jealous. So she kept reminding Draupadi that she wasn't Krishna's real sister, and that she wasn't important because she was adopted. This made Draupadi very unhappy, for she loved her brother Krishna. She was always especially kind to him, he was kind to her too.

"It's not fair," Subhadra complained to Krishna. "You're much nicer to her than you are to me. And I'm your real sister, and she's only adopted, so it ought to be the other way round. You ought to like me better."

"But she's much nicer to me than you are," said Krishna. "So of course I'm nicer to her."

One day, Krishna cut his hand. It was bleeding very badly, and hurt a lot. He tried to mop up the blood, but it just seemed to be getting everywhere.

Subhadra came into the room where Krishna was, and saw what had happened.

"I suppose I'll have to get you a bandage," she sighed. "Or you'll just get blood all over the place." And she wandered off.

She was away for a very long time, Krishna did not know what to do. He knew that if he went off to look for a bandage himself, the blood would just drip everywhere. And it would be difficult to tie the bandage because the cut was in an awkward place.

After a while, Draupadi came in. She saw what had happened.

"Oh! Poor Krishna!" she cried. "Look at your hand! Let me bandage it up!"

At once she tore a strip of cloth from her beautiful sari, and bound up the cut. Her kindness and thoughtfulness seemed to stop the pain, as well as the bleeding.

Who do you think acted more like a sister? Was it Subhadra, who was Krishna's real sister? Or was it Draupadi, who was adopted?

Activities for Raksha Bandhan

1 Make simple puppets so that the children can use these to dramatize the story of Raksha Bandhan above.

2 Talk about brothers and sisters. Discuss the questions at the end of the story. Sometimes you hear it said that all people are our brothers and sisters? What does that mean? Ask the children to write poems or stories about their own brothers and sisters. Do they always like them? Sometimes? Never? Why

do they feel this way?
3 Work on plaiting, using coloured wool. Use three different colours, and show the children how they can be woven together to make simple wrist bands.
4 Since it is the tradition for brothers to give sisters presents of sweets at this festival, this is another appropriate time to try making some. Children could work out ways of wrapping them as presents for their own families. As the Day of the Coconuts festival also falls at this time it would be appropriate to make coconut ice.
5 Talk about the occasions when children have felt they needed someone to look after or protect them. What happened? Ask the children to work together to think of a simple story, real or imaginary, about someone who was in some sort of danger or difficulty – getting lost in a shop or in a crowd, left behind on a bus, carried away by a dragon to a strange and frightening land – but who was rescued by a sister, brother, or friend.
6 Talk about, write about, and draw pictures of families. Make graphs to show who has older brothers and sisters, who has younger ones and so on. Is there anyone who has no brother or sister? Who would they choose to be a brother or sister?

POEM
This is a poem about not being a perfect brother or sister. It is probably quite true to life, and might help children discuss what they really feel, instead of what they think they ought to feel!

Sometimes
*Sometimes I share things,
And everyone says
'Isn't it lovely? Isn't it fine?'*

*I give my little brother
Half my ice cream cone
And let him play
With toys that are mine.*

*But today
I don't feel like sharing.
Today
I want to be alone
Today*

*I don't want to give my little brother
A single thing except
A shove*
(by Eve Merriam, **The Tinder-box assembly book**, A & C Black 1982)

POEMS
I'm the youngest in our house, Michael Rosen; *For sale*, Shel Silverstein; and *My brother*, Dorothy Aldis, both from **The Tinder-box assembly book**
Road of peace, Paul Robeson; *My noisy brother*, Kashim Chowdhury, both **Wheel around the world**
SONGS
The whole world in his hands, **Look away**
The ink is black, **Love, work and hope**

Weddings

About weddings

Weddings are important in almost every culture. A wedding usually involves a legal contract, in which a woman and a man promise to live together for the rest of their lives. It can also be a religious ritual. If people are married according to the rules of their religion it is usually because they accept that their marriage needs to be blessed by God. It is also a family or even a community festival, which brings people together to celebrate an event everyone believes is important.

A Jewish wedding

As in many other societies, a wedding among Jewish people is seen as the uniting of two families, so the views of everyone involved must be considered. On the day of the wedding, the bride and groom, who have been fasting all day, stand in the synagogue under a canopy decorated with flowers. Here the wedding ceremony takes place. This includes the bridegroom giving the bride a ring, and the rabbi blessing the couple seven times. At the end of the ceremony, the bridegroom stamps on a wine glass, as a reminder to everyone of the destruction of Jerusalem, many centuries ago.

A Christian wedding

In the USA and in many Western European societies, the idea of marriage as a union of two families is not as obviously important as it is in other cultures. This is not the case, however, in many other parts of the Christian world. A Christian marriage takes place in a church, with a priest conducting the ceremony. He will have spent some time with the couple earlier, discussing with them the idea of marriage and what it means to them. During the ceremony, the couple promise to live together and to care for each other for the rest of their lives, and to symbolize this, the couple exchange rings. Some Christian churches accept divorce as permissible, though never welcome, while others, such as the Roman Catholic Church, do not allow it.

A Muslim wedding

In a Muslim marriage the unity of the two families is considered most important. It is believed that the futures of more than just the two people concerned are at stake. The bridegroom begins by approaching the bride's family to discuss the marriage, though the last word is with the bride, who can refuse to marry.

The ceremony is very short, and takes place in the home or the mosque. The imam (religious leader) and men from both the families conduct the wedding, which involves the couple agreeing to the marriage.

The important part of the ceremony is the signing and witnessing of the marriage contract. It is possible for the ceremony to take place with the bride and the groom in separate rooms, or even without the bride being there at all. Divorce, though allowed, is considered to be a very evil thing.

A Hindu wedding

In traditional Hindu society, families arrange marriages with special reference to the couple's horoscope. The two people involved may not even meet until the wedding day, for it is the opinions of the families, rather than of the individuals, that matter. The horoscope will, it is believed, show whether the couple are compatible or not. An astrologer is also employed to decide on what day the wedding should take place.

A Hindu bride may take days to prepare for the occasion. She will have her hands and feet painted with henna. Muslim brides from India and Pakistan also do this.

The ceremony takes place in a courtyard, or even a part of the street that has been blocked off, but not in a temple. It is performed in front of a fire, into which the bride and groom pour offerings of rice and butter (see picture). The most important part of the ceremony is the moment when the bride's sari is tied to the groom's shirt and the couple walk round the fire seven times.

A Sikh wedding

Here again, families are more important than individuals, and it is the families who make all the arrangements.

A Sikh wedding is held in the temple, during the morning worship. The bridegroom, wearing a muslin scarf, sits in front of the Sikh holy book, the Guru Granth Sahib, and the bride enters, dressed in red. She wears gold jewellery and will have her hands and feet painted like a Hindu bride. She will have a string of pieces of dried coconut around her neck, as a symbol of good luck. Someone will read a suitable passage from the Guru Granth Sahib and then, when the couple have bowed to his holy book, the bride's father ties the woman's dupatta (scarf) to the man's muslin scarf. A special hymn, known as the Lavan hymn, is sung as the couple walk four times around the Guru Granth Sahib.

The wedding – a story

This is a story about a wedding in a Greek Cypriot family in London.

"Last year, my cousin Maria got married, and I had a really important part in the wedding. It was my job to hold one of the candles.

But let me start at the beginning. My name's Artemis, and most of my family come from Cyprus. When Maria got married, quite a few of our relations came over here, and we went to the airport to pick them up. Everyone was so pleased to see everyone else, that it was like a party long before the wedding.

On the big day, I had to go round to Maria's house to get ready. Our friend Stefanos is a hairdresser and he was doing her hair. He did my hair too.

When it was time for the wedding to begin, we went into the church ahead of Maria and her new husband, Chris. By 'we' I mean me, and my cousins Nicky and George. George and I carried tall candles, all decorated with ribbons, and Nicky had a basket of confetti. The children who carry the candles and confetti aren't bridesmaids and pages. The bridesmaids in our church have to be grown up because they have to help pay for the wedding.

The wedding happened round a special table in the church. We had a bishop and a priest taking the service. It was very long because everything has to happen three times. The rings have to be exchanged three times and we had to walk around the table three times, with Maria and Chris behind us.

During the service, Maria and Chris had to put on special white wedding crowns. All the bridesmaids and best men – there were lots of each – had to change these crowns around from Maria's head to Chris's head, three times of course.

After the service, everyone signed their name on a long white ribbon, which was fixed to Maria's crown.

After we left church we all went to have a proper Greek meal, with all my favourite food. We had kebabs and rice, and lots of other things. There was plenty of music and dancing. When Maria and Chris danced, all the adults pinned bits of money to Maria's dress, as a wedding present.

I danced too, and so did the other children. We had such a good time. I hope I'm invited to another wedding very soon."

Activities on a wedding theme

1 Draw pictures of a Sikh, Hindu or Christian wedding. This might be the occasion for some interesting collage work, using some of the different kinds and colours of fabric used to make wedding clothes. Add 'gold' jewellery and tissue paper flowers as necessary.
2 Ask children who have been to a wedding, or taken part in one, to describe it.

SONGS
If you will marry me, **Granny's yard**
Nana Kru, **African songs**
MUSIC
Wedding March (Mendelssohn)
Celebratory music from Africa and Asia (various collections)

149

Birthdays

Birth

Children may be surprised to learn that not everyone in Britain thinks that birthdays are important. But although everyone does not celebrate birthdays, the moment of birth and the subsequent acceptance of the newborn child into the community are almost always important and treated as an occasion for celebration.

Christians usually baptize children in the name of God soon after they are born. The baptism, or christening, is a church ceremony which welcomes the child into the Church after the baby has been symbolically washed and given a name.

Muslims make sure that the first words a child hears are those of the Adhan, the basic beliefs of the faith: "I bear witness that there is no god but Allah, and Muhammad is the Prophet of Allah."

These words are whispered into the child's right ear soon after birth. Naming takes place seven days later, in a ceremony in which the child's hair is shaved off and its weight in silver is given to the poor. On the same day, in another ceremony, a baby boy will be circumcised.

In the Jewish religion baby boys are named and circumcised eight days after birth, in an important ceremony known as Brit Milah. Girls are named on the Sabbath after they are born, when the father announces the child's name in the synagogue.

For Hindus, birth is the occasion of the re-entry of a soul into the world, rather than the first arrival. Nevertheless, the moment of birth is very significant as the horoscope the priest casts for the child is based on the exact time of the baby's arrival. Having cast the horoscope, the priest will tell the parents what syllables they must use in the child's name. Later on the baby's head will be shaved, to symbolize the removal any bad influences left over from the child's previous life.

Sikh babies, like Muslim ones, hear the words of their faith before anything else, as the first words of the Sikh holy book, the Guru Granth Sahib, are whispered into the child's ear. Naming comes a few weeks later when, in front of the congregation in the temple, the baby's tongue is touched with a sword which has been placed in the sacred drink of sweetened water, known as amrit.

Birthdays and saints' days

Birthdays are not celebrated everywhere. In much of Africa, for example, they are considered of such little consequence that children may not even know their exact age, or what day is the exact anniversary of their birth.

In Chinese tradition, everyone celebrates their birthday at the same time, for people consider themselves to be a year older with each new year, regardless of the date on which they were actually born.

Even in Europe, birthdays are not always celebrated. In predominantly Roman Catholic countries such as Poland, it is the custom to have your own personal birthday-like celebration on your saint's day, or name day, instead. People are almost invariably named after a saint or a religious festival. When that saint's day comes round, it is a very special occasion, for the saint is your patron, who looks after you throughout your life. Children get cards and presents and hold a party on their saint's day, just as children in Britain do on their birthday (see picture).

A birthday story

Frances is a small badger, who features in a number of books by the American writer Russell Hoban. This adapted extract comes from a book called 'A birthday for Frances', in which Frances's younger sister Gloria has a birthday party, and Frances is a little jealous.

Albert was the first friend to arrive and he and Frances sat down in the living room while they were waiting for Ida.

"I am thinking of giving Gloria a Chompo bar for her birthday," said Frances. "But I am not sure. I might and I might not. I had to spend two weeks' pocket money on it. And anyway, little sisters are not much good."

"No they are not," said Albert. "They can't catch. They can't throw. When you play hide and seek, they always hide in places where part of them is sticking out."

"They take your pail and shovel too," said Frances. "They pull the button eyes off dolls that have button eyes. They break your crayons so that there are no long ones left in the box. They put water in your mud pies when you don't want them to. I don't think many of them deserve a Chompo bar."

Frances's mother came into the room.

"Here is Ida," she said. "Now the party can begin."

"Where are the presents?" said Gloria, as they sat down at the table.

"First," said father, "we will bring out the cake, and I will light the candles. Then we will sing 'Happy Birthday to You.' Then you will make a wish and blow out all the candles. Then you get your presents."

"I know what to wish," said Gloria.

"Don't tell it," said Ida.

"It won't come true if you do," said Albert.

"Here comes the cake," said mother.

She put it on the table and father lit the candles. Then everybody sang 'Happy Birthday to You'.

150

Frances did not sing the words that the others were singing. Very softly she sang:
"*Happy Chompo to me*
Is how it ought to be –
Happy Chompo to Frances
Happy Chompo to me."

"Now," said mother to Gloria, "make your wish and blow out the candles."

"I want to tell my wish," said Gloria.

"No, no!" said mother and father and Albert and Ida.

Gloria made her wish inside her head and blew out all the candles at once.

"Hooray!" said everybody.

"Now your wish will come true," said mother.

"This is what I wished," said Gloria. "I wished that Frances would be nice and not be cross because I hid her pail and shovel last year. And I am sorry, and I will be nice."

"She told," said Ida. "Now her wish won't come true."

"I think it will come true," said mother, "because it is a special kind of good wish that can make itself come true."

"Is it time for the presents?" said Gloria.

"Yes," said father.

Father and mother gave Gloria the paint box and the tea set and the plush pig. Albert gave her the little tiny truck. Ida gave her a little tiny china doll. Frances had wrapped the Chompo bar in pretty paper and tied it with a ribbon, and she got ready to give it to Gloria.

"What is it?" asked Gloria.

"It is something good to eat," said Frances, "and I will give it to you in a minute. But first I will sing 'Happy Birthday to You', because I did not really sing it before."

Some birthday activities

1 Make a pinata. These are very popular in the USA, but they come from South America. Originally, a pinata was a cheap, pottery jar filled with sweets and decorated to look like a bird or an animal. You can make one with card or paper. It hangs from the ceiling from a rope. The idea is that children take turns to be blindfolded and to hold a stick. They try to hit the pinata and break it open.

2 Write birthday poems, or draw presents. What would you most like to get for your birthday? What would you most like to be able to give?

POEMS
Between birthdays, Ogden Nash, **The Tinder-box assembly book**
Birthdays, traditional; *Solomon Grundy*, traditional, both in **Seeing and doing**
A SONG
Birthday song, **Tinderbox**
MUSIC
African rhythm and instruments (Volume 1) **Lyrichord** label (LLST 7328)
3rd movement from Haydn's *Trumpet Concerto*

One World

About One World

We look at the theme of One World through One World Week, which is, as its name implies, a week-long event. Its aim is to try to get people to think about the interdependence of all living things throughout the world. It is a time for thinking positively about the way other people live, not just about the hardships they suffer, in terms of lack of food, water, shelter and so on. It is also a time for finding out about what the rest of the world has to offer in the fields of art, music, technology, and so on from other countries.

One World Week was first thought up by the Churches Committee of the World Development Movement. But it is not supposed to be a predominantly Christian event. Indeed, the whole point of it is to demonstrate that people of different faiths and cultures share the world and depend on each other.

When is it?

One World Week is always planned to fall in the week in which October 24, United Nations Day, occurs. It also coincides with the Week of Prayer for World Peace.

But is it a festival?

One of the aims of One World Week, the organizers say, is "to celebrate the richness and adventure that belonging to one world offers us". It can be seen as a 'whole world' festival, drawing together the ideas celebrated in so many other festivals that occur throughout the year in so many parts of the world.

The week can provide an opportunity for children to learn about these different festivals, and the different cultures these represent as part of a whole, rather than as isolated curiosities – the ingredients that make up an exciting and colourful world which we can all share.

The organizers have put together a book of ideas for celebrating One World Week, describing the ways in which local groups can participate, and learn while they are doing so. Each year, a different aspect of 'One World' is emphasized, but you don't have to stick to the one suggested. In 1985 it was 'Recipes for Justice – Food for the World'. The book has ideas for all age groups. Some are suitable for young children, some will need some adaptation before they can be used. For addresses of the One World Week offices from where you can order the book, see below. An important part of the whole concept is to learn by enjoying yourself, so it should be celebrated as a festival of different cultures and ideas.

Ideas for One World Week

It's a good idea to prepare for this festival well in advance. Pick the theme you intend to concentrate on right at the beginning of term, and work on researching and presenting the different ideas in a grand display during the week itself. Local churches and groups interested in world development may already have plans in which you can take part, so make some enquiries early on.

Research into helpful local contacts who can come and talk to the children, show slides or demonstrate some suitable activity during the week itself. Such people might be former residents of other countries, or students here for only a year or so. The following are a few ideas, but the possibilities are limitless:

1 Have a festival of festivals, with pictures or displays about world festivals. You could pick a theme such as harvest festivals, or springtime festivals, or just choose favourites the children have celebrated in the past.
2 With older children, and the help of a local supermarket manager, plan a 'supermarket raid'. If you can arrange to do this after closing time, it will be easiest, but otherwise choose a slack time of day. Pick out from the non-perishable items, foods from as many different countries as you can find. Some schools have been allowed to set up a special display during the week, with a map to show where the different items come from.
3 With younger children, discuss food, where it comes from, how it is made, and how it arrives in the shops. Make booklets about the various parts of a meal, with pictures of the crops growing, being harvested, and so on.
4 With the help of parents, the children themselves and international cookery books, display a selection of foods from different parts of the world and let everyone have a taste. Oxfam, among others, publish an international cookery book with recipes from different parts of the world available. Use pictures to show what the crops look like and where they grow.
5 Introduce children to games from other parts of the world. UNICEF publishes a pack called 'Games around the world' and Oxfam publishes a booklet called 'Games children play around the world'.
6 Work on a 'junk' project, perhaps making a 'junk home corner'. People in many parts of the world depend on items we throw away to provide cooking utensils, tools, clothes and much more. Provide a few basic materials such as carefully opened tins (with no ragged edges), pieces of cloth, boxes and so on, and get everyone's imagination working to think

of practical uses for them all.
7 Think about waste and pollution. What happens when water gets polluted, especially in places where there are no taps, or rubbish is left lying around to attract flies and disease?

The outline of a play
This play involves one or two 'consumers', a shopkeeper, and assorted farmers from various parts of the world, plus animals, pickers, and so on.

Consumers: *We just want you to know that we can manage all by ourselves. We don't need any help from anyone.*
They pick up their shopping bags and go to the shopkeeper.
First consumer: *I'd like some milk, please.*
Shopkeeper: *I thought you said you could manage all by yourself.*
First consumer: *I can! I can pay for the milk.*
Farmer steps forward, followed by a cow: *But you need us, just the same.*
Cow: *Mooo! You dooo!*
Second consumer: *Well, I'd like a packet of tea. You don't need cows for that!*
Tea picker steps forward, with a basket: *But you do need me! My fellow tea pickers live far away in India, and you'll never meet them – but you still need them, and me …*
And so on.

ONE WORLD WEEK OFFICES
These are at:
One World Week,
PO Box 1,
London SW9 8BH

One World Week,
Interchurch Centre,
48 Elmwood Avenue,
Belfast BT9 6AZ

One World Week,
41 George IV Bridge,
Edinburgh

Wythnos Un Byd/One World Week,
Coleg Trefeca,
Aberhonddu/Brecon,
Powys LD3 0PP

BOOKS
The Centre for World Development Education, 128 Buckingham Palace Road, London SW1 9SH can provide lists of materials suitable for a variety of age groups, including infants. Among the materials they stock are five sets of 'Stories from overseas', published by the Malvern Oxfam group, suitable for children aged five and upwards. The Centre also has slides, posters and much more. Write to them, or telephone 01 730 8332/3 to get lists of materials and order forms.

POEMS
The wheel around the world, a children's song from Mozambique, translated by Chris Searle; *Road of peace,* Paul Robeson; *Old woman's song,* Edward Bond, all from **Wheel around the world**

SONGS
May there always be sunshine, **Tinderbox New Day, Love, work and hope**

Index

General Index

Aaron 114-115
Abraham 14
Adam and Eve 58
Aeroplanes 98
Aesop 82
Africa 50-51, 54, 72, 82, 126, 150
Ahazareus 136-137
Air 90-91
Alfred the Great 54
Ambulances 98
Antiochus 52, 130
America, North 10, 12, 24, 26, 34, 108, 134, 144, 148
   South 19
Animals 11-12, 15, 17, 24, 30, 32, 40, 48-49, 57, 59, 64-65, 68, 74-75, 85, 91, 110
Australia 28, 54
Autumn 12, 14-16, 50

Baboushka 34
Bali 146
Bells 32-33, 40, 108, 116
Bethlehem 18, 106-107
Birds 12, 15-16, 46, 49, 51, 64-65, 67-68, 95-96
Blindness 84-85
Brahma 58
Braille, Louis 84
Brazil 134
Bread 14, 18, 20-21
Bread, Matzah 114-115
Buddha, the 34, 138-139
Buddhism 52, 138-139
Burma 138
Buses 46, 98

Canada 19, 54
Candles 52-53, 106, 130-131, 138
Cars 11, 18
Cats 24-25, 73-74, 76
Charities 28-29, 139
China 8, 14, 19, 42-43, 51, 96, 110-111, 138, 150
Christianity 40, 52, 66, 68, 106-107, 116, 119-120,122-123, 126, 134-135, 148, 150
Christmas 15, 34, 36-37, 40, 50, 52, 106-107, 116, 122, 127
Churches 18, 22, 26-27, 116, 144, 148, 152
Clothes 10-11, 19, 28, 33, 49, 92-93, 100-101
Columba 32
Confucius (Kung Fu Tzu) 8-9
Conservation 12, 58, 139
Cowboys 22
Crops 19-20, 26, 62, 74, 124
Czechoslovakia 15

Dance 8, 14, 26-27, 42, 74, 120, 127-128, 134, 140
Darling, Grace 22
Deafness 86-87
Demeter 48
Deserts 12, 36, 40, 62, 113-114, 125, 135
Devaki 58
Dionysius 7, 44
Disabled people 84-87
Dogs 16, 30, 73-74, 98, 141
Dragons 42-43
Drapaudi 88, 146
Dr. Barnado's Homes 78

Ears 8, 86-87, 100
Eden, Garden of 58
Egypt 64, 66, 80, 114-115, 124
Eli 86
Elijah 114
England 108, 116, 120
Eskimos 100
Esther 136-137
Eyes 8, 84-85, 100

Families 28, 80-81
Farms and farming 14, 18-19, 31, 69, 74-75, 95, 128
Fasting 66, 132, 134, 136, 139
Feasting 66, 106, 134, 136
Feet 88, 89
Firemen 98-99
Fireworks 22, 110, 128, 134
Fishing 22-23, 26, 32, 90, 94
Flowers 12, 18, 48, 66, 74, 94, 96-97, 116, 133, 138-139, 144-145
Food 12, 14, 16, 18-20, 26, 28-29, 40, 52, 56, 59, 64, 98, 100-101, 106, 108, 110, 114, 125-127, 140-141, 152
France 34
Friendship 8, 12, 14, 16, 24, 26-27, 40, 74, 94
Fruit 12, 18-19, 96

Gabriel, Angel 40, 132
Gardens 10
Germany 34, 68, 106, 116
Grandparents 10-11, 14
Greece 44, 68, 116, 130
Gurdwaras 56
Guru Gobind Singh 56, 140-141

Guru Granth Sahib 140, 148, 150
Guru Hargobind 92
Guru Nanak 140

Hades 48
Hagar 62
Haman 136-137
Hands 88-89
Harvest 16, 18-19, 22, 26, 114, 118, 122, 124-125, 128-129
Hearing 8, 33, 86-87
Herod 106-107
Hinduism 40, 42, 52, 58, 88, 118-119, 128, 146-148, 150
Hiranyakasipu 66, 118-119
Holicka 66, 118-119
Holidays 94-95
Homes and houses 16, 26, 59-60, 63, 78-79, 100, 110
Hong Kong 101
Hospitals 28
Hunger (famine) 18, 20, 26, 62, 64

India 19, 28, 34, 42, 46, 56, 58, 66, 74, 76, 92, 118, 128, 138-140, 146, 148
Insects 67, 76-77
Iraq 28
Ireland 142-143
Isaac 14
Ishmael 62
Islam 112-113
Israel 12, 124
Italy 34, 116

Jacob 64
Jains 76

154

Jamaica 96
Japan 40, 96, 101, 108, 138
Jerusalem 107, 116-117,
    122-124, 130
Jesus Christ 36, 40, 68, 90,
    106-107, 116-117, 122-123,
    134-135
John the Baptist 134
Joseph, son of Jacob 64
Joseph, father of Jesus 36,
    106-107
Judaism 14, 52, 66, 106,
    114-115, 124-125, 130-131,
    136-137, 148, 150
Judas 117

Kampuchea 138
Kansa 58
Khalsa, the 140
Kindness 28-29, 34, 36, 48, 56,
    72, 74-75
Kings, the Three (also Wise Men)
    36, 106-107
King Wenceslas 48
Krishna 58, 66, 88, 119
Korea 138

Lakshmi 52, 128
Lifeboat 22-23
Lighthouse 22-23
Loneliness 16, 28

Maccabaeus, Judas 52, 130
Mary, mother of Jesus 36, 40,
    106-107
Mecca (Makkah) 62, 112, 132
Mexico 108
Midas, King 44

Middle East 28
Migration of birds 15, 50-51
Miracle plays 122
Money 8, 12, 19, 23, 28, 46, 54,
    62, 80, 94, 108, 110-111, 136
Moon 10-12, 14-15, 42, 48, 50,
    132
Morris dancing 120
Moses 66, 80, 114, 124-125
Mosques 26-27, 45, 148
Mother Teresa 28
Muhammad, the Prophet 40, 62,
    112-113, 132, 150
Music 22, 42, 74, 83-84, 87, 127,
    134-135
Muslims 40, 45, 62, 66, 92, 112-
    113, 126, 132-133, 148, 150

Naomi 18, 122
Nazareth 106, 134
Netherlands 34, 96, 106, 134
Nigeria 126
Nightingale, Florence 56
Noah 64
Norway 34
Nursing 28, 30, 56, 98

Old age 10-11, 49, 96, 98
Olympus, Mount 44
Oxfam 28, 152

Pakistan 148
Persephone 48
Peru 28
Pilate, Pontius 117
Poland 106, 150
Police 98
Pollution 23, 63, 153

Postman 98-99
Prahlada 66, 118-119
Presents 34-36, 52, 128, 130-133,
    147, 150-151

Rama 42, 128-129
Ravana 42-43, 128-129
Red Indians 10-12, 24, 26-27,
    108
Rivers 23, 26
Robbers 28, 46, 117
Romans 29, 106-107, 116
RNIB 85
RNLI 23
RSPCA 139
Russia (Soviet Union) 34, 106
Ruth 18, 122-123

Saints, patron 106, 142-143, 150
St. Lucia 52-53
Samuel 86
Saudi Arabia 132
Save the Children Fund 28-29
Schools 8-9, 11-12, 14, 46,
    54-55, 72, 94, 98-99
Scotland 40, 108
Sea 22-23, 27, 94
Seder, the 114-115
Seeds 11, 13-18, 96
Seeing 8, 84-85
Sharing 9, 18, 80-81
Shepherds and sheep 14, 18,
    30-31, 36, 106-107
Ships and boats 11, 22-23, 64,
    94-95, 98
Sikhism 56-57, 92, 140, 148,
    150
Singing 14, 24, 26, 29

Snow 12, 34, 48-49
Spain 19, 22, 96, 106, 116
Springtime 66-67, 96, 114, 118
Sri Lanka 138
Storms 22, 32, 58, 90-91
Subhadra 88, 146
Summer 60, 94-95
Sun 8, 18, 45, 50, 60-61, 72, 90
Switzerland 40
Synagogues 26-27, 123, 136,
    148, 150

Taiwan 101
Teachers 14, 92, 98-99, 112
TEAR fund 28
Temples 26-27
Thailand 138
Tibet 138
Trains 46, 98
Trees 12-13, 15, 24
Travel 15, 46-47, 56, 98
Tsao Chun 42, 110-111

UNICEF 152

Vasudeva 58
Vegetables 15, 19
Vishnu 66, 118-119, 146

Wales 108, 142-143
War 14
Whittington, Dick 33
Winter 12, 16, 26, 34, 48-49, 50,
    60, 66-67, 96
Witchcraft 24-25, 52
Wizards 25

Yams 126-127

155

Festivals/Celebrations Index

Advent Sunday 40

Baisakhi 140-141
Baptisms 81
Birthdays 41, 53, 150-151
Bullock's Festival 74

Caribbean Carnival 66-67, 134
Chinese Moon Festival 14
Chinese New Year 42, 110-111
Christmas 15, 34, 36-37, 40, 50, 52, 106-107, 116, 122, 127

Diwali 40, 42, 52, 128-129

Easter 68-69, 116-117, 122, 134
Eid-ul-Adha 112
Eid-ul-Fitr 76, 81, 112, 132-133
Epiphany 106
Esther, Fast of 136

Flower festivals 96

Ganjitsu 40

Hallowe'en 24
Hanukah 52, 130-131
Harvest Festival 18
Hijrah 40, 112-113
Holi 66-67, 112, 118-119
Hogmanay 40, 108-109
Holy Week 116

Islamic New Year 112-113

Lailat-ul-Qadr 132
Lent 66, 134, 144

Mardi Gras 66-67

156

Marriage 148-149
May Day 67, 120-121
Midsummer's Day 60, 94
Mothering Sunday/Mothers' Day 67, 81, 144-145

New Year 14, 40, 43, 52, 108-109
New Year for Trees 12

One World Week 152-153

Palm Sunday 116
Passover 66-67, 114-117, 122
Pentecost 122-123
Purim 136-137

Raksha Bandhan 81, 88, 146-147
Ramadan 66, 112, 132-133
Rosh Hashanah 14, 40

Sea festivals 22
Shavout 122
Shrove Tuesday 66-67, 112, 134-135
St. Patrick's and St. David's Day 142-143
Sukkot 124-125

Thanksgiving 26

Valentine's Day 67

Weddings 81, 148-149
Wesak (The Buddha's Birthday) 138-139
Whitsun 122-123

Yam Harvest 126-127

Projects/Activities Index

African masks 127
African model village 59
animal masks 17

balloon-seller 65
bell decoration 33, 109
bells, bottle 33, 109
bendy figures 99
'big and little' patterns 73
bread 21
bubble patterns 91
butterflies and caterpillars 77

calendar 15, 41
calypso music 135
candle clocks 53
candles 53, 129
carnival costumes 135
chapatti 21
Chinese objects 43
Christingle 37
circuit, electrical 33
coin collection 11

David and Goliath figures 31
doll 49
dragon, Chinese 43
dragon collage 142
drama
    krishna dance-drama 119
    members of a family 79
    miracle play 123
    nativity play 106
    One World Week play 153
    Passover play 115
    puppet drama 137, 146
    Purim play 136-137
    story of Buddha 139
    story of Esther 137

story of Guru Gobind Singh 141
story of Rama and Sita 129
story of St. Patrick 143
dyeing 93

Easter bonnets 69
Easter decorations and cards 117
Easter eggs 117
eggshell seed box 67
Eid cards 133

fancy-dress dance 135
fans 43
Father Christmas 37
'feely' box 89
fish and chip shop 23
fish mobile 23
flower garlands 139
flower posy 63
flowers, decorating with 121, 123
flowers, pressing wild 97
flowers, from yoghurt cartons 97
fruit and nut displays 17
fruits and vegetables, drawing 19

games from other parts of the world 152
gift tags 35
grandparents' day 11

harvest displays 125
hedgehog 17
house, a 3D, 79

insects, collecting 77
inventions display 61

'junk' project 152

lamps 129
language work 25, 73, 83, 87
lantern 43
leaf patterns 13
lion 75
lion, for the lion dance 111
litter project 59

mathematical activities 31, 65, 73, 77, 81, 85, 89, 147
maypole 95
maypole dance 121
mobiles 19, 23, 51, 61
moon cakes 15
moon chart 11
moving person 83
musical instrument 87, 127
Muslim religious artefacts 45

nativity scene 37
necklaces 65
New Year project 41

owl 57

parathas 141
parcels 35
paste graining a tree 13
patterns, Islamic 113, 133
peacock, hand-printed 51
percussion instruments, rattles 127
pinata 151
plaiting 147
plates of model food 27
portraits, painting 55
printing blocks 133
puppetry, shadow 25
Purim cakes 137

rainfall gauge 63
Red Indian head-dress 11

'ring around the world' 101
road safety talk 47
Roman soldier 29
rug design 133

scientific experiments 13, 31, 33, 44, 47, 53, 61, 63, 65, 77, 91
seaside collection 95
seed growth chart 13
seed pattern pendant 15
seeing double pictures 85
sequencing patterns 65
shadow clocks 61
shamrock motif 143
Shape house and family 81
soldier 69
star, five-pointed 45
street scene 47
sun bird mobile 61

target chart 19
twigs collection and drawings 49, 67

visits
  farm 95
  museum 11
  old people's home 29
  park 13, 17, 51
  police or fire station 99
  seaside 95

weather chart 41
weaving mat 55
welcome poster 9
wigwam 27
windmill 21
witch 25
wood display 13
wrapping paper, designing 131

Story, Song and Poem Index

Action rhyme 8, 82
Action song 78
Adam and Eve 58
Aesop and his master 82
Al-Hijrah 112-113
Alfred learns to read 54
Animals, years of 110
Atri, bell of 32
Autumn song 14
Ayesha finds a friend 94

Baboushka 34
Baisakhi Day 140
Bernard the helper 98
Big waves and little waves 22
Birds 50
Birthday story 150
Blackbird 50
Blind boy who helped others 84
Blind boy who loves music 84
Blind man and the lame man 84
Boy who cried wolf 30
Boy who disliked school 54
Boy who loved to learn 8
Bright star (Christmas play) 36
Buddha, the 34, 138-139
Builders, the two 78
Bullock's festival 74
Bushytail 16

Calendar rhyme 40
Cat and the tortoise 74
Chinese New Year 42
Chinese moon festival 14
Chinese twins 80
Church mouse 18
Cinder Joe 72
Clever sister 80
Columba rings the bell 32

Creepy crawly caterpillar 76

Darling, Grace 22
Diwali 42
Down at the station 46
Dr. Barnardo's Homes 78

Easter 116-117
Easter egg 68
Easter rabbit 68
Easter story 68
Eid-ul-Fitr 132-133
Esther, Fast of 136
Every day 18

Feet 88
First snowdrop 96
Five and twenty masons 78
Five little spacemen 60
Florence and the shepherd's dog 30

God made the world 58
Good morning 8
Good night 84
Greek myth 48
Greeting song 8
Grey squirrels and the red squirrel 16
Guru Nanak 140-141

Hagar and Ishmael 62
Hanukah 130-131
Hargobind's cloak 92
Hay time 94
Holi 118-119
House upon a rock 78
House with the golden windows 60

If 72
Indian boy and the robbers 46
Insey winsy spider 62

Jack Frost 48
Jains 76
Jesus and the storm 90
Johnny Appleseed 12
Joseph and the coloured coat 64
Junaid Baghdadi, a kind man 28

Kind man and the wolf 40
King Wenceslas 48
King who wanted gold 44
Krishna 88, 119, 146
Krishna saved the world 58

Lady with the lamp 56
Land of the silver birch 26
Lent 134-135
Lion and the mouse 72
Little bird in Africa 50
Little old lady 10
Littlest camel knelt 36

Mahagiri the elephant 76
May Day 120-121
Me 82
Monster and the red doors 42
Mother Teresa 28
Mothering Sunday 144-145
Mouse, frog, and little red hen 20
Mr Singh's turban 92
Muhammad and the well 62
My dog 74

Naughty little lamb 30
New moon 10
New year 109
New year for trees 12
Noah and the rainbow 64

Passover 114-115
Peapod 10
Pedro 94
Penn, William 26
Piccolo and the baby bird 50
Pilgrim Fathers 26
Poor boy gives a present 34
Poor traveller 46
Postman 98
Purim 136-137

Rama and Sita 128-129
Red Sea crossing 124
Ruth 18, 122

St. David 142
St. Lucia 52
St. Patrick 142-143
Sarah's baby 14
Simnel cake 144
Singing game: two in a boat 22
Snowdrops 96
Sol, the sun god 60
Someone 56
Sometimes 147
Special job for everyone 82
Sukkot 124-125
Sun and the wind 90
Susu Chatterbox 86

Tall trees 12
There was an old witch 24
Traveller calls at night 56
Tsao Chun 42, 110-111
Two in a boat 22
Two little ears 86

Wanda the kind witch 24
Wash day 92
Wedding 148-149
When a little boy listened 86
Whitsun, the first 122-123
Wise king 88
Witch in the wood 24
Woodman and his axe 44

Yam harvest 126-127

Acknowledgements

The publishers have made every effort to trace the ownership of all copyrighted material, and to secure permission from holders of such material. They regret any inadvertent error, and will be pleased to make the necessary corrections in future printings.

Thanks are due to the following for their kind permission in allowing us to reprint material (copyright holders appear in **bold**):

Nadia Bakhsh for an extract from *Eid Mubarik*, published by Cheetah Books, Ajaib and QRB Publishers; **Bell and Hyman Publishers** for *The Blackbird* by Phyllis Drayon, *If* by P.A.Ropes, *My Dog* by C.Nurton, *Feet* by Irene Thompson, *The Wind* by Dorothy Gradon, *Tall Trees* by Eileen Mattias, *Every Day* by Mary Osborn, *Wash Day* by Lilian McCrea, and *Snowdrops* by Mary Vivian, all in The Book of a Thousand Poems; **Mrs Bennett** for *The Little Old Lady* in The Book of a Thousand Poems; **A&C Black** for *Sometimes* by Eve Merriam in the Tinder-Box Assembly Book, and *The Postman* by Clive Sansom from The Book of a Thousand Poems; **Blandford Press Ltd** for *Florence and the Shepherd's Dog*, and *The Kind Man and the Wolf* from Stories for Infants; Child Education for

A Bright Star, and *A Greeting Song* by Christine Telfer; **The Commonwealth Institute** for *Yam Festival* by Dominic Effiom; **Faber and Faber Ltd** for an extract from *A Birthday for Frances* by Russell Hoban; **Hamlyn Publishing**, a division of Hamlyn Publishing Group Limited, for *Little Pedro* from 366 Goodnight Stories; **Harrap Ltd** for *Birds* by Natalie Joan from Lilts for Little People; **David Higham Associates** for *There are Big Waves* by Eleanor Farjeon from The Book of a Thousand Poems; the **I.L.E.A.** for *The Land of the Silver Birch* from Sing A Song 2; **Longman Group Ltd** for *Wanda the Kind Witch* from Reading with Rhythm by Taylor and Ingleby; **National Sunday School Union** for *Jack Frost* by C.E.Pike from The Book of a Thousand Poems; **The Religious Tract Society** for *Haytime* by C.M.Lowe; **The Society of Authors** as the literary representatives of the estate of Rose Fyleman for *The Donkey* from The Book of a Thousand Poems; **The Society for Promoting Christian Knowledge** for *Every Day* by Mary Osborn, an extract from Good and Gay; **The Literary Trustees of Walter de la Mare and The Society of Authors as their representative** for *Someone* from The Book of a Thousand Poems.

The author wishes to acknowledge the following for their help and encouragement in the preparation of this book: the staff and children of The Cedars Infant School, Blackburn; her family; and all the children she has taught in previous schools who have unknowingly evaluated much of the material, and without whom the book would have been impossible.

The publishers, and author of the Festivals section, wish to thank the following for their assistance with the preparation of the Festivals section: Leonora Davies, musical adviser to the ILEA; Rabbi Sybil Sheridan; Dr S.Darsh; and the Haringay Multicultural Resources Department Centre.

The publishers also wish to thank Ellen Rust, head teacher, and the staff at the Kingsgate Infant School in London for their help and co-operation in the shooting of the cover photograph.

Editor: Stephen White-Thomson

Design: Sally Boothroyd

Production: John Moulder

Festivals text: Jenny Vaughan

Artists: Julio Osorno
(Terms One, Two and Three)
Suzanna Rust
(Festivals section + pages 1, 2, 3, 7, 71 and 103)

Main text © Doreen Vause 1985

Festivals text © Simon & Schuster 1985

Illustrations © Simon & Schuster 1985

All rights reserved

First published in 1985 in Great Britain by
Macdonald & Co (Publishers) Ltd

Reprinted 1987, 1989, 1990, 1993, 1994

Third and subsequent impressions published by
Simon & Schuster Education
Campus 400, Maylands Avenue
Hemel Hempstead, Herts HP2 7EZ

Printed and bound in Portugal by
Printer Portuguesa
Indústria Gráfica, Lda

British Library Cataloguing in Publication Data
Vause, Doreen
   The infant assembly book
   1. Schools – Prayers   2. Schools – Exercises
   and recreations
   I. Title
   377'.I BV283.S3
   ISBN 0 7501 0140 7